~>ANTIQUE~<
TOYS AND DOLLS

Studio Vista · Christie's
London

ANTIQUE
TOYS AND DOLLS
Constance E. King

Acknowledgements

In writing this book I was especially fortunate in having at my disposal all the issues of *The Toy Trader,* first published in 1908 (and never before used as source material), and I would like to thank the present editor Greville Bogard for this facility. Among firms which kindly allowed access to catalogues were Chad Valley Ltd, Dean's Rag Book Company and William Britain's. It was a special delight to meet and talk to Lili and Francis Bing, who remembered their childhood in Nuremberg when their family factory was at the peak of its production, and to look through their catalogues. For assistance in obtaining photographs I would like to thank the staff of the Bethnal Green Museum, the Victoria and Albert Museum, Christie's (South Kensington) Ltd and the Margaret Woodbury Strong Museum, New York. I am especially grateful to Robert Hallmann, who photographed the battered as well as the beautiful and elegant toys with humour and sensitivity, and to John and Betty Harvey-Jones, who allowed him to take pictures of their discriminating collection. My husband Andrew not only read the manuscript but purchased many of the items that are illustrated, and he is very especially thanked.

All pieces illustrated in this book are from the author's collection unless otherwise indicated.

The half-title page illustration shows a clockwork chauffeur-driven motor landau with folding seats marked 'Velleda' on the bonnet and on the wheels 'Lehmann' with a 1913 patent. Length 24 cm. (9½ in.). (Christie's, South Kensington.)

The contents page illustration shows a highly-coloured group of small tin toys. The unmarked cockerel once had real feathers in its tail. *Circa* 1920. The bird pecks the ground when the key is wound and the two late 19th-century ducks bob up and down as they roll along because of an eccentric wheel. The snail was made *circa* 1950 and is marked 'Lehmann Noli no. 915. Made in Western Germany'. Size of cockerel 6·5 cm. (2½ in.)

A caption for the illustration on the title page is given on page 82.

A Studio Vista/Christie's (South Kensington) book
published by Cassell Ltd,
35 Red Lion Square, London, WC1R 4SG
and at Sydney, Auckland, Toronto, Johannesburg,
an affiliate of
Macmillan Publishing Co., Inc., New York

ISBN 0 289 70834 6

Designed by Sandra Schneider
Filmset and printed by BAS Printers Limited, Over Wallop, Hampshire.

Contents

Introduction	6
Early toys	8
The toy horse	26
Tin toys	46
Optical toys and the model theatre	81
Dolls in adult form	96
Child-like dolls	124
Soft toys	146
The miniature world	177
Board games and jigsaw puzzles	210
Toy animals and their settings	232
Appendix: on collecting	248
Bibliography	250
Index	253

Introduction

The development of toys is a subject that reaches as far back as the history of civilization itself. In writing this book I have therefore selected those aspects that most interest modern collectors, who are unlikely to buy many items made before the late eighteenth century and are largely uninterested in acquiring Oriental toys or toys of a folk nature. Though certain groups of enthusiasts now collect items made quite recently, such as 'Dinky' cars, railways and dolls of the thirties and forties, these toys are not generally to be found in collections of antiques. In a few cases, however, as with tin and soft toys, the collector's boundaries are becoming extended; in my accounts of these areas I have therefore included a few later toys if their manufacture made a substantial contribution to the development of the subject.

The manufacture of very high quality toys is necessarily connected with the lives of richer children until the late nineteenth century, when mass production methods and better pay for artisans meant that even children from quite humble homes could afford attractive playthings. Cheaply made rag or carved wooden toys owned by the very poor cannot be documented, as they were usually so crudely made that they were soon discarded.

Germany was the greatest producer of toys before the First World War, though there was also a sizeable French manufacture. In England the main emphasis was upon large toys, such as dolls' houses and rocking horses, or upon items of exceptionally high quality, such as poured wax dolls. In America there was at first an almost complete reliance upon imported playthings. The American toy industry developed rapidly after 1860, and although a few individual makers created, for instance, highly collectable rag dolls, the main contribution was in the field of heavy iron toys and moneyboxes. In both England and America before the First World War, most toys sold continued to be of German origin.

Collectors should turn to one of the books listed in the Bibliography for a comprehensive list of the makers' marks on dolls and toys. Many toys, such as arks, farms, horses, dolls' houses and some soft toys, are completely unmarked and acquisitions have to be attributed on the evidence of their characteristics alone.

I have not thought it valuable to attempt to supply guidelines to the escalating prices in today's antique markets. Certain collecting fields, such

Opposite A delicately modelled figure of the Infant Jesus. When the lever at the side is pulled the arms are raised in blessing and the eyes open. Made in France, *circa* 1860, and marked 'Deselas'. Height 38 cm. (15 in.).

as dolls and tin toys, are so popular that prices have risen out of all logical proportion to the workmanship employed in their manufacture, and they are valued purely on rarity and ephemeral charm. The steadily growing band of toy enthusiasts evidences the contemporary suspicion of articles of so-called intrinsic worth and points to a more emotional and whimsical appraisal of the artefacts of past generations.

Early toys

Ancient toys

THE commercial manufacture of toys is a practice that is of considerable antiquity. Even among the remains of ancient Egyptian and Greek civilizations, discoveries are made of objects once played with by children that are not individual, unique creations but the work of craftsmen supplying in some quantity a basic demand for playthings. Egyptian children, for instance, were familiar with such fundamental toys as balls, dolls and pull-along animals. Perhaps the best-known toy of this early period is a wooden crocodile whose under-jaw is moved by pulling a string that runs through the nose. A similarly activated tiger, with glass eyes, originated in Thebes in 1000 B.C., and both illustrate how ancient is the use of simple movement in playthings. At the British Museum is a group of clay figures showing scenes from Egyptian everyday life, such as a woman kneading bread and then rolling it; and items such as balls were put in tombs for the amusement of the dead.

Children playing with toys are often shown in the scenes painted on Greek vases; the perfect body united with a perfect mind had to be developed from childhood, and this period of life was therefore revered and children were popular subjects for artists. Paintings of very young children sometimes show them riding simple hobby horses, while an Attic vase, dating to 400 B.C., shows a toy cart with long handles and very big wheels that is obviously an ancient forerunner of the mail carts that were so popular in the nineteenth century.

Babies were sometimes amused with earthenware rattles in animal form, like the pig from the second century B.C. that was found in Cyprus. At the Festival of Eleusis, objects thought to be the favourite toys of the infant Bacchus were carried in procession, while the dedication of toys at puberty to Zeus, Hermes and Artemis has also provided written references to early playthings. The earthenware dolls of the Greeks have survived in some quantity: they were very simply shaped and the limbs were articulated by cords at the shoulders and thighs. Boys played with model warships and were also encouraged to build their own toy boats and carts as well as model houses. The development of the very complex automata of the nineteenth century can also be traced from this early period, for they have antecedents in the moving statues used to awe the common people.

A pair of articulated earthenware Greek dolls dating to the 5th century B.C. The faces and hairstyles were well modelled and the breasts and buttocks clearly defined. Height of largest doll 15 cm. (6 in.).

Roman children, like the Greek, dedicated their toys at puberty to gods—to Jupiter, Mercury and Diana—and their cradle toys at an earlier age were offered to Bacchus. Miniature furniture exists from both the Greek and Roman civilizations, but while the probability is that the pieces were toys, it is impossible at present to prove this. There are also many small military figures that seem to be toys and it is generally considered that the flat, single-sided lead figure of a horseman on a stand found at Rosegg, as well as an equestrian Julius Caesar, form a very early thread in the development of the tin soldier. In Roman times girls played with both rag and clay dolls, and craftsmen carved exquisite articulated wooden figures.

Medieval and Renaissance toys

Documentary evidence, as well as actual examples, increase significantly, especially in France and Germany, from the twelfth century. Small clay figures, horses and mythological beasts, all thought to be toys, are attributable to the thirteenth and fourteenth centuries; some of them were discovered under the streets of old Strasbourg. In the ruins of Osterburg Castle in the Rhône mountains toy utensils were found that can be approximately dated, for the castle was built in 1200 and destroyed in 1270. Illuminated manuscripts sometimes provide useful information about toys: in a French psalter of 1300 a boy is shown playing with a fife and drum while a girl rides a hobby horse. An English manuscript of the fourteenth century (now in the British Museum) shows a man and a boy whipping a top; the whips are short sticks with several knotted lashes, and the top, like many depicted in illustrations of this period, is surprisingly large. The top was one of the many sorts of toy once played with by adults, and the English antiquary John Brand relates how a town top was kept in each village 'to be whipt in frosty weather that the peasants might be kept warm

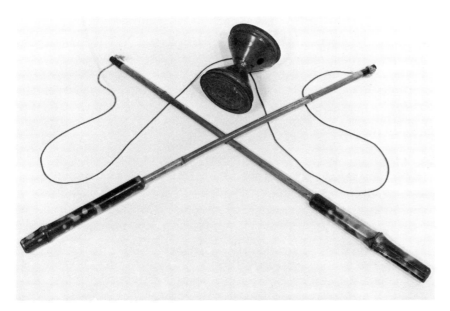

The ever-popular game of Diabolo, of ancient origin, where the spool is run on string between two sticks. This example whistles. Marked on spool 'Le Gracieux. F. G. Paris. Depose'. For Fernand Gratieux. *Circa* 1910.

by exercise and out of mischief when they could not work' (*Popular Antiquities*, 1777). Large tops of this type were whipped in turn by several men. Another game of adult origin was cup-and-ball, which so absorbed Henry III of France that he carried the toy even when out walking. His courtiers obediently followed the fashion, as did other adults, and when the craze was over it became a nursery pastime. A German manuscript of 1405 explains how a boy should construct a kite, describing the colours for its decoration and the most effective means of flying it from horseback.

The earliest graphic representation of a toy battle occurs in the twelfth-century *Hortus Deliciarum* of the Abbess Herrad of Landsberg, where children are shown manipulating figures by strings to make them strike at one another with swords. The *Weisskunig* by Hans Burgkmair, dating to 1516, shows the boy Maximilian I playing with articulated jousting figures at a table. The figures were pushed by hand and some skill was needed to unseat the opponent. This was obviously a princely toy as the horses were richly equipped and the figures costumed in miniature armour. In the same year Maximilian himself ordered from Kolman, a helmet-maker and master smith of Augsburg, two knights, armed with lances and mounted on wooden horses, which he presented to the ten-year-old Ludwig II of Hungary. This reference is of great interest, for it indicates both the name of the craftsman and his place of work—detailed information that up to this period is always lacking. The jointed knight at the Bayerisches Nationalmuseum at Munich, believed to have been made around 1550 and originally the property of the Holzschurer family of Nuremberg, was most probably one of a similar set. It is costumed very correctly and carries the family coat of arms. Both the neck and the legs of the horse are jointed for added realism and it is provided with a horsehair tail; the knight doll is also jointed. There is a comparable knight in a Paris collection and they are both thought to derive from the same manufacturer. A number of miniature suits of armour have also survived, and probably formed the costume of similar jointed figures.

By the end of the sixteenth century the production of specially commissioned princely toys was still occasionally documented, but more interesting to most collectors is the evidence of incipient commercial manufacture in Europe around this time. As early as 1578 the Council of Nuremberg had authorized pewterers and jewellers to make tin figures as children's playthings, thus firmly establishing in the area the practice of manufacturing toys in tin. At first guild regulations often hampered production, for the workers in each guild could only make items appropriate to their own particular skill; thus, although a pewterer could make soldiers, he could not make a wooden fort to put them in. In 1572 the Elector of Saxony ordered a hunt from Nuremberg for his twelve-year-old son, consisting of wild boar, dogs, huntsmen, roebucks and wolves, all carved in wood. Nuremberg was able to establish itself as a toy-making centre because of the abundance of wood and the proximity of lead mines, in combination with its position near the medieval trade routes across

Europe. The great fairs held on Church feast days ensured ready markets for toy-sellers; other toys were distributed by pedlars. Ideas in toy-making were quickly passed on throughout Europe, with the result that similar items were constructed in various countries.

Seventeenth-century toys

In a copperplate by Jacob von der Heyden, printed in Nuremberg in 1632, children are depicted skipping, stilt-walking, playing with dolls, riding a well-made hobby horse with the front legs in a jumping position, as well as flying kites and playing with knucklebones and whipping tops. Much of our knowledge of the aristocratic toys of the later Renaissance is gained, however, not from pictorial sources but from the accounts of the childhood of Louis XIII of France, who was born in 1601. Louis was placed under the care of a devoted doctor, Heroard, who recorded the Dauphin's progress in considerable detail, so we know, for instance, that before the age of seventeen months he owned a hobby horse, a windmill and a whipping top, as well as a toy fiddle; and at twenty-two months he was given a tambourine and a drum. At the age of two years and seven months, the future Duc de Sully presented him with a carriage full of dolls. Before he was three he was enjoying military games, as well as tennis and mall. He 'danced and sung at the coming of Christmas' in 1604 and watched the Yule log being lit. He received as gifts a ball and 'some little baubles from Italy including a clockwork pigeon'. Although his reading lessons began at three years and five months, and he was writing at four, he continued to play with dolls at the age of six. Among his possessions was a 'German cabinet' (presumably similar to the Nuremberg cabinet dolls' houses) and a doll dressed as a nobleman wearing a scented collar. When he was seven he was admonished to forget his childhood: 'You are a big boy now, you must stop playing the waggoner, you are no longer a child.' It was in the same year, however, that his mother Marie de Medici presented him with a miniature army made by Nicolas Roger and composed of three hundred silver soldiers. Another of his silver toys was a ship on gilded wheels propelled by the wind in the manner of the land-ships of Holland. The silver army was augmented with lead figures he made himself, as well as war machines, including cannons 'soldered with Spanish iron which fired without bursting'. Presumably it was these home-made toys that he played with in the forts he built in the Tuileries gardens.

On the death of Louis XIII his toy army passed to his successor, who added to it another of silver in 1650. In order that his son should own the finest set, Louis XIV instructed his minister Colbert in 1672 to write to his brother reminding him of an army with figures and horses 'that I asked you to have produced by the most illustrious makers of Augsburg and Nuremberg'. This army was made by Jacob Wolrab with additional automatic devices made by the goldsmiths, silversmiths and compass-makers Hans and Gottfried Hautsch from the designs of a well-known fortress engineer named Vauban. It seems that these new regiments could retreat, march to left and right, double their ranks and lower their weapons, while the pikemen attempted to knock the cavalry from their horses. Another army was made of cardboard by Henri de Gissey, designer to the King's ballet troupe.

Interesting commercially made toys were becoming more readily available by the end of the sixteenth century, when dolls of all sizes, correctly costumed, as well as trumpets, helmets, drums and hobby horses with prancing forelegs, could be bought from market stalls. Military figures, engraved on wood and brightly coloured, were published in Augsburg at the end of the seventeenth century by J.Ph. Steudner. Many seventeenth-century prints show children indulging in games of chance for money, a practice that was not yet shocking to adults since the games of childhood did not begin to become completely divorced from grownup amusements until the eighteenth century. As card games were so popular with children, it was an obvious progression to instruct them through their use, a practice which had originated in the late sixteenth century. One early example, which few children could have found enjoyable, was a pack published in 1603 by Andream Strobl in Bavaria, which taught Bible stories with the aid of three hundred pages of text for each copper-engraved suit! Some interesting instructional games in card form were sold by Henri le Gras in the mid-seventeenth century. One was founded on fables, gods and

An English miniature beechwood day bed. Late 17th century. Length 28 cm. (11 in.). (Bethnal Green Museum.)

demigods, and heroes of antiquity, and each figure was provided with a short history. Another was entitled 'Le Jeu des Rois de la France', and had a description of the reign of each monarch beneath his portrait. 'Le Jeu des Reines Renommées', with portraits of queens and heroines, was another set in the series, supplied with two hundred fine plates prepared by Stefano della Bella. Even military science was taught by means of cards, as in 'Le Jeu des Fortifications' issued in Paris. The grammatical playing card also makes its gloomy appearance in the seventeenth century; one set published in London is described as being 'ingeniously contrived for the comprising of the general rules of Lillie's grammar'.

Another originally adult pastime that was eventually to be used as a toy was the magic lantern, which was invented by Athanasius Kircher around 1640; its principles were outlined in his book *Ars Magna Lucis et Umbrae*. Kircher was a scientist and Jesuit priest, but he was also a skilled showman with such a power of arousing and terrifying his audiences that he was thought to be a sorcerer. The lantern was simple but effective: a screen of translucent silk was placed between the viewers and the lamp, and the figures projected from sheets of glass could be made to advance and retreat quite frighteningly. In 1719 the magic lantern could still be described in a dictionary as an 'Optical machine which enables one to see in the dark, on a white wall, many spectres and frightful monsters of a sort that those who do not know the secret believe it to be done by Magic Art'. Much less frightening were the peep-shows or perspective boxes set up by the raree men in the village square, through which the countryfolk were urged to view exciting contemporary scenes.

Among other toys dating from the seventeenth century are several fine continental cabinet-type dolls' houses. These were equipped with pewter, brass and copper miniatures mainly of German origin. Some of their furnishings were commercial, while many were especially made for the individual houses and are the work of fine craftsmen. These cabinets, particularly in Holland, were mainly an adult amusement; well-known painters were employed to decorate the walls and even paint a chimney-board to be put in the fireplace during the summer.

Eighteenth-century toys

The eighteenth century is above all the period of the fine English baby houses, some of which are so lavishly equipped as to be the province of adults. The finest carpenters and cabinet-makers combined to create the often complex models that are frequently an amalgam of all the specialist skills of the time, with fine silver miniatures and embroidered linen. Nostell Priory baby house, for instance, in Yorkshire, was probably designed by James Paine who also worked on the great house itself, upon which the façade of the baby house was loosely based. A baby house was a prized family possession and was sometimes taken with a girl when she married; one example of this is to be found in the case of Sarah Lethieullier, who originally owned that most elegant house now at Uppark, Sussex.

The excellently constructed door of an 18th-century Baby House that once belonged to the Gardener family. The door once locked and the panelling is correctly made. Height to cornice 32 cm. (12½ in.).

A cast-iron hob grate decorated with classical figures, dating from 1780. A correctly made miniature possibly intended for a doll's house. Height 17 cm. (6¾ in.).

A Georgian style, front-opening Baby House with a lock. English, *circa* 1810. Width 121 cm. (48 in.). (Bethnal Green Museum.)

Fortunately, both of these two excellent baby houses can still be viewed in the country houses that were their owners' homes. Quite apart from the fine craftsmanship of the furnishings, the variety of dolls available at the time can be seen to range from quite simply made carved wooden dolls to the most elegant of wax ladies, beautifully attired. Sometimes a type of doll more commonly associated with another period can be seen in a dated baby house, but in its correct setting it can be more precisely dated. The importance of such houses to collectors, therefore, cannot be over-emphasized.

Commercially produced houses of much simpler construction were also available in the eighteenth century, but actual examples are uncommon and they are known mainly from prints. Extremely cheap tin furnishings were imported from Germany and sheets of paper furniture for baby houses were made in Strasbourg, a town more usually associated with its vast output of model soldiers.

The kitchen of an 18th-century Baby House
showing the original dresser, grate and spit rack.
The pedlar doll, *circa* 1825, is unusually small. The
papier mâché maid dates from 1840. Width of room
38 cm. (15 in.).

A craftsman-made miniature bureau of oak veneered
with walnut and inlaid with boxwood. English, late
18th century. Height 23 cm. (9 in.). (Bethnal Green
Museum.)

The Knave of Clubs from a set of wood-block printed and hand-coloured court cards dating to 1709. A similar pack was printed by Hall & Son for George III. (Victoria and Albert Museum.)

A Strasbourg printer by the name of Seyfried (Alsace, of which Strasbourg was the garrison town, was a traditional printing area) occupies an important place in the development of the manufacture of printed toys. Seyfried originally published a series of small, well-engraved, finely coloured sheets to represent the uniforms of the Garde d'Honneur, and this venture was followed in 1766 by a set showing the mounted troops of the Régiment Orléans Cavalerie. The latter are thought to be the earliest Strasbourg engravings expressly designed for cutting. In 1786 Jean Frederic Striedbeck set up a factory in the town for the making of correctly dressed cardboard soldiers and these were eventually sold either plain or coloured.

The earliest German lead figures of soldiers also date from the eighteenth century. The basic elements of mass production became obvious in the work of Johann Gottfried Hilpert, a tinsmith's son, who initially made toys of genre subjects such as tradesmen and farm scenes. His early figures were of pure tin, which gave excellent detail but was soon replaced by lead alloys. Apart from the manufacture of miniature armies, such as the troops of Frederick the Great, the Hilpert family also made single figures such as 'Voltaire' or the 'Prince de Ligne', marked on the base 'J.G. Hilpert 1778'. The Hilperts marketed their soldiers in the chip or matchwood boxes obtained from Berchtesgaden that were also used by doll-makers and makers of toy villages and farm animals. They issued a catalogue so that specific items could be ordered by shopkeepers all over Europe.

There were far more children's toy shops in the western world by the end of the eighteenth century than ever before, and the success of the German merchants depended on an efficient marketing chain. One of the traditional areas for the manufacture of folk-type wooden toys was Oberammergau, and by the end of the century there were Oberammergau merchants in most countries. The skill of the painters there was well established and toymakers from other parts of Germany sent their unpainted wares to the town for decoration, to benefit from the characteristic Oberammergau technique of making the paint remain fresh and bright, qualities that can still be seen today in eighteenth-century examples.

Berchtesgaden is another area with a long toy-making tradition and the ivory-carvers of this part of Germany were highly famed. The agents' notes and sample-books of the seventeenth and eighteenth centuries record a large number of wooden toys and ornaments. Carl Martin Plümicke visited the agent Anton Wallner in 1791 and described some of the stock that was available, including birds on bellows, sedan chairs, bugles and trumpets, a donkey and a stag on wheels, a horse with a rider and a foal, as well as numerous other 'tinkle toys' and wooden figures.

The area of the Groden valley was involved in woodcarving from the sixteenth and seventeenth centuries but it was only in the second half of the eighteenth century that small Berchtesgaden-style toys began to appear. Some of the Sonneberg workers in the mid-eighteenth century experimented with a type of composition substance, but it soon deteriorated and it is difficult to assess the quantity manufactured as so few specimens have survived.

In the eighteenth century the use of cards as a vehicle of instruction continued to be popular. One typical example was the 'Nouveau Jeu d'Officiers', with each card showing a soldier in uniform, published in Geneva in 1774. The 'Geography of England and Wales, accurately delineated on fifty-two cards including the boundaries, extent, products, manufactures etc. of each county' was published by J. Wallis in 1799, while 'Events in the Reign of Queen Anne' showed 'The glorious victory at Hochstet whre ye French and Bavarians lost 40,000 men'.

Card-playing was such an accepted part of eighteenth-century life that even the furnishers of baby houses found it essential to supply miniature packs. The making of cards had become a skilled profession and card-makers' guilds had been established. The Germans' skill in wood-engraving gave them a great lead in the middle range of the market and a considerable number of types were printed by Andreas Benedictus Gobl, though the finest cards, for the use of nobles, were printed from copper plates. In England card-making was becoming heavily taxed and the game increasingly frowned upon, for family fortunes were sometimes lost in a matter of seconds. Few children benefited from this gradual aversion among adults however: a set of 'Various Employments' depicting and describing skills and crafts, published in Pennsylvania towards the end of the century, continued the relentless cramming of facts.

Dice-throwing table games such as 'The Royal Game of Goose' and 'The

The Knave of Hearts from an English 18th century pack. The Arum lily-like object held in the left hand was in earlier packs a truncheon. By 1830 this had become a feather. (Victoria and Albert Museum.)

Here take my hand and with it grasp my heart
Love leads the way from you I nere will part

Vain are their hopes who to Magicians go
Decrees of Fate and Destiny to know.—

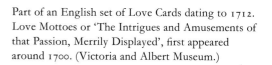

Part of an English set of Love Cards dating to 1712. Love Mottoes or 'The Intrigues and Amusements of that Passion, Merrily Displayed', first appeared around 1700. (Victoria and Albert Museum.)

The Game of Matrimony, also known as Pope Joan.
The central section has a decorated cover and the
board swivels on a stand. Late 18th century.
(Victoria and Albert Museum.)

'The New Game of Ladies Costumes and of Ladies
Hairdressing dedicated to the Beautiful Sex'. It was
intended mainly for adults and was played with dice
and counters. Because various ladies are so beautiful
the player remains ensnared for a turn. On
becoming 'A Little Mother' on 23 the player has to
return to the couturier at 5 for new clothes. *Circa*
1778. (Victoria and Albert Museum.)

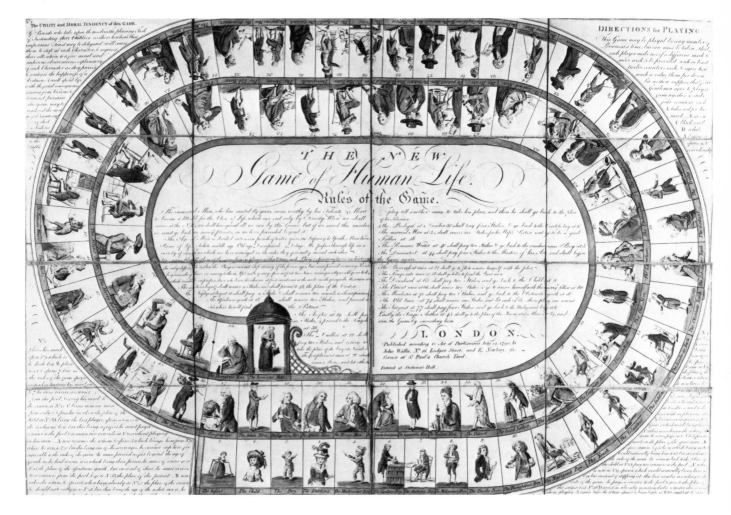

New and Most Pleasant Game of Snake', both published between 1680 and 1690, were originally intended for adult amusement. In order that the child should not fall into bad ways later in life through a too early familiarity with dice, a small spinning-top with flat sides, known as a totum or teetotum, was substituted in children's versions of such games. The first use of race games to inculcate morals is attributed to the Abbé Gaultier (1746–1818), a French *émigré* who ran a school in London and taught with the aid of his own type of geographical text-book, *The Abbé Gaultier's Complete Course of Geography by Means of Instructive Games*.

A similar game that was particularly devised for children was 'A Journey through Europe', published in 1759 by John Jeffreys and sold by Carrington Bowles from his shop in Saint Paul's Churchyard. In 1770 this game was followed by Thomas Jeffreys' 'Complete Tour Thro' England and Wales'. Though some of these games, especially the woodcuts of the early eighteenth century, have great appeal for adults of today, who find the strange information and moral strictures amusing, it is doubtful that they could have long engaged a child's attention. 'Bowles's European Geographical Amusement', with no pictures but just a map with printed columns, was even more dismal than average. By the end of the century, however, new standards of attractiveness were being set. Pictorial games were by this time usually water-coloured. It is these tinted games that are

'The New Game of Human Life' published by John Wallis, No. 16, Ludgate Street, and E. Newbery, according to the Act of Parliament 14 July 1790. A hand-coloured engraving mounted in sixteen sections on linen, it takes the form of a race played with counters and a dice or teetotum. Size 68 × 47 cm. (27 × 18¾ in.). (Victoria and Albert Museum.)

'The New and Favourite Game of Mother Goose and the Golden Egg'. Published on 30 November 1808 by John Wallis & Son, Warwick Square, London. The ancient origin of this game is lost but the first known English edition was published by H. Overton in 1750. Played with counters and teetotum. (Victoria and Albert Museum.)

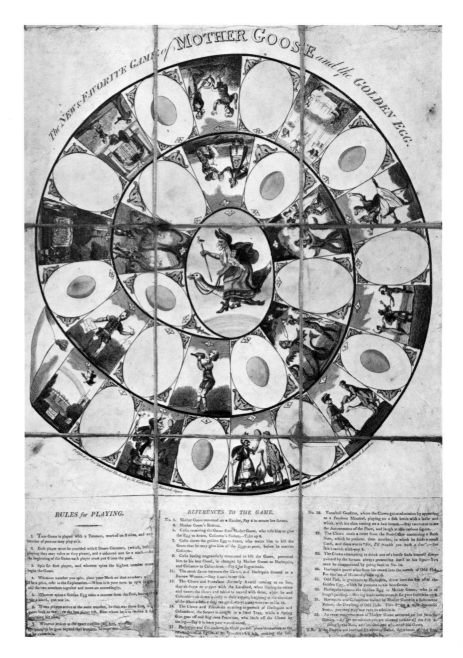

particular favourites of collectors, though many have suffered through being framed and hung in a harsh light.

Both table games and card games had originated as the pastimes of adults, but with the growing awareness of a child's educational needs in the eighteenth century, a completely new invention appeared—the dissected puzzle. It is generally considered that John Spilsbury, a cartographer and engraver by trade, was the inventor of this, for the 1763 edition of the *Universal Director* lists him as 'Engraver, and Map Dissector in wood, in order to facilitate the teaching of Geography. Russell Court, Drury Lane'. The paper maps were mounted on mahogany board, and one of Spilsbury's trade cards lists thirty different versions at various prices, including 'America in General', 'Ancient Geography' and 'Sweden and Norway'. The pieces were cut along county borders and some are extremely difficult to assemble. The cheapest were contained in chip boxes, while those that came in square wooden boxes were two shillings more expensive.

After the death of John Spilsbury, his widow continued to publish his maps. However, she was apparently not so interested in puzzles, and this side of her husband's business was acquired by Woodman and Mutlow by 1772. Other publishers swiftly pirated Spilsbury's idea. It was at this time mainly seen as a device for maps, such as that published in 1772 by Robert Sayer: 'Africa. Divided into its several regions and laid down accurately to the most exact observation'.

Engravings illustrating John Gilpin and published from 1785 were probably the first dissections intended purely for amusement, though popular broadsheets were also cut into puzzles of the lighter kind. 'Before and after Marriage', published by John Wallis, seemed tailored for a parent's sense of humour rather than a child's: depending on which way round it was viewed, one saw either a happy or a decidedly bad-tempered couple. Another series, containing 'Lessons for the Young and Old in Industry, Temperance, Frugality etc.', was published by Bowles and Carver and consisted of twenty-four scenes showing subjects such as 'The sleeping fox catches no poultry', drawn by the caricaturist and portrait-painter Robert Deight. Dissections with much larger pieces were especially made for younger children, such as William Darton's 'Miscellanies for the Instruction of Infants', published at the end of the eighteenth century and including pictures such as that of a ferocious dog near a house, accompanied by the lines, 'K for kennel. A kennel for a Dog to sleep in Is too Dirty for a Child to creep in.' More serious information, it was quickly seen, could also be imparted by the dissected puzzle, as in 'The Chronological Tables of English History for the Instruction of Youth', where details of each reign were supplied beneath the appropriate picture. William Darton had issued a similar dissection a little earlier, but that was so difficult to assemble and contained so much very boring information that it could have had little popularity with either adults or children. At this time the teaching of Christian morality took precedence over all other forms of instruction, even in puzzles, and among the ethical dissections of the 1790s were Wallis' 'Key to the Old Testament' and the same manufacturer's 'Pilgrim's Progress'.

After the continual inculcation of facts by such means, children must

'The Little Artist'. A pasteboard box and squares on which are line engravings. Inside the box are miniatures of each of the paintings on the squares. An early example of magnetism. When the box is placed over the squares the miniature replica appears on the easel. Austrian, *circa* 1775. Height 12 cm. (4¾ in.). (Bethnal Green Museum.)

A carved wooden doll that was found in the 1920s behind a wainscot in the Beehive Inn in Scarborough. Dated *circa* 1820. Height 33 cm (13 in.). (Collection Betty Harvey-Jones.)

Opposite right A carved wooden doll that belonged to Elizabeth Gordon, *née* Enderby, born 1792, and mother of Gordon of Khartoum, wearing the original costume and believed to be of Breton origin. The arms are jointed to the body with wire and it has brown glass eyes. A cockade was once worn in the hat. Height 25·5 cm. (10 in.). (Collection Betty Harvey-Jones.)

Opposite left An effective and gracefully carved oak-stump doll wearing the costume of the late 18th century. There is no evidence of this figure ever having been part of a piece of furniture; it was almost certainly a doll. Height 23 cm. (9 in.). (Collection Betty Harvey-Jones.)

have turned to their dolls with some relief. Many contemporary references indicate that dolls were enjoyed by small boys as well as girls. The majority, in both the seventeenth and eighteenth centuries, were made of turned and carved wood, though standards varied widely, from some with realistically shaped bodies and heads to others that were almost skittle-shaped with crudely made limbs. The few examples of papier mâché dolls which survive from the last quarter of the eighteenth century are interesting because they are so completely different, in both construction and feature, from those made in Germany in the early years of the following century. The difference is in fact so great that it seems probable that the earlier dolls were made in England, especially since some are found on jointed wooden bodies very similar to those seen on the English woodens of the period.

A very beautifully carved ivory doll with a black painted, tapered spot on the head, and a wire and fabric body with ivory lower arms and legs, wearing an open robe and petticoat of 18th century silk trimmed with gold thread and lace. Late 17th or early 18th century. Height 18 cm. (7 in.).

Typical wax dolls of the late 17th century, with painted features, costumed in silk and gold lace and assembled to represent the Virgin and Child, modelled to waist level in wax only and with paper underskirts. In their original paper-lined box-like frame. Size of frame 27 cm. (11 in.).

Dolls for baby houses were often made of wax, since it enabled the small features to be modelled with greater realism than in wood, and here again the variation in quality is large, ranging from very fine miniature portraits to simple round heads with small bead-like eyes.

There was some considerable export of dolls from Europe in the eighteenth century and the British government found it necessary to support the native industry by imposing taxes on imported dolls. American children at this time were forced to rely for their better toys on the English and German makers, though the quantity imported was not large. The Reverend John Higginson wrote in 1695 that toys might sell in New England if they were sent in small quantities. In 1713 there were already a few shops specializing in the sale of playthings, usually in addition to their main line of trade; William Price, for instance, who in 1743 offered English and Dutch toys for children, was primarily a seller of prints and maps. English, Dutch and German settlers all brought with them their native methods of toy manufacture and many toys that are considered to be early

American examples are almost indistinguishable, except sometimes by the wood, from European toys, especially those made in Germany. Charles Shipman, an ivory and hardwood turner 'lately of England' but now working in New York, listed among his products 'ivory counters engraved with the alphabet and figures, and cup and ball games'. In 1785 another immigrant Englishman, William Long, a cabinet-maker and carver, offered 'Rocking Horses in the neatest and best manner, to teach children to ride and to give them wholesome and pleasing exercise'.

The important American metal toy industry was also founded in the mid-eighteenth century, by men such as Edward Patterson, an Irishman who took his brothers and sisters with him to the new country and settled in Berlin, Connecticut, where they began to make simple tinware from imported tinplate. At first their wares were hawked from door to door but soon the possibilities of selling toys from a waggon as far afield as Canada were seen. Another early toy-maker was Henry Stiegel of Pennsylvania, who set up an iron foundry in 1758 and also owned a glass-works that produced some toy pieces.

With the exception of printed games and dissections very few eighteenth-century toys have makers' marks, and they are judged purely on their quality and attractiveness. Age is often scarcely taken into account when collectors value an item, and examples from this early period of collectable toys frequently fetch less at auction than a piece by a known maker dating from the late Victorian era.

'The Newly Invented Musical Game. By His Majesties Royal Letters Patent. Dedicated by Permission to H.R.H. Princess Charlotte of Wales'. The box is mahogany, with boxwood borders. It opens flat to represent a keyboard. The ivory and bone pieces are engraved with musical notation. English, *circa* 1801. Size 43 cm. (17 in.). (Bethnal Green Museum.)

The toy horse

Though hobby horses with formed bodies are usually associated with the 17th and 18th centuries, a few were made as late as the 1920s, as shown in this birthday card.

A group of 'Strong Toys' made by Hugo Roithner & Co. of Schweidnitz and advertised in *The Toy Trader* for January 1909. A rocking horse in the form of a chair for a very young child is included. (By courtesy of *The Toy Trader*.)

THE toy horse remained an essential part of a boy's life until the early twentieth century, and ranged in type from the huge craftsman-made examples that furnished the nurseries of country houses to the simple home-made hobby horses with woollen manes that were owned by the poorest children. In an age when it was necessary that adult skills should be learned in childhood, the young were encouraged to ride wooden steeds and play with mounted soldiers. 'The honourablest and most commendable games that ye can use are games on horseback,' wrote James I of England to his young son, and the degree of adult approval for these toys is evidenced by the large sums parents spent on them.

In addition to the mounted knights that were provided for table tournaments, there were also carousel tourneys in which two knights rode in a circle on hand-turned platforms and tilted at a ring suspended from a pole. Such figures appear in the early catalogues of Hieronymus Bestelmeier of Nuremberg, dating back to the late eighteenth century, and they were still sold in the Regency period, though by this time very outmoded.

Hobby horses

Although hobby horses were created in vast numbers from a very early period, only rarely have they survived, presumably because of their fragility. At the conclusion of the Thirty Years War in 1650, over a thousand small boys rode their hobby horses to the residence of the Duke Piccolomini and were given silver Peace Pennies decorated with hobby horses to commemorate the occasion. This type of toy remained the province of the poorer child, though better examples with realistically carved heads and well-shaped half-bodies are sometimes seen in prints. The very simple hobby horses were popular fairground gifts and were sometimes made more attractive by gilding and tinsel. The general standard, again judging from graphic representations, declined during the nineteenth century and the sole improvement seems to have been the addition of wheels to give a smoother ride. Walter Crane's illustration of the Lowther Arcade suggests the range of such horses available to the child of the 1870s, and it is obvious that the elegant prancing horse of the seventeenth century had degenerated into a variant of the cheap barrel type with a silhouette head crudely jointed

HUGO ROITHNER & CO.,

Manufacturers, SCHWEIDNITZ.

Best Finished WOODEN TOYS
Games, Swings, Chutes,
See-Saws, &c., &c.

Sample Show Room—
TOY HALL, 90, Goswell Road, London, E.C.

Telegrams—"To-morrow, London."
Telephone—9284 Central.

NEW SAMPLE COLLECTION READY JANUARY 20th, 1909.

A lithographed paper head mounted on wood, marked 'F. Carter. Patent', with a metal clip on the neck for fixing to pole. *Circa* 1900–1910. Height 33 cm. (13 in.). (Bethnal Green Museum.)

to the chest, while some hobby horses were merely heads attached to poles.

Realistic horses

Hobby horses required a considerable imaginative effort from their riders, but there were also more lifelike toy horses. The practice of making a toy realistic by a skin covering is of some antiquity. In 1591 a letter was sent from young Balthasar Paungartner asking that there be brought back for him from Frankfurt Fair a horse covered in goatskin. In return for this gift he promised to be 'a good boy'. Another reference to skin-covered horses occurs in 1674, when the woodcarver Matthias Schutz made up a bill for horses supplied to a German prince for the feast of St Nicholas and itemized twelve toy horses with proper skins.

Nuremberg cabinet houses are very rich sources of information on the development of the realistic horse, and in the Stromer House, made in 1637, there is a stable holding two well-carved horses and a cow, the black painted manes of the horses being rendered with great vigour. Similar, rather over-fed horses can be seen in another Nuremberg house dating to the end of the seventeenth century; here they are provided with a hay-box and correctly made grooming brushes. In the Kress house of the same period (now in the Germanisches Nationalmuseum, Nuremberg) the horses are given an exquisite fabric and leather saddle that is a most correct miniature. Model stables were popular toys throughout the eighteenth and nineteenth centuries and appear in many trade catalogues. The lithographed walls in late examples are highly decorative, and the horses were by this time often made of a substance such as Elastolin rather than wood. Some of the most decorative stables were created in America by the R. Bliss Manufacturing Company of Pawtucket, Rhode Island, established in 1832. This firm, which specialized in wooden novelties, toy tool-chests and lithographed toys, began to manufacture stables in 1895, and the firm's name was often printed over the stalls. The 1911 catalogue describes the stables as all-wood and lithographed in colour, and mentions that the horses were imported, in all probability from Germany. The buildings are brightly printed and often have turned wooden pillars, while the hay lofts have opening doors.

Considerable realism was often given in the nineteenth century to groups of horses to be mounted together on a wheeled platform. In a painting by Raffaele D'Auria, *The Six Youngest Children of Francesco 1*, dated 1831, there is a toy of this kind with one horse looking apprehensively back over its shoulder while the other rears up—an arrangement which must have created a very real problem of balance for the craftsman. The style of this model is typical of work produced by the Oberammergau craftsmen.

A Bliss stable, dated 1895–1907. Each wing has a double stall on the ground floor, and the upper storey is a hay-loft with hinged double doors. The stable has red and blue walls, a red roof and red interior. Height 39cm (15½in), width 65cm (25½in). (Margaret Woodbury Strong Museum.)

An early 19th-century carved elmwood horse of the most delicate construction with painted detail. Horses became much heavier in shape as the century progressed. Height 51 cm. (20 in.).

A painted wooden model of a horse-drawn bus. *Circa* 1820. The interior is decorated with prints and a royal coat-of-arms. The sides of the coach are marked 'Wonder' and it is pulled by carved wooden horses. Inside are seven Grödnertal-type passengers. It is contained in a wooden box inscribed Basil Robert Wood. (Christie's, South Kensington.)

A painted wooden coach from the Berchtesgaden area of Germany. 19th century. Length 28 cm. (11 in.). (Bethnal Green Museum.)

Another finely carved single specimen of the same period wore a richly embroidered blanket and the children who owned it had placed about its neck a rich garland of flowers. It is a characteristic of this period that a good horse was admired, almost adored: the desire of every provincial British child was to be taken to Astley's Circus in London and families competed for a 'spanking turn-out'. The English were highly respected for the quality of their equipages; and curricules, buggies, barouches and landaus were all copied as toys. Several stage-coaches survive from the early nineteenth century and are evocative of the time when young aristocrats gave up all to become coach-drivers and even filed down their teeth so they could spit through them like 'swell dragsmen'.

Many of the finest equipages were made by the German woodcarvers, particularly those in Berchtesgaden and Oberammergau. One catalogue of 1800 even mentions a surprisingly sophisticated wooden coach and two galloping horses driven by clockwork. The variety of horse-drawn transport made in just a single area can be seen at the Folk Museum at Oberammergau, where coaches and carts with typical peasant decoration in brilliant primary colours are displayed in profusion, together with carved figures in seated positions representing drivers and passengers. The local decorators seem to have favoured blue as the colour for coats, and some of the passengers have amusing characterization. The finest pieces in this museum are the large individual horses, some of which were never painted, so that the full skill of the craftsman can still be seen. One horse, with a finely carved mane, turns its head to stare, while another paws the ground restlessly. There is one particularly clever example standing with one foot lifted from the base and the neck arched down and bent to one side—surely one of the most exquisite wooden horses ever made. The

balance was maintained by the device of carving the horse against a tree-trunk and the whole figure stands on a wheeled base. Very large toys such as this one are only very occasionally seen in Britain, for they were probably far too large for export in quantity. Large camels, donkeys, elephants and wolves, all about 90 cm. (3 ft) high, were made by the same group of craftsmen, who appear to have been responsible for the fine pieces described above, while lesser-skilled workers, often at their kitchen tables, made the cruder coaches and waggons. The obvious difference in quality suggests that there were two different markets: clearly both peasants and princes were supplied by the Oberammergau craftsmen.

Early Russian toys exhibit nothing of this duality of standard, and surviving examples are of the simplest peasant type. A horse, for instance, would simply be cut in outline and then made attractive by gay decoration of flowers and leaves. As early as the ninth century, near the Volkhov river, there were households making wooden toys, though the industry did not expand until the seventeenth century when large quantities were carved around Moscow, as well as in Moscow itself at the Armoury. Horses, being such an essential part of life, were among the most popular subjects and range from some that appear to have been hewn from wood with great force and speed, so that an almost abstract quality is conveyed, to others, perhaps in the form of a coach and horses, which are so like the Bavarian work that confusion as to origin would seem inevitable. Much of the toy-making in Russia was concentrated around the monasteries, but it is often virtually impossible to know the exact origin of individual pieces. At the Troitse-Sergeyev monastery toys were both carved and painted, whereas in Bogorodskoye only carving was effected and the toys were taken elsewhere for decoration, so that a single toy can exhibit the work of two craftsmen.

When metal clockwork toys were widely introduced, the horses pulling the carriages continued for some time to be made of wood, presumably because it was so much more realistic than pressed metal.

A well-preserved model of a stage-coach in the Bethnal Green Museum, London, dated around 1840, is made very substantially out of half-inch timber, and is occupied by several dolls with their labelled trunks on the roof. Other examples have survived intact even to the luggage, and it is possible that the child owners treated their toy coaches with the same reverence that caused adults of the period to leave their carriages at home when they visited Brighton, lest the sea air should damage their appearance.

The small horses carved in England in the nineteenth century specially intended for pulling carts and carriages were known as 'White Mice' by the men who made them. The English toy-makes were far less concerned than the Germans about scale, and their horses are often found harnessed to vehicles of quite disproportionate size. The variety of vehicles pulled, however, is large, for the nineteenth-century increase in service traffic was reflected by the replacement of the rural or military toys of the eighteenth century by milk floats, water and coal carts, mail vans and horse-drawn

A push-along wooden horse with metal wheels and a turned wooden handle. *Circa* 1905. Marked on plaque 'Hamleys 200–202 Regent Street'. Height 56 cm. (22 in.).

trams. Large toys of this type were often made in the country of sale as they were so costly to import.

One of the most respected British makers was Patterson Edwards, Wood Toy Manufacturers, of the Old Kent Road, London, who in 1908 advertised horses and carts, gig horses, pole horses, pram horses, galloping horse gigs, express carts, pole carts, beech horses and hobby horses, a list that gives some idea of the variety of models that was necessary at the time. The beech horses stood on wheeled stands and were of the simple barrel type with the heads cut in outline and the decoration consisting mainly of applied strips of paper. The horses and carts were much more substantial and the milk floats made in correct detail.

A visitor to the Patterson Edwards factory in February 1909 commented in *The Toy Trader* that 'The average wood toy takes a month to produce on the system employed in this factory', and went on to explain that the making of toys was completely different from any other sort of trade because from commencement to finish the methods employed in each factory were entirely original. Toy-makers entered the factory as boys, learned a particular branch of the business and were then almost forced to stay with the firm, for their knowledge would be of little use elsewhere in the toy trade.

Another British firm which was a large producer of what were described in the trade as 'Strong Toys' was the Midland Tent and Strong Toy Company of Birmingham, who offered a very similar range to that of Patterson Edwards but also showed an engaging horse on wheels that

A horse-drawn water cart of carved wood painted in red and blue. Late 19th century, British. Length 61 cm. (24 in.). (Bethnal Green Museum.)

A skin-covered pull-along horse with metal wheels. *Circa* 1880. Height 29 cm. (11½ in.).

A pull-along skin-covered pony with a farm cart that has a removable back board. *Circa* 1875. Length 76 cm. (30 in.).

pulled a steam train. Charles Morell in 1896 were offering skin-covered horses in a stable with loose box, carriage, fittings and clothes for the driver—an expensive toy that was also available in cheaper versions.

The esteem in which English-made horses were held in America is indicated by the fact that one of the earliest makers of these toys in the New World, William Long, described himself prominently as a 'cabinet-maker and carver from London'. In general, the settlers in the new country were too busy to manufacture toys on a large commercial scale such as was possible in Germany, though there was naturally some small local manufacture of both rocking and hobby horses. There were also travelling toy-makers, usually of German origin, who carved simple animals on the spot for their young customers. There were specialist toy shops in America from 1713, but they were mainly stocked from European sources. Even when Henry Schwartz opened his Baltimore toy shop in 1849, he was at first forced to rely on foreign imports of the larger craftsman-made toys, although the market was soon supplemented with inventively constructed horses made by such men as Jesse Crandall.

Fine model stables with their accessories were made in Sonneberg in the early twentieth century by Louis Lindner and Sons, who could provide 'skin-covered animals, large and miniature'. Another German producer was F. Graeffer of Schleiz, who advertised 'Wood, skin and plush rocking horses and horses on wheels. Novelty pasteboard horses (compressed pasteboard, feather-light, very durable and unbreakable, elegant shapes)'. Erste Schweizerische und Spielwarenfabrik of Langenthal in Switzerland made 'Papier mâché stable animals, wild animals of all descriptions and carts of all kinds', as well as special fur, imitation fur and varnished rolling and rocking horses. This company, like several of the British firms, could supply life-size show horses that were used as window exhibits by both tailors' shops and toy-sellers.

Rocking horses and velocipedes

Of all the various types of toy horse, the rocking horse is the most loved, though in a child's feelings towards the larger versions affection was often combined with awe. Diana Holman Hunt (in *My Grandmother and I*, London, 1905) remembered her encounter with her father's old rocking horse that was kept in an attic: 'When my torch caught him in its beam, I was shocked by his evil expression. His ferocious upper lip snarled and twisted over huge chipped yellow teeth. His nostrils were red and flared.' Posed imperiously on their curved rockers, many horses do exude quite an aggressive air, and probably taught the small child something of the respect he would later need in dealing with a living horse. In some families the rocking horse was an essential companion; thus we read of Queen Victoria's children insisting on taking their skin-covered rocker with them on each trip to Osborne House, the royal residence on the Isle of Wight.

A few seventeenth-century rocking horses have survived, though in a somewhat battered shape. There are no references to rocking horses before this date. The early method of construction involved attaching two boat-shaped planks to either side of the lower half of a horse's body. In an

A strongly-carved horse on curved rockers. Early 19th century. Complete width 215 cm. (85 in.). (Bethnal Green Museum.)

A boy's Christmas presents painted by an unknown Viennese artist in the early 19th century. The rocking horse in the foreground has the early type of board sides. The well-made carriage was obviously sold without a matching horse. (Germanisches Nationalmuseum, Nuremberg.)

example reputed to have belonged to Charles I the complete body is raised from the boat-shaped base and provided with a seat, while the lower body and legs are painted on the base's solid sides. Several early horses are known with traces of this type of design still visible on the base, and there is even one that is further decorated with a painting of two standing children. The finest examples were given most realistically carved heads, with a great deal of care lavished on the representation of a luxurious mane, and padded leather-covered seats. For very small riders a foot-rest was sometimes provided on the shoulder, though in contemporary prints the horses, even when ridden by young children, are usually seen with the riders seated cowboy-style with dangling legs. A wooden horse that was made in this manner (now in the London Museum) has a gun-holster for the rider. The means of construction used in these examples was obviously the simplest, as it avoided the difficulties of carving horse's legs, which would have had to be thin but extremely strong. It was a method that, because of its practicality, continued to be used occasionally in the nineteenth century for cheaper horses. In the small nursery of the Stromer doll's house in the Germanisches Museum, Nuremberg, is a delightful miniature horse made in this way, and because it has been contained in what is virtually a cabinet, it is in much better condition than any others that have survived. It is painted dapple-grey and has a painted mane but a horsehair tail, and the legs are painted in outline on the green, solid, boat-shaped sides.

A few horses with legs carved in the round date from the seventeenth century, such as the fine example purchased by the Duke of Bedford, a horse which is carved with as much sensitivity as is seen in the best Oberammergau examples. This horse is of great interest as it gives a good indication of what the best-quality toys of the period were like. It is carved almost more like a model than a toy, with two legs raised from the base, and is mounted on a platform standing on curved rockers. At some stage a metal support was added to relieve the strain on the cleverly balanced construction.

The standing horse on slender carved rockers was the natural development from the horse with painted sides; it was only necessary to cut away the section between front and back legs for an embryonic standing horse to emerge. Collectors once thought that the earliest examples of this type stood with their hoofs attached to the very ends of the curved rockers, but prints of children at play show some horses that were fixed with their legs on a central platform or stretched half-way along the length of the rockers. Almost all the horses in eighteenth-century illustrations are equipped with stirrups, so that a small child could accustom himself to the riding position. One of the few recorded makers is William Gabriel, Rocking Horse Maker of Goswell Street, recorded in the Heal Collection of London trade-cards and working in 1784. Most eighteenth-century examples are elegantly made, though there were a few of the barrel-type construction. By the Regency period the rockers had become much heavier and often ended in a flamboyant decorative swirl. Manes and tails of English and American horses were by this time almost invariably made of hair, which looked more realistic to a child and was cheaper than carving. The saddle was still frequently non-detachable, with the leather merely nailed in place, a type of construction that Maria Edgeworth thought most unsuitable, since the child could learn little from such a toy. She would have found the work of the German woodcarvers much more satisfactory, as the horses were more frequently made so that real saddles could be used. A number of miniature rocking horses were made for export at both Oberammergau and Berchtesgaden, and these stood from 13 to 15 cm. high (5 to 6 in.), some being of the early plank type with carved tails. In one example a construction of this kind stands on a box-like base. A variety of

Good-quality skin-covered rocking horses were an indispensable piece of equipment in a Victorian photographer's studio. Quite poor children, who could never have owned such toys, are frequently posed with them. This photograph from a family album of the 1890s. (Bethnall Green Museum.)

larger horse seen only in Oberammergau stands on curved rockers which turn suddenly upwards in the middle to give the body of the horse extra support.

The development of the toy horse in America is particularly associated with the work of Benjamin Crandall, who is believed to have examined a rough wooden model originating in Germany and decided that he could produce much better horses for American children. At first stuffed skin-covered horses were made, but these were soon abandoned in favour of carved wood. Crandall showed great ingenuity in the designing of different types, and produced oscillating, leaping and spring horses among other sorts. To capitalize on the popularity of the leader of the 'Rough Riders' in the Spanish-American war, a model called 'Teddy's Horse' was made. Jesse Crandall, working for the same firm, often found that very young children fell off the conventional rockers, so he patented a design in 1859 with two horse-shaped boards with a seat safely sunk between them, a model that later became known as a 'Shoo-fly' and was the most typically American style of rocker. It was this firm that made the finest velocipedes and won the gold medal at the Philadelphia Exhibition of 1876. All sorts of variations on the velocipede design were made, including a 'Cantering Tricycle' that moved up and down. Another American toy-maker, Schwartz, advertised in its catalogue in 1878 a rocker upholstered in enamel cloth; this fine steed was known as 'Pegasus' and sported the necessary splendid wings.

An unusual nineteenth-century invention was a horse that stood on springs concealed in a coffer-like stand and could move up and down as well as swing back and forth. Another rather strange variation of the basic rocker, with a vigorous trotting action that was presumably intended to develop the child's muscles was made by R. F. and W. Kendrick of Loughborough, Leicestershire. This horse was rather like a scooter in form and was made to be pushed along by an older child or an adult. The child sat on a plank-like seat that was attached to a bellows at the front. The horse's head was just in front of the seat and there was a handle for the child to hold. As the toy was pushed along, the rider was bounced about by his own action on the bellows in the manner of a slow trot. The firm was so proud of this rational toy that its name was displayed on a white plaque at the front. Few manufacturers bothered to mark toys of this type, and the rare marks that are found are often printed on circles of tin that have rusted too much to be read.

Velocipede horses first made their appearance in the mid-nineteenth century, the best-known being the finely decorated example that once belonged to the Prince Imperial of France. Earlier versions have very slim bodies that are not always well shaped and frequently have a rather mean appearance. A few, dating from the 1860s, have extremely attractive decorative cast iron work and the horses are often skin-covered. Early wheels were often of wood bound with a metal tread, but these were generally replaced in the 1860s by metal wheels with spokes of the same material. As the century progressed the construction became much heavier, and the velocipedes made in the Edwardian period have squat, plump bodies. Early models were propelled by handles fixed to the head and were

A carved wooden velocipede of the tricycle type with handlebar steering. *Circa* 1895–1900. Height 86 cm. (34 in.).

ANTIQUE TOYS AND DOLLS

steered by the feet, but by the early twentieth century the standard tricycle construction was usual. The Star Manufacturing Company of Davis Street, London, made tricycle horses with rubber-tyred wheels and fine carving, as well as a cheaper version that was just as robust but not so well carved. Patterson Edwards also included velocipedes in their range, and theirs were quite magnificent, with padded saddles and very realistically carved bodies. The records of the Patent Office abound with various improvements to the basic design of the velocipede, although few of these were put into practice commercially.

Some of the finest British horses and horse-drawn vehicles were made by George and Joseph Lines, whose factory was the largest in the country. A few of the Lines horses still carry their original mark, which incorporated a thistle, while the many toy milk-floats with the words 'Thistle Farm' on the side also originated at this factory. Pieces marked 'G. & J. Lines' can be dated as pre-1933, although the Lines brothers themselves broke away from their parent company in 1919, and their 'Triang' mark is still used today. An astonishing range of sizes and types of horses was made, and interestingly, the firm also carved fairground horses. The sign over their factory in the Caledonian Road read 'Velocipede Horses, Rocking Horses. Also horses for fairs and steam circuses and life-sized show horses'. In 1895 they were still producing 'old style' curved rockers, some as long as 226 cm. (89 in.). At the Lines factory the head and body of the horse would be carved in yellow pine and the legs in beech for strength. During the summer months the bodies were assembled and undercoated, then painted, dappled and fitted with harness, and finally attached to rockers just before Christmas. Better quality stands were polished but the cheaper ones were brightly painted.

Spring or safety rockers are mentioned as early as the 1870s, though the majority of those constructed in this way date after 1900. Lines continued to produce old-style horses on curved rockers, such as those offered by the London store Gamage's in their 1913 catalogue; among these was the 'Scots Greys Rocking Horse', with detachable cavalry harness, shoe-cases, valise, holsters, martingale, saddle cloth and military bridle, standing nearly 150 cm. (5 ft) high.

However, from this time it was spring horses that were most popular. One of the most amusing pre-First World War horses made by Lines was the 'Wobbling Goblin, where by an arrangement of springs, the little rider imparts a natural trotting motion'. The well-carved head was set into an ottoman-shaped base that was both padded and fringed, with wheels at floor level. At the same time Lines were still making velocipedes with iron wheels alongside the modern rubber-tyred versions. A most complex toy of this period was their 'Galloping Gig', propelled by pedals and chain and with horses that appeared to trot as the toy moved along. Push handles were supplied for this to enable someone to take over if the child became too tired. Earlier versions of this toy, without the pedals, were intended to be used purely as push chairs.

A fabric-covered horse with metal lugs through the body so it could be suspended from ropes. Such horses were popular in the early 20th century. Length 86 cm. (34 in.).

A very realistic carved wooden skin-covered horse that was converted from a rocker to a pull-along by the removal of screws. *Circa* 1880. Height 75 cm. (29½ in.).

Opposite top A tin tram with porcelain-headed passengers. A simple but effective pull-along toy probably of German origin. The tin horses are dappled and the tram is painted red, yellow and green. Length 41 cm. (16 in.). (Collection Betty Harvey-Jones.)

Opposite bottom An attractively coloured 'penny toy' of the type that was hawked on city pavements. The cab is green and black and the horse is dappled. Unmarked. *Circa* 1900. Length 11·5 cm. (4½ in.).

In 1908 the Crown Prince of Germany was impressed by a dirigible rocking horse that had been invented by a Berlin photographer and he bought it for his eldest son, Prince William, as a Christmas present. Four wheels were attached to the rocking horse and these ran on rails laid down in the room. By means of the rocking action the horse was set in motion and could be directed along the rails at 'the whim of the young horseman'. The firm of Steiff made a particularly effective wheeled horse in the first decade of the twentieth century that was covered with a skin of silky plush and supplied with a saddle and stirrups. Of added interest was its steering apparatus, controlled by a ring protruding from the horse's neck, so that steering was a little like that on a bicycle.

Horses in tin

Tin began to assume importance as a toy-making material for mass production early in the nineteenth century and model horses were quick favourites. The makers of tin flats in the eighteenth century had created a number of scenes and situations in which the horse was the most important creature, such as the 'Boar Hunt' made by the Hilperts of Nuremberg in 1770 that showed typically stylized horses. Johann Friedrich Ramm of Lüneberg made a number of hunting scenes and menageries, while horse-drawn transport was a speciality of Georg Spenkuch of Nuremberg. The early tin fire-engines were, of course, horse-drawn and some continued to be made in this way until 1920. The amazing variety of late nineteenth-century horse-drawn transport can be witnessed in the London Museum's famous collection of 'penny toys', most of which originated in France and Germany, though some were made in England, in particular by the Reka Company of Wimbourne Street, London, whose penny metal toys and novelties included delivery vans and donkeys as well as their better-known model soldiers.

Ludgate Hill was the particular centre of the 'penny toy' trade, and the shopkeepers here resented competition from vendors who sold from the pavements. A report in *The Toy Trader* for 1908 commented: 'Now again

A group of mid-19th century Nuremberg flats. Height 4 cm. (1¾ in.).

that Christmas is at hand, Ludgate Hill again has asserted itself as the happy hunting ground of the itinerant toy vendor and though the number is reduced, there still remains a small army of these toy sellers. Their prices average one penny each and for a shilling one can purchase quite an interesting collection of novelties. These include miniature rocking horses, gollywogs and other mechanical devices too numerous to name.' Thousands of customers came to Ludgate Hill from all parts of London, and it was not an unusual sight to see a messenger with a large sack start from the top of the hill and buy items from each vendor in turn, presumably for use on Christmas trees. The traditional supplier of these so called 'penny toys' (that sometimes cost considerably more than a single penny) was J. W. Lawrence of 112 Houndsditch, who always maintained a huge selection.

The successors of these cheap toys were the metal figures made by William Britain, who included vast numbers of horse-drawn transport as well as mounted soldiers among his toys. The figures are almost invariably well made and painted, and the hunting scenes were particularly decorative.

William Britain's Hunting series 'The Meet No 234'. The horses and dogs are marked but the figures in this boxed set are not. It is very colourfully painted. *Circa* 1947.

Opposite top 'Tally Ho', a group of hounds and huntsmen from William Britain's Hunting Series. *Circa* 1930.

Opposite bottom 'Penny toys': some copied contemporary transport as in this limousine with a flywheel mechanism painted in red and yellow and with a blue running-board. *Circa* 1905. Length 7·5 cm. (3 in.).

Tin toys

'The Brookland': a tin motorist on a tilting circular track. Key-wound at base. The car is red and the driver wears a blue uniform. *Circa* 1905–1910. Height 18 cm. (7 in.).

WOOD was an excellent material for the manufacture of strong toys that could withstand the rough play of several generations, but as changes in the adult world, especially in the area of transport, began to occur more quickly, a child became more and more unlikely to want the toy that had pleased his father. Even children living in country districts soon became aware of new vehicles on the roads and railways. Metal became a much more suitable material for making accurate models, since advertisements, coach-lining and the costumes of passengers were much easier to print on a smooth surface. In early tin models of the mid-nineteenth century there is sometimes a mixture of wood and metal, but toys made completely of metal appeared on the market in quantity from about 1880 onwards.

The earliest toys of pressed tin were made in the Nuremberg area and frequently took the form of model kitchenware, a product with which the region is particularly associated. The Hilperts, who worked in the town since 1775, made toy coaches and tin fairground scenes, as well as the soldiers for which they are most famed (see page 204). The town attracted toy-makers because of the workers' low wages and the number of skilled clock-makers, whose techniques could be diverted into the construction of mechanical toys. The making of wooden toys with simple mechanisms was

Rachet-driven tin dog that rolls along on concealed wheels while the paws move up and down. *Circa* 1880. Length 20 cm. (8 in.). (Collection Betty Harvey-Jones.)

A pull-along copper and brass train whose detailed construction would suggest live steam but there are no working parts. *Circa* 1880. Length 46 cm. (18 in.).

traditional here and it was a logical progression to manufacture good tin models. The Germans were able to produce toys so cheaply that at first the British and Americans hardly bothered to compete; the standardization of parts, the use of basic mass-production techniques and the careful use of every scrap of tinplate ensured the maintenance of a German monopoly.

In most countries the duty on mechanical toys was levied on weight, which meant that although American makers created excellent iron toys they would not have been viable on the world market. Taxation on weight is one of the reasons why so many tinplate toys are fragile and rely for much of their appeal on the surface decoration, which at first was painted or stencilled. Improvements in lithographic techniques in the last quarter of the nineteenth century enabled the manufacturers to decorate even the cheapest of toys with an abundance of colour. The new technique also meant that individual batches could be decorated to suit the importers and carry slogans and advertisements appropriate to that country.

Nuremberg was truly the toy centre of the world in the nineteenth and early twentieth centuries, the principal output consisting of metal toys of infinite variety, the commonest being tin soldiers, toy engines and boats. In 1908 12,000 people were employed in toy-making at Nuremberg and Fürth, about one half of this number being women and girls, whose wage

The 'Flip-Flap' fairground machine. The toy is key-wound so that the cars touch the ground on either side of the central tower. In the cars sit figures of well-dressed gentlemen. On the yellow base is a stick-on label reading, 'Moko. Made in Germany for Moses Kohnstam & Co. of Fürth'. *Circa* 1907. In 1908 a new 'Flip-Flap' worked by a Dynamolith was introduced. Height 33 cm. (13 in.).

was only half that of the men. The majority were employed in large factories such as that owned by Bing, but there were also hundreds of concerns employing from half a dozen to a hundred persons and it was not unusual to find factories in which, besides the proprietor and his wife and children, only two or three extra men were employed. 'The workshops, with their so-called trade secrets, are generally very strictly guarded and it is a very difficult matter to gain admission,' wrote the States Consul at Nuremberg (*The Toy Trader,* November 1909). One third of the entire production went to the U.S.A., but 'With the exception of the largest three factories, none of the Nuremberg factories exports directly to the United States or to any other country. The entire export business is in the hands of commission merchants, who buy for their customers, pay for the goods, attend to packaging and shipping and assume all risks of collection.' Though we now connect the German toy industry with well-made toys, an irate report from the Leipzig fair in 1909 complained about the number of clockwork mechanical toys that failed to operate, 'either through faulty construction or being badly fixed up. In one showroom over eighty per cent of the pieces shown could not be made to work.' (*The Toy Trader*, March 1909)

The German toy industry, by the early twentieth century, was very dependent upon the U.S.A. and depressions in that country rapidly caused German factories to close temporarily, or at least workmen to be dismissed. The value of toys imported into America from Germany in 1908 was $7,250,000 while far down the scale, France was the next largest importer with only $180,472 in the same year. There are continual reports in the trade magazines of the period of the difficult times encountered by the Germans because of the fluctuations in American demand.

The importance of presentation was fully realized and splendid exhibition pieces were staged at all the trade fairs. In Berlin in 1908 the

Warenhaus Tietz of Nuremberg installed a complete metal toy factory in their toy department, where six metal-stamping and -pressing machines, worked by electricity, produced composite parts for the so-called 'Tietz Toy Motor'. 'The attending work-girls simply turn a crank and one sees the metal body, wheels, etc., cut out and assembled and the motor given a trial run.' A great deal of effort was also put into innovations in order to keep ahead of the market. In 1908 novelties in the production of the Nuremberg and Fürth manufacturers included Zeppelin airships, flying birds and a cats' band where cats drummed and played the clarinet and trumpet, the sounds being produced by a musical box in the base.

The process of making tin toys was often lengthy, and the lacquered goods often took from seven to ten days for the complete finishing of the operation. In the early twentieth century time was saved by placing the toys in electrically heated drying chambers, where they were made perfectly hard in eight hours.

With the introduction of tin toys, another area of Germany had moved to the forefront as a manufacturer. The rise of Württemberg occurred not from any proximity of materials but purely, it is thought, because factory owners were aware of the hard-working temperament of the Swabians. The founding of the German Empire in 1871 and the final granting of free trade, as well as the rapid growth of the German railway system, all encouraged the manufacturers to increase their output. There are no towns especially associated with toy-making in this region, and products are famed because of their brand-names rather than their town of origin. The output was sold direct to retailers, and the fashion for this form of direct marketing, used to very great advantage by Bing, had begun here.

One of the most important companies to emerge in this part of Germany was the famous firm of Märklin, which began production, as makers of miniature kitchenware, in 1859. Caroline Märklin, wife of the founder Theodor Friedrich Wilhelm (1817-1866), helped to organize sales and travelled widely across South Germany and Switzerland—one of the first recorded female sales representatives. Despite the efforts she made after her husband's death, it was left to their two sons Eugen and Karl to set the business on the way to success. In 1888 they changed the firm's name to Gebrüder Märklin and by this time they were producing simple carts, boats and 'Russian wheels' (a variety of the ferris wheel) in addition to the toy kitchenware. Their model clockwork railway, introduced in 1891, that ran on a figure-of-eight shaped track was revolutionary, as other firms had previously made only pull-along carpet trains or 'floor runners'. The Märklin train could be extended by further lengths of rail and this development was the beginnings of the vast toy railway systems that filled so many Edwardian homes.

The success of the Märklin brothers was so great that they felt it necessary to move to larger premises in Markerstrasse, Goppingen, and there was another move only five years later to even bigger premises that are still the nucleus of the firm today. In 1892 Emil Fritz came into the business, and after this date the firm was known as Gebrüder Märklin and Co. Their early catalogues show attractively coloured carpet trains with wire wheels, some of them running on circular tracks, as well as a vast number of horses and traps. There were also many boats, one in a *chinoiserie* style with a Mandarin sitting under a canopy. The variety of horse-drawn transport was at first very great and included trams, water carts and a number of carriages. Some of the more splendid coaches were given silk-padded seats, though in most the seats were of pressed tin. One of the more amusing Märklin toys was a model of a boy with a whip and toy horses attached to a belt at his waist, a toy that was popular in a child-sized version. Farm carts, model factories, fire-fighting teams, push-along wheels containing bells, and even small trotting horses, were all made in brightly decorated tin. After 1895 there was a vast increase in the number of trains and trams produced. Among the early rolling stock were animal waggons, tilting sand waggons, double waggons for wood, and beer waggons. Line-keepers' houses with barriers and signalling apparatus were also offered by 1895. Much of the Märklin work shows more restraint than that made by Bing, their powerful Nuremberg rivals, though in the creation of their splendid railway stations Märklin lavished just as much care as Bing. The toy museum at Nuremberg has a particularly fine example of a Märklin train; this model, an 0-2-2, was made in imitation of a train of the 1870s but was actually produced in 1898, a discrepancy that shows how difficult it is to date toy trains purely by appearance. Among the superb displays of working models at the 1909 Leipzig fair, that of Märklin was generally considered the most splendid, as we learn from the *The Toy Trader* (March 1909):

> New locomotives, in clockwork and for steam and electricity were there shown in almost innumerable quantities and in a bewildering range of sizes and qualities. To show how up to date the firm keeps things in this department we noticed models of the very latest engine recently produced in England, exact to scale and finished in correct colours. Their trains vary from the very cheapest to models of luxury, suitable for putting under a glass case and presenting as a triumph of the model maker's art.

Märklin's railway equipment became more complex in order to compete with the other German companies and some of their complete landscape settings, with a predictable castle on a hill and a tunnel running through it, are highly decorative. One setting had a town at the foot of the hill with a park containing a bandstand and a fountain, as well as the station. Figures for peopling the stations, some made of papier mâché, were sold separately. Steam-driven toys also appeared in profusion and Märklin's steam-powered water-mill, containing water-wheel, sandbags, two pools of water and several magnetic figures, was complex even for a firm that specialized in such exercises. Some of their windmills and water-mills were completely open so that the interiors could be seen with all the equipment in operation.

Märklin fire-stations were very well equipped and sometimes included a

A Stuart open tourer of heavy tinplate made by
Märklin, *circa* 1908. (Bethnal Green Museum.)

practice jumping-tower with a group of firemen at the bottom holding a
blanket. The first sheet metal cars seem to have appeared simultaneously
with those of Bing, in 1904, and though often lighter in construction they
were perhaps more attractive on account of their decoration. The firm
again changed its name in 1907, this time to Gebrüder Märklin et Cie, the
name it still carries today. In 1909 flying machines were produced, among
them a new model that was suspended from an overhead track and executed
several different manoeuvres in mid-air. An especially fine toy for
Märklin's later period (now in the toy museum at Nuremberg) is a double-
cylinder fairground engine made in 1926 and pulled by two wooden cart-
horses—an interesting feature, since horses of pressed tin would have been
more usual at that time.

The Nuremberg firm whose products are among the most popular with
collectors is that of the brothers Ignaz and Adolf Bing, who established a
company in 1865 to manufacture kitchenware and, later, toys. Ignaz had
worked as a traveller in tinware and being aware of the potential market for
this product he decided with his brother, who also lived in Nuremberg, to
establish a company to supply the immediate area. The Bings' first works
was at Karolinenstrasse, and the name of the firm at this time was
Nürnberger Spielwarenfabrik Gebrüder Bing (Bing Brothers' Nuremberg
Toy Factory). In the early 1890s other finishing workshops were opened, as
well as a factory for the manufacture of enamelled toys at Grünhain in
Saxony, though the warehouses and administrative offices were united in
one building in Nuremberg. In the opinion of the surviving members of
the family, it was this centralization, together with the family flair for
business administration, that was responsible for the Bings' great success in
the early years of this century.

In 1895 the firm became a limited company with Ignaz as chairman of the
board, and it was now known as Nürnberger Metall- und Lackierwarenfab-
rik vorm. Bing A.G. (Nuremberg Metal and Enamelware Works). The
firm was among the first in Germany to recognize the importance of good

Opposite Toy gramophones. The round example decorated in yellow and green has a good quality motor for a toy and plays 6 inch records. The Pigmyphone carries the Bing Werke trade mark and the British patent No. 221734. It is key-wound through the turntable and has a two speed motor. The lid of the box is brightly decorated with birds, children and notes. Both *circa* 1930. Pigmyphone box 15 cm. sq. (6 in. sq.).

Opposite 'Bingola II' with the Bing Werke trade mark and 'Made in Germany', coloured in red, gold and cream. It has infinitely variable speed up to 78 rpm. Art Deco styling seldom influenced children's toys to this extent. Length 26 cm. (10 in.).

worker-management relationships, and there were trades-union representatives in all their factories. According to contemporary trade magazines, groups studying methods of business efficiency in the early twentieth century regularly visited this concern. The brothers themselves were not in any way involved in the actual design of the toys and their interest was purely in the administrative side of the business.

The firm complemented the skill and inventiveness of its designers with a willingness to experiment with the new ideas that were often suggested by shop-floor employees. *The Toy Trader* (January 1909) commented: 'Let any visitor pick up any article he may come across and he will find that, irrespective of price, the finish, style and workmanship are, in every individual case, perfect; there is something in the construction, appearance and finish of their products which places Messrs Bings' goods on the highest pinnacle of excellence.' At this time 4,000 full-time workers were employed. The Bings had won the highest honours at exhibitions, such as that in Nuremberg in 1882, Barcelona in 1888, Chicago in 1893 and the World Exhibition at Paris in 1900, and in recognition of the firm's achievement Ignaz Bing was nominated Councillor of Commerce by the Bavarian government.

The firm's export success—it was their boast that their toys could be bought anywhere in the civilized world from the Sudan to Alaska—was mainly dependent on the huge warehouses set up in various countries, so that products did not rely for sales upon general warehousemen. Their first London warehouse was at Chiswell Street, but this quickly became too small and they moved to Ropemaker Street. Each room in the Ropemaker Street warehouse was divided into aisles and in one a huge display of clockwork locomotives was set out with rolling-stock of all descriptions. Lines, crossings and switches were all neatly packaged in boxes, so that the retailer could conveniently stock his shelves with Bing toys just as they came from the warehouse. As many toys at this time were still sold loose, this type of packaging was much appreciated. One department of the warehouse was devoted purely to repairs, and even tiny cogs could be supplied from stock for any damaged piece. Only retailers could visit the warehouses and catalogues were also restricted to shopkeepers, which is why it is virtually impossible to locate specific editions. In the warehouse there was also a department dealing with designs made to the specification of firms requiring promotional or gift-type items. In a large tank, battleships, torpedo boats and submarines could be seen manoeuvring.

The earliest Bing toys are the most decorative of their output and there is a noticeable simplification after 1900. However, some of their key-wound figures, such as dancing bears, organ-grinders, negroes, and ferris wheels with musical boxes in the bases, continued to be made very much in the nineteenth-century style. A number of complete scenes, such as a military band marching against a background showing a mountain landscape with a fort in the distance, were key-wound.

The firm's battleships, though functional, were at first given ornamental

scrolling on the prow, but this detail is not seen in catalogues after 1912. Finest-quality tin boats were sold in cardboard presentation boxes with a seascape background, so that on lowering the front flap of the box the child saw his new toy perfectly displayed. One of the more interesting 1906 battleships was given a torpedo door in the hull through which actual torpedoes could be fired. Names such as 'Moltke' and 'Wilhelm' were painted on the boats intended for home sale, but boats for Britain and America were given names appropriate to those countries. By 1912 a considerable range of ocean liners was available, some of which were modelled after the Cunard liner *Mauretania*. These came in two sizes, the 41 cm. (16 in.) version driven by clockwork and the 65 cm. (25½ in.) steam-driven version with four lifeboats. Some of the steam-powered boats were as small as 42 cm. (16½ in.). The largest clockwork liner measured 99 cm. (39 in.) and was fitted with ten lifeboats. The awakening interest in functional design at this time can be seen particularly in the smooth lines of the motor boats. Steam model racing-boats supplied with brass steam boilers and oscillating brass cylinders, simple paddle-steamers costing remarkably little, and a whole range of gunboats, were all supplied by Bing. The 1912 catalogue also shows some amusing divers: 'They dive into the water and rise to the surface again by air being blown into a rubber tube!' An improvement on the firm's basic submarine, described as the 'Navy Model', was introduced around this time: 'Automatically diving and rising to the surface, imitating in a surprising manner the movements of the large prototypes'. New armoured cruisers were also appearing, again driven either by clockwork or steam. Possibly the most exciting of these were the

A Bing submarine marked on the bow 'G.B.N' in a diamond shape, key-wound through the conning tower which is then sealed with a screw. It travels just below water with the conning tower showing. *Circa* 1909–1912. Length 24 cm. (9½ in.).

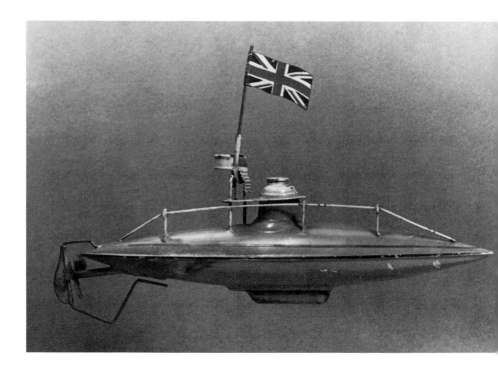

automatically firing gunboats: 'After winding up the clockwork the boat is put on the water. It will go straight ahead for some distance, then, as if intending to attack an enemy, will suddenly fire a shot. After this, the boats sizes 1 and 2 will sail on in a circle whilst boat size 3 will turn around and steer back to the original starting place.' The largest size, firing two shots at intervals, was 49.5 cm. (19½ in.) long. In the years just before the First World War, both torpedo-boats and destroyers with torpedo tubes were understandably popular. The largest destroyer was nearly a metre (40 in.) long and was available in both a steam-driven version and a slightly more expensive clockwork version. One of the most amusing of the pre-war model boats was a fully furnished houseboat, complete with Chinese lanterns and potted plants. For those more interested in constructing their own boats, there was a complete range of parts for steam, electric and clockwork. Cards of figures for peopling these boats were also available in several sizes. One of the more adventurous toys in 1906 was a land-and-water automobile, which was basically a simple boat mounted on car wheels with chauffeur sitting under an ornate canopy with two passenger seats behind.

Before the First World War toy motor-cars were still very decorative, with buttoned seats and bright colours. Several types were made by Bing, ranging in quality from some that were very substantially made in iron (and have therefore stood a good chance of survival) to others of pressed tin. The chauffeurs of the 1906 coupés were provided with rugs in real fur, while a spare rubber tyre hung from the roof. Tin garages sometimes came complete with both an open-top and a saloon car. In 1912 the 'New Model Motor Brougham' appeared, with two electric lights powered by a dry battery. Some of the lorries carried the Bing symbol on their removable tarpaulins, as well as being stamped as usual on the body-work itself. The initials 'G.B.N.' must have become as familiar as the alphabet to many American and European children.

Of all the Bing products it is their trains, especially those powered by steam, that arouse the great passions of enthusiasts. Bing was engaged in their manufacture from the 1880s, and by 1898 railway accessories, including signals and distantly controlled points and barriers, were available. At the Paris Exposition Universelle in 1900 the firm mounted a good display, and among the exhibits was a fine 4–2–2 miniature Midland Railway engine. There was considerable rivalry between Märklin and Bing in the introduction of correct models and the most complete range of accessories, which meant that an almost uneconomic variety was produced. The springs of clockwork trains often had only a short life and the catalogues gave dealers detailed instructions on fitting new ones. Construction kits for trains were sold in some number as well as loco lanterns and all varieties of rolling-stock. The very finest steam-trains were made for window displays in gauge 2. One, made only in Midland Railway livery, represented an express train with reversing gear; this was available in gauge 3. In 1912 Bing marketed the 'New Model Express Steam

Locomotive'. The catalogue description is as follows:

> Entirely reconstructed and brought up to date. This is the first really good model of an eight wheeled steam locomotive in this small gauge 'o'. Two fixed cylinders and reversing gear. Japanned brass boiler, new flame guard, new improved steam jet oiler holding a large quantity of oil which continually oils the working cylinder. New gas generating lamp, tender with imitation coal: $14\frac{1}{2}$ inches (36.8 cm.) long with tender.

Some of the rolling-stock was extremely detailed, such as the 'Express Mail Van', inside which could be seen post-office workers sorting mail, complete with sorting board and piles of letters. Also advertised were express sleeping and dining cars, petrol waggons, crane trucks and even car-transporting trucks, one of which carried an open tourer and a saloon car. A cattle truck contained model animals. More sophisticated than the 'Express Mail Van' was the 'Royal English Mail Van', which was equipped with post bags and receiving net, and received and delivered mail bags automatically.

Many of the engine sheds and railway stations were highly ornate, and there was much use of pressed surface decoration and brilliant printed colours. Even when intended for foreign sale, many of the stations still resembled the fairylike buildings of Bavaria, an effect heightened by the candlelight that glowed through the open windows. Some of the largest stations were almost like dolls' houses, with opening doors, glass windows and figures seated at tables while they waited for trains. The 'Superior Railway Station', completely Bavarian in concept, was provided with a mechanical signal bell, two sheltered halls, coloured glass in the windows and an arc light to illuminate the scene. Another pre-war masterpiece was an all-automatic signal box. On turning a crank, a signal bell sounded and a tin watchman stepped out of his house, the signal bar went up, the barrier was closed and the watchman saluted the passing train; the signal then dropped, the barrier rose and the watchman returned to his hut.

For any boy with an interest in mechanics, a stationary engine was an essential. The first full-size stationary engine was that made by Thomas Newcomen near Coventry in 1723, but it did not appear in toy form in any quantity until the 1840s. Miniature engines, made in great variety after 1865, could be linked to working models such as ferris wheels, ornamental water fountains, forges, windmills, simple moving tin pictures contained in a shallow box, or complete tin scenes, such as the one made by Bing in which an Alpine train runs up a hill while water runs down. Tin factories were available, some complete with workmen. In one model the stationary steam-engine was enclosed in a boiler room, while a grinder and other tools were powered by it in a separate workshop. Steam-engines could also be coupled with dynamo plants and electric lighting. Their importance cannot be over-emphasized, since so many small toys were designed to be powered in this way.

Possibly the finest Bing toy expressly designed for steam power was a model brewery worked by a 'Superior' steam-engine. All the machinery that would be found in a real brewery was carefully reproduced, including the mash-charger, mash-cooler and brewery vat. Another Bing factory, enclosed under a roof, contained shafting that worked a lathe, a grindstone, a drilling machine and a hammer. Individual tools could be purchased separately, so that the boy could assemble a large factory built to his own design. Some of these working models were suggested as suitable for instructive pupposes, for they were made to the most exact specifications and built up from castings and finely japanned fittings. Among the tools for Bing's 'Superior' model were sensitive drills with conical steel pulleys and fretsaws with adjustable tension.

During the First World War, Bing, like so many toy-makers in England, was diverted into the war effort, although the management remained very active and a large number of factories all over Germany were added to the company's holding. In 1917, to service the numerous semi-independent subsidiaries still trading under their own brand-names, a distribution company known as Concentra (Continental Distribution Centres) was set up. Bing's tin toys and trains continued to be marked 'G.B.N.' until 1919,

A vertical steam engine with the original Carette box, linked to a Bing water mill that works a simple hammer forge. There is a shallow depression in the base for water. Marked 'G.B.N' in diamond shape. Forge 12·5 cm. (5 in.) high.

A small-scale tinplate clockwork table train that is unmarked but contained in the original box with a Bing Werke trade mark. *Circa* 1920. Size of engine 9 cm. (3½ in.).

when the name was changed to 'B.W.' (Bing Werke). Ignaz Bing died in 1918 and in 1919 his son Stephan Bing became Director-General. The very large number of factories owned meant that it was becoming increasingly difficult to supervise operations personally in the manner that had led to such great successes. Eventually serious differences of opinion arose between Stephan Bing and the supervisory board, and the family severed their connection with the firm in 1927, although it continued to bear the Bing name. However, Stephan Bing's service contract was good for another ten years yet, and in consideration of this, compensation payments were made to him. In return he accepted a restrictive covenant not to start manufacturing trains in competition with Bing. After the loss of the family link, the lack of positive central control, combined with the depressed state of the world economy, created serious difficulties for the firm, and in 1932 it was put into compulsory receivership. This nullified Stephan Bing's covenant and he at once began to manufacture 'Trix Trains' in Nuremberg, while his son Francis produced an English version in conjunction with Bassett Lowke at Northampton in 1933. The Bing empire, meanwhile, was split up among a diversity of firms. In 1932 for instance, Fleischmann took over the equipment of the model ship department, and Karl Bub bought the equipment for making model trains.

Lehmann and Carette
Although the collector looks chiefly to Bing or Märklin for high-quality products, the more whimsical and amusing toys are frequently the work of Lehmann, a firm that was founded in Brandenburg in 1881 by Ernst Paul Lehmann. Initially this firm made metal boxes, but eventually branched out to make toys, including all types of clockwork-driven vehicles. These are often very flimsy in construction yet have a strong appeal, which relies heavily on the quality of the surface decoration. The frightened bride, jumping up and down in a basket-type trailer drawn by her daring young husband's motorbike, and the naughty boy who dangerously drives the car

that he has stolen, are both very typical of Lehmann. These toys were in full production by 1914, though for continued patent protection they were again registered as late as 1927. Erratic movement was first introduced in 1908, and this was used in Lehmann's 'Zig Zag', which consists of two figures in a car with 13 cm. (5 in.) wheels, vainly attempting to control the wayward vehicle by means of a steering device. Subjects such as the 'Alabama Coon Juggler', the 'Tut Tut Automobile', a mechanical beetle that flaps its wings as it walks along, a nurse bathing a naughty baby, and a climbing monkey, are all typical of the firm, and are decorated with characteristic abundance. However, in toys of contemporary vehicles the decoration was more restrained, so that their cars are usually in accord with the actual designs of the period. A similar economy of design is seen in 'Gustav the Miller' which first appeared in 1897, together with the less common 'Climbing Nigger' which carries a coconut and is based on the same principle, though very differently decorated.

Two Lehmann climbing monkeys. The example on the left is unmarked and has a flocked jacket. The colourfully lithographed monkey is marked 'Lehmann' on one arm and 'Tom' on the other. On the waistcoat is the firm's trademark and 'Made in Germany'. Height 20 cm. (8 in.).

An amphibious car made by Lehmann with 1905 and 1906 patents. On the front of the car is a list of towns including Berlin, Paris, Liverpool, New York, Toronto, Bombay and Moscow. Clockwork driven. Also marked underneath 'Auto Uberland Und Wasser'. Length 24 cm. (9½in.). (Collection Betty Harvey-Jones.)

In 1914 Lehmann introduced a mechanical airship show that ran for an hour and was composed of dirigibles and aeroplanes, each with a propeller and passenger. A ball revolved in a tower and balloons and airships flew around it. The same firm's 'County Fair Tower' was also very attractive and showed four motor-cars running through gilt arches and four pendant airships circling the tower at the top. The toy museum at Nuremberg has a particularly fine display of Lehmann toys, including a pre-war aeroplane in a box decorated with a print of the plane flying over the Lehmann factory, and a number of 'erratic' toys, such as a farmer riding a dancing pig and a London hansom-cab dating from 1908. The latter is particularly ingenious: the driver steers an erratic course while two distraught ladies, one named Lise Lotte and the other Laura, bounce around inside. Laura carries an umbrella and attempts to beat the driver with it through the open roof, while a dog sits in the front and begs. The museum has an example of a motorcyclist, in red knee-socks and a grey hat, that is unusually well-balanced and travels without outriggers, as well as a 'Journey to the Pole' showing Roald Amundsen raising and lowering his hat while an umbrella-like globe, with a map of the Northern Hemisphere, revolves above him.

Eight hundred people were employed by Lehmann in 1921. In the same year Johann Richter, a cousin of the founder and a man full of lively ideas and innovations, became a partner, and after the death of Ernst Paul Lehmann in 1934 he took charge of the entire business. In 1949 the factory was sequestered without compensation by the Russians.

Another of the great German toy manufacturers was the firm of George Carette, founded by an *émigré* Frenchman in Nuremberg. Before 1900 it concentrated mainly upon a range of tin and brass toys that were mostly hand-enamelled. In the early period many examples of 'Storchbein' (Storklegs) trains, so-called because of their high wheels, were made in brass. After the introduction of photolithography in 1895 there was rapid expansion and special work was undertaken for Bassett Lowke in England. Carette severed his personal link with the business just after the outbreak of the First World War, although the firm continued trading until 1917; its most important period, coinciding with Bing's best years, stretched from 1900 to 1914. After the company's break-up their models were taken over by other firms, and Carette cars, for example, later appeared with Karl Bub trade-marks. Bassett Lowke continued to produce Carette locomotives and rolling-stock in the post-war period. Even during its peak years Carette was never as customer-conscious as Bing. Repairs, for instance, needed to be sent to Nuremberg for attention, and any received in the last three months of the year could not be dealt with until the following year, because of the seasonal rush.

Carette, like Bing, were proud of those among their models that could be regarded as 'educational appliances'. Some of their steam-engines were of the most complex type with crosshead shafts and fixed 'double action slide valve cylinders'. Their range of models designed to be powered by a steam-engine, though not as large as Bing's, was impressive, and included an organ-grinder with an organ of eight notes, a working fire-engine complete with firemen, a miner in a coalmine and a butcher in his shop in addition to the usual factory setting. As with the other major manufacturers, the cheapest factories stood on a simple tin base, whereas the finer versions, with working figures, were enclosed in a structure. A smithy, with a moving figure and japanned horseshoes hanging from nails on the wall, is an idiosyncrasy of this firm and is not seen in other catalogues. Drummers, acrobats, a blacksmith's shop and a joinery, as well as windmills and water-wheels, could all be linked to a steam-engine and were sold in numbers as great as Bing provided. Their range of model railway equipment rivalled that of Bing, although they did not supply parts for the construction of engines. Their 'Central Fire Brigade' is so similar to that made by their main competitor that there seems to have been some pirating of ideas: the Carette model, like the Bing version, was made with a door that sprang open when a lever at the side was touched. Their fire-fighting equipment, however, was much smaller. Carette's range of waggons, London buses, aeroplanes, and motor-cars, some of which were as large as 33 cm. (13 in) was fairly impressive, but in the 1914 catalogue both cars and aeroplanes were omitted.

Below and opposite left 'Gustav the Miller', a toy that folds neatly into a box with German, Dutch and English instructions. Marked 'Lehmann' on box, on top of tower and on the flour sack. The weighted sack is hung from a hook at the top of the tower and this activates the sails, causing Gustav to climb up, receive the sack on his head and climb down again. This toy was sold from 1897. Height 48 cm. (19 in.).

Above A tin 'Busy Lizzie' who mops the floor by a swinging motion of the arms has a spotted red dress and a blue apron and is key-wound. The base is marked 'Made in Germany. British patent applied for. U.S. patent applied for. D.R.P.A. Busy Lizzie'. *Circa* 1920. Height 16·5 cm. (6½ in.).

Above right 'Berline De Voyage', a clockwork car of mild pressed steel, painted in green and red and thought to be based on a Mercedes. Made by Carette. *Circa* 1910. Length 38 cm. (15 in.). (Bethnal Green Museum.)

A colourful steam roller of fairly lightweight tin, marked 'Made in Germany'. It is key-wound to roll to and fro and has printed strapping on the boiler. In the fire-box is a battery-powered electric light. The wheels are printed in cream, red and black. Early 20th century. Length 30 cm. (12 in.).

The 'R 101' made of silvered tinplate with a yellow propellor. Marked 'Made in Germany'. To be hung by cord from the loop at top, key-wound and circled by the movement of the propellor. Underneath is a holder for a battery and a bulb. The configuration is thought to resemble the Zeppelin more closely than the R101. *Circa* 1932. Length 37 cm. (14½ in.).

A red sports car marked 'Hessmobil 1020' on the bonnet and with the Hesse symbol on the door. The flywheel is activated by the crank at the front of the bonnet. *Circa* 1910. Length 20 cm. (8 in.).

Tin toys in France

The production of tin toys in France was also considerable, and among those most popular with collectors are the amusing clockwork figures made by Fernand Martin, based on characters seen in the streets of Paris. These won thirty gold and silver medals in Europe and America, including those in Barcelona and Paris in 1886 and 1889. The figures are often costumed in fabric, which is probably why they appeal to collectors of automata as well as tin.

The firm was founded in 1880 with over two hundred employees and its own foundry, and at one stage the annual production of mechanical toys was as many as 800,000. Unlike other French manufacturers of the period, who often utilized old tinplate, Martin used only new metal. He eventually became President of the organized French toy industry, and also belonged to a very early group of toy collectors that included Henri d'Allemagne and Léo Claretie, both of whom are well-known to toy collectors for their exploratory books on the subject. In 1908 Martin donated a collection of the toys he had manufactured over thirty years, together with their patent specifications, to the Conservatoire des Arts et Métiers, and this collection is invaluable to students of the firm's work. As all the pieces have been individually dated by Martin, we know for instance that to some extent he used rubber bands to drive models throughout the firm's period of manufacture, that steam-rollers with flywheel mechanisms were made in 1883, and that in 1901 there was a very large output of clockwork figures that performed simple actions.

Another well-known French firm was Jouets de Paris, believed to have been founded in Paris in 1899 as the Société Industrielle de Ferblanterie, a name that was changed to Jouets de Paris in 1928, after which date the toys were marked 'J de P'. Around 1932 the name was again changed, this time to Jouets en Paris. The firm copied all the great cars of the period. Typical of their output was the 'Hispano Suiza', 52 cm. (20½ in.) long with a mechanical double-spring engine and electric lighting; models of the Hotchkiss, Delaunay, Belleville and Delage motor-cars were also well made. Their finest cars were built in the twenties and included the popular Citroën, while their Rolls Royce was among the most splendid. The Delahaye fire-engine, made in 1930, was provided with a meths-fired steam boiler. The Delage racing-car, claimed in the catalogue to be the prettiest racing-car ever, had forward and reverse drive, a handbrake, and sheet-metal wheels with imitation spokes. J.E.P. toys are popular with collectors because they are particularly well-made as realistic models, whereas most toy-makers were content with vague impressions. The firm was also helpful in clearly marking its work.

Another of the very collectable French toy-makers was the firm of Charles Rossignol, founded in Paris in 1869. The firm made a range of trains and motor-cars and, after 1920, a series of Paris buses, marked 'C.R.'. Their Renault taxi, made in 1914, is a particular favourite because of its realistic shape and colouring.

A tinplate tourer with the Renault badge on the radiator. Painted in dark blue and with red coach lining, it has forward, reverse and neutral gears and steering by steering wheel. Marked in red on base 'Automobiles J de P. Breveté s.g.d.g. Paris. Made in France', also stamped on rear axle assembly. *Circa* 1929. Length 34 cm. (13½ in.).

Cars of French origin are popular not only because of their intrinsic qualities but also because some were made in large numbers, to promote full-size cars (the belief being that if a child owned a model Citroën he would want a real one when he grew up). Among the Citroën toys was the 1923 'B2 Taxi' with a cane body and rubber tyres. André Citroën, when he launched the 1923 5 horse-power Citroën, simultaneously made a 1 : 11 scale model in sheet metal. The 'B2 Torpedo', an open four-seater with a four-door body, was an extremely popular toy in the twenties. The 1929 'Coupé C6' was the most elegant of the luxury range, with electric headlights, opening driver's door and steering operated by the driver's wheel. The 'B14' car, sold in 1927 and also available in a taxi version, was possibly the most attractive of all, with its four opening doors, winding windows, rear suspension springs, wheel embellishers and working steering-wheel; it is of added interest in that it was their first model to be provided with real tyres. The 1929 Citroën 'C6' went even further in the direction of authenticity, for it was fitted with genuine Michelin tyres. In 1932, when a road-sweeper and water-sprayer was manufactured, this also was made as a toy, with a screw-top water tank.

A stationary engine by Ernst Plank marked 'E.P.' on the instruction envelope. On the yellow and black base an enamelled plaque reads 'Viaduct'. The oval silver plaque carries the words, 'A. W. Gamage's Ltd. Holborn, London. Made in Bavaria'. The original Gamage's bill for 3/6., dated 21 March 1911, is also contained in the box, together with funnels, etc. Spirit-fired. Height 23 cm. (9 in.).

Tin toys in Britain

British involvement in the manufacture of tin toys before the First World War was very slight. Among the few examples were the model steam-engines made by Smith, Bailey and Co. of Hockley Street, Birmingham, together with a variety of parts for model-building and for vertical, horizontal, beam and marine engines. Another firm with a long history was Stevens Model Dockyard, which was founded in 1843 in Aldgate, London, and issued catalogues of components for the construction of model steam-engines and ships. Model steam-engine parts were sold on cards ready for assembly. From the late 1880s the firm marketed some toys of German origin, and the clockwork submarines in their 1906 catalogue look like those made by Bing. The company was a fully-fledged commercial concern with a full staff of skilled workmen who would make special models to order. Many of their toys were in mixtures of wood and metal, for example a model square-topsail schooner with a copper bronze 'bottom'. The catalogue for 1906 offers 'Every description and size steam boat, torpedo boat, cruiser, submarines and battleships, ships and boats ancient and modern made to order. Estimates on application. Steamboats repaired.' For their boats the company produced a wide range of fittings, including sailors, wheels and signalling equipment. In addition, complete vertical steam-engines, model cranes and all sorts of guns were sold, as well as trains. Their English locomotive engines were issued with a telling warning in the catalogue: 'NOTICE: Bogus scale locomotives of English railways stamped out of tin and made in Germany and puffed up by misleading advertisements are NOT SOLD BY THIS FIRM.' Among the steam

locos made by Stevens Model Dockyard were the 'Swift', the 'Fury' and 'Boadicea'. The Pullman cars were of polished mahogany.

A similar range of products was supplied by J. Sutcliffe, established in 1882 in Leek, Staffordshire, with the purpose of making parts for the home construction of stationary and locomotive steam-engines as well as finished examples, including a number of tinplate toys. The firm has continued to produce models for a very specialist market, in the traditional manner and often using the old machinery, to the present day. Another, similar company was John Bateman, founded in 1774 to produce components for the manufacture of steam-engines but after 1879 turning to the building of model steam-locomotives. 'Bateman and Companies Museum of Models' occupied five houses and claimed to offer the largest selection of working models in the world.

Although there were few brightly decorated tinplate toys produced in Britain, much energy was put into the creation of amusingly designed tin containers, often in the form of toys, such as babies in prams, coaches, motor-cars, pieces of furniture and delivery vans that were often marked with the names of biscuit makers and confectioners. Even as late as the 1930s

A dark and light grey destroyer marked on the stern with a red and gold transfer printed label 'Sutcliffe Model. British Made', also with an impressed 'Sutcliffe' in an oval. *Circa* 1920. Length 43 cm. (17 in.).

A Macfarlane Lang & Co. biscuit tin with effectively printed decoration in rich colours and with two printed delivery men in the cab. A simple pull-along type of toy with printed wheels. *Circa* 1920. Length 19 cm. (7½ in.).

A brightly-printed paddle steamer that is key-wound from the funnel and marked 'Made in England'. *Circa* 1930. Length 24 cm. (9½ in.).

a large number of such tins were made in the same, now decidedly outdated idiom, for example the kitchen range issued by Huntley and Palmer. Though some of the tin containers were probably made in Germany, it is likely that the majority were made in Britain as the native manufacturers were becoming increasingly skilled. In the thirties very acceptable printed toys in tin were made by Wells and Chad Valley.

The most respected British manufacturer of trains was Bassett Lowke and Company, founded in 1899. They began, like several other British firms, by making rough castings for home construction of model engines. At the Paris Exposition Universelle of 1900, Wenman J. Bassett Lowke was impressed by the Bing stand and in conjunction with Stephan Bing undertook to market realistic Bing locomotives, made to British specifications. Lowke's designer Henry Greenly was entrusted with the design of true models, which were made in Germany, initially by Bing but later by Carette. In Bassett Lowke's shops models appeared in sizes from 6·3 cm. (2½ in.) upwards advertised annually in the illustrated catalogues and the model railway handbooks. From 1919 the Northampton works was enlarged for the manufacture of items previously obtained from Germany, with the result that the withdrawal of Bing caused no break in supply. The manufacture of model trains ceased in 1953 after Bassett Lowke's death, although models for industry continued to be made in Northampton.

Very accurate model trains were also produced from the 1930s to the present time by James Beeson, a model-maker who made British locomotives mainly in gauges 0 and 1 with either electric or clockwork movement. Good locomotives were made too by Stewart-Reidpath of Kent,

A high-wing monoplane printed in turquoise and cream and representing a small passenger-carrying plane of the late 1930s. It is key-wound from the side of the cabin to move along the ground. Length 21 cm. (8½ in.).

a firm that was among the pioneers of oo railways. Another maker of true-to-scale model railway equipment was Mills brothers, Model Engineers Ltd, whose trade-mark stated 'Milbro True to scale models for reliability'.

The first Hornby clockwork trains were made in 1915 in gauge o, marked with the trade-mark 'MLDL' for Meccano Limited, Liverpool. Their trains were mass-produced, however, only after 1920, and from this date were known as Hornby Trains, the first electric versions of which were made in 1925. In 1938 gauge oo trains were introduced by this firm under the name of Hornby-Dublo. Hornby is also particularly known for its Dinky Toys, introduced in 1933, three years before Frank Hornby's death.

A breakdown lorry marked 'Made in England. Wells, London' with the original price ticket of 5/11d. It is brown, yellow and cream.
A red sports car marked 'Mettoy. Made in Great Britain'. Both *circa* 1935. Length of breakdown lorry 29 cm. (11½ in.).

An unmarked key-wound metal trotter that is probably of American origin. The coloured driver with a whip in his mouth, wears a red cap. Length 19 cm. (7½ in.). (Collection Betty Harvey-Jones.)

Tin toys in the United States

American production of tin toys had begun in the eighteenth century with the Pattersons of Berlin, Connecticut. By 1820 Connecticut had become established as the centre of the tin toy industry, with at least five factories, possibly aided, like Nuremberg, by the traditional clock-making of the region. Turners of Meriden made use of local waste engineering scrap for toys. From Connecticut the industry spread rapidly to Philadelphia and New York. The American toy-makers were quick to utilize new inventions and only a year after the introduction of clockwork toys in Germany, George W. Brown of Forestville was putting clockwork into small engines. Many of the American designs were based on the knowledge of *émigré* French and German workers, though the affinities between the work produced in those countries and work from America are not as great in tin as in traditional wooden toys.

The middle years of the nineteenth century saw the establishment of several American toy factories. Among them were Benjamin T. Rooney's Tin and Sheet Iron Ware and Stove Manufactory, of Attleborough, Pennsylvania, boldly claiming to produce 'Everything in the tinware line that has ever been thought of'; Francis Field and Francis, also known as the Philadelphia Tin Toy Manufactory, making 'japanned and tin products superior to any imported'; and S. O. Barnum and Son of Toledo, Ohio, who specialized in toys with metal wheels. Henry Schwartz opened his Baltimore toy store in 1849, and this shop sold quantities of American-made goods, though initially reliant on imported German products. The wheeled bell toys, such as those made by all the German makers, were for some unknown reason sold more in the American market; Marshall Field's toy catalogues show a fine variety of these, including a pull-along cat-and-dog fight, Cinderella in her chariot, and a very charming 'Daisy' riding in a horse-drawn sledge and clutching a doll, all with cheerfully ringing bells and chimes.

Of all American makers Ives is the best-known, with its slogan, 'Ives Toys make happy boys'. This firm began production in 1868 when Edward

Ives made movable dancing figures that were turned by a spiral turbine impelled by rising hot air from a household stove. Another early Ives toy was a man rowing a boat with two oars. The firm grew rapidly and produced a wide variety of tinplate toys, including figures worked by clockwork, as well as the trains for which they are best known. The American fondness for cast-iron toys is reflected in the work of this firm; after the late 1880s it used this material in particular for trains of the floor runner type. In 1901 Ives introduced his German-inspired gauge 0 clockwork trains that ran on rails, and electric trains in this gauge were introduced three years later.

Top An American-made cast-iron pull-along train probably made by the Ives Blakeslee & Williams Co. of New York, as a similar example is shown in their 1893 catalogue. Bears the initials 'N.Y.C & H.R.' for New York Central and Hudson River Railroad. Each section is made in two halves, riveted together and electroplated. Complete length of train with coaches 152 cm. (60 in.). (Bethnal Green Museum.)

Above left An American cast-iron money-box. The gun is fired when the soldier's foot is pressed. Marked on base 'Creedmore Bank'. *Circa* 1880. Length 25·5 cm. (10 in.).

Above A cast-iron money-box made in U.S.A. marked on base 'Pat. Pendg & Patd' Feb. 2nd 1875'. A lever at the base releases the spring on the gun so the coin shoots into the bear. Size 25 × 20 cm. (10 × 8 in.). (Bethnal Green Museum.)

A bread-cart pulled by a tinplate walking girl that is operated by winding thread around a weighted pulley. The girl walks on a revolving wheel of legs and a similar patent was granted to Henry C. Work of Brooklyn, New York. (Christie's, South Kensington.)

Many of the iron toys made in America were constructed in outdated designs, and examples made in the last years of the nineteenth century would suggest a much earlier date on purely visual evidence. The strong shapes of trains seem appropriate for manufacture in this material, but other quite delicate constructions, such as ponies pulling phaetons, dog carts and elegant surreys with the drivers in livery, were also created in iron. Model stoves in great number were also made, with names such as 'Jewel Range' or 'Pet', models that are so attractive and collectable that they are now much reproduced. Toy banks were also frequently made of iron and in such great numbers that the collecting of money boxes is a particularly active field in the United States, as there is such a variety of good examples, often with the most ingenious mechanical and sometimes musical movements. One of the most amusing is 'Professor Pug Frog's Great Bicycle Feat', showing a frog riding a bicycle while Mother Goose sings and a clown stands by the drum-like bank. Various banks of simpler construction involved placing the coin on a gun, in a tambourine, or even in an eagle's beak: by the pressing of a lever or the turning of a handle the coins were deposited inside.

The American toy trade saw a further great expansion in the early twentieth century, the value of manufactures classed as toys rising from $1,500,000 in 1880 to $5,500,000 in 1905. There was an accompanying increase in investment capital from $1,000,000 in 1880 to $5,000,000 in 1905. Whereas in the 1880s there were one hundred and six factories, by 1905 there were a hundred and sixty-one, with the number of persons employed rising from 1,000 to more than 4,000 by the later date, with the greatest increase in the field of wood and metal toys. Surprisingly there was even some export of toys to Germany, which received 56,000 dollars' worth of American imports while the U.K. received 231,000 dollar's worth.

However, despite American activity in toy manufacture at this time, it should be remembered that the industry was still in relative infancy, and was not to attain its real boom in production until the 1920s. As late as 1903, when the American toy trade magazine *Playmates* was first published, there were still only just over one hundred established toy manufacturers in the country, and the initial prospects for the magazine were not optimistic (although in fact it was to continue in circulation until the present day). In 1914 one half of the toys sold in America still originated in Europe. After the First World War the American manufacturers found themselves in a position to forge ahead, ensuring that there would never again be such dependence on imported toys. From then on European firms became less adventurous in comparison with makers such as Louis Marx, who was prepared to represent current screen and cartoon characters in tin for the delight of young fans. The Marx toys were brightly decorated and cheaply made to appeal to the mass market. They were sold by direct mail and from the counters of cheap chain stores, and are now popular with collectors because of their strong period effect and the ingenuity of their construction.

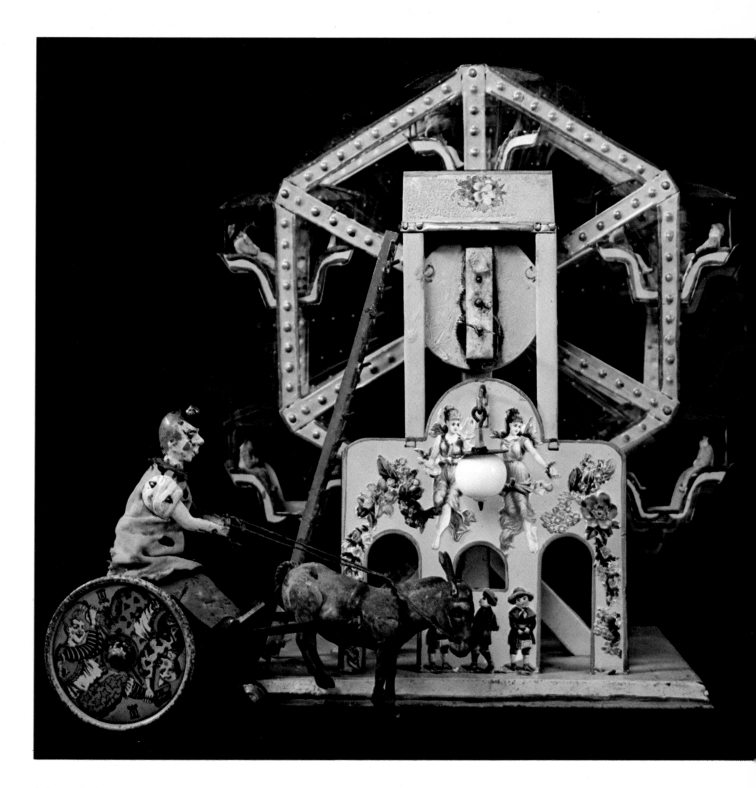

A ferris wheel with a simple musical box movement that plays as the key-wound wheel revolves. The passengers are made of composition. In the foreground is a Lehmann bucking mule, showing the typical brightly-printed colour on the wheels that also carry the 1908 patent mark. Both clown and donkey lurch as the toy moves along. Unmarked but probably German, *circa* 1890. Height 31 cm. (12½ in.).

Above A fire station marked 'G.B.N.' for Gebrüder Bing of Nuremberg. When a lever at the side is pulled the station doors fly open, a bell rings and a fire escape, pump and a salvage corps tender all rush out at once. Height 24 cm. (9¼ in.).

Opposite above The excitement of live steam. A model made by Gebrüder Bing of Nuremberg and marked 'G.B.N.' on tender and 'HI' inside the driver's cab. In 1913 Gamage's catalogue referred to an identical Midland Railway steam train that was priced 10/6d. Gauge 1, oscillating cylinders, meth. burner. Length 35 cm. (14 in.).

Opposite below 'The Royal Scot' made by Bassett Lowke during the 1930s. Centre rail electric, 'o' gauge. In original L.M.S. livery. Length of engine 9·2 cm. (11½ in.).

A milk float with a brass royal coat-of-arms on the side. Horses of almost identical type were linked with a variety of tradesmen's carts. The milk-man is an Armand Marseille and the assistants are Simon and Halbigs, the smaller of the walking, head-turning type. Length of horse and cart 61 cm. (24 in.).

Model cars were produced after 1904 by the majority of tin toy-makers, but this example is very attractively printed. Unmarked but possibly by Carette. Length 31 cm. (12½ in.). (Collection Betty Harvey-Jones.)

A group of late 19th-century tin toys. The man with
the wire spectacles skates sideways while raising and
lowering his arms, while the lady moves rigidly
along on wheels concealed under her skirt. This is
activated by a flywheel mechanism. The key-wound
conjurer taps the dice with a wand, the box lid lifts
to show the empty interior, he taps it again and this
time when the lid is lifted a head is shown inside.
All are unmarked. Length of skater 20 cm. (8 in.).

Group of characters from a child's Punch and Judy
set, made of carved pine. South German, *circa* 1875.
The assured painting of the heads is typical of the
work of Bavarian toy-makers. Punch stands 50·8 cm.
(20 in.) high.

'The Compliment. A movable figure with a great variety of changes.' There are six different heads and torsos. Hand-coloured, made by G. W. Faber. Height 22.9 cm. (9 in.).

Magic Lanterns of the finer type were usually adult parlour items rather than toys for small children as is obvious by the workmanship seen in this brass-finished Edwardian example. (Collection Robert Hallmann.)

Optical toys and the model theatre

THE interests of adults and children probably converge more in the field of optical toys than in any other, as so many of these items began their development as amusements for the sophisticated and were eventually relegated to the nursery.

Peep-shows and panoramas

Peep-shows originally entertained the educated, who appreciated the skilful simulation of perspective by various means, but by the early nineteenth century they had become a much less exclusive form of entertainment, though the dividing line between toy and parlour amusement is often difficult to define, except in the case of such obviously adult-directed gadgets as the alabaster 'peep eggs', with scenes changed by a simple wire device and viewed through a double convex lens. Until the mid-nineteenth century in Europe and America showmen known as 'raree men' travelled the countryside with peep-shows. Their scenes were contained in a box that stood on folding legs for ease of transport, with several peep-holes so that a few children could view simultaneously. The top of the device was sometimes ornamented with a group of carved figures. Having set up his stand, the showman would cry out to the fascinated children standing nearby: 'Thousands of lives have been lost and thousands of pounds have been spent acquiring knowledge which you may cheaply attain. Have none of you got a halfpenny?' He would often find it necessary to exhort the children not to breathe on the viewing glasses, or they would need almost continual wiping. In *Sargeant Bell and his Raree Show* by G. Mogridge, published in England around 1845, the showman includes scenes such as 'Victoria Visiting the City', 'The Tournament of the Field of the Cloth of Gold', 'The Epping Hunt' and 'Battle of the Pyramids'. The pictures in shows such as these were changed by pulling a string, and sheets from model theatres were sometimes included, presumably as dividers between the more spectacular events. Those most often appearing on the market were originally sold by book sellers, folded into a convenient size: when extended at arm's length and viewed through peep-holes, very lively representations of current events were observed. Among the most commonly found is that published by C. Moody in 1851, 'Telescopic View of the Great Exhibition'; another that was probably

Opposite Late 19th-century colour slides were often both attractively coloured and amusing, as in this scene from Goldilocks and the Three Bears. In the foreground is a typical child's Magic Lantern marked on the box 'F.N.N.' for Fritz Neumeyer of Nuremberg. It contains the original oil lamp. Height 21 cm. (8¼ in.).

'Polyorama or Endless Changes of Landscape, one of a set of three hand-coloured etchings that can be arranged in a variety of scenes. It is similar to a set published by Hodgson and Co., London, in 1824. Size of cards 14 × 7 cm. (5½ × 3 in.). (Bethnal Green Museum.)

'Days in Catland with Louis Wain'. A Panorama by 'Father Tuck', very lavishly coloured with amusing scenes. The figures are contained in an envelope at the back of the folder and slotted into place. Raphael Tuck. *Circa* 1895. Length 27·5 cm. (10¼ in.) (Collection Betty Harvey-Jones.)

commemorative is 'Thames Tunnel', very cleverly made in two layers so that by viewing through the central holes at the top the spectator sees a panoramic scene of London, while a look through the lower pair of holes reveals the tunnel under the river. Some of the peep-shows were completely hand-drawn, such as one sold in 1815 entitled 'Run Neighbours Run, All London is Quadrilling It'. Some represented geographical subjects ranging from 'The Road to Rome' to 'St Leonard's on Sea, Sussex' (a rare example).

Toy panoramas were a simple form of moving picture, painted as a series of scenes on a roll of paper that could be viewed through a frame. In this category those representing the coronation of George IV are certainly the most commonly found in Britain. Of more interest to collectors, however, are subjects such as 'A Satirical Panorama of a Mis-Spent Life', in twelve hand-coloured scenes, each divided by eight lines of verse and stretching to some 864 cm. (340 in.). A wide variety of contemporary incidents was depicted: for example there was a bird's-eye panoramic lithograph of the funeral procession of the Czar Alexander, and even a 'Moving Panorama of the Route of the Overland Mail to India from Southampton to Calcutta', printed in lithographed colour in 1840.

The model theatre

The model theatre is often thought to have derived from the sheets of Nativity scenes and sets of figures that were produced at both Augsburg and Strasbourg in the eighteenth century for the amusement of children. Another theory, however, suggests that this amusing toy developed from the popularity of prints of theatrical characters that could be cut out and were eventually provided with simple scenes in which to strike appropriate dramatic attitudes. What is known for sure is that around 1800, J. F. Schreiber of Esslingen began to produce children's theatrical scenes, followed some ten years later by coloured sheets. The 'Schreibersche Kindertheater', including notes and construction details as well as sheets of figures, were sold until the beginning of the First World War in German, French and English versions and enjoyed considerable popularity. The development of the German model theatre was also influenced by the Viennese publisher Trentsensky, who issued over two hundred sets of sheets and two hundred and forty-three sets of figures for forty-one titles. Around 1825 Trentsensky's 'Big Theatre' was issued, using the new technique of pen lithography, and by 1860 this was provided with forty-one plays, together with the appropriate sets and two hundred and forty-three figures. Trentsensky's 'Mignon-Theater, or Complete Apparatus for the presentation of the main features of popular plays from the repertoire of the Vienna theatres, with faithful representation of décor and costumes' was published in 1830; however, these more closely resemble costume plates than settings for model theatres, and because of their faithfulness to detail they are documents of considerable importance in theatrical history.

There was a substantial production of model theatres in Germany from the early nineteenth century, not only by Schreiber in Esslingen but also by Riemschneider, Gustav Kuhn and Oehmigke in Neuruppin. In Berlin.

An engraved paper battle-scene from a set of six which fit into a proscenium front. Late 18th century. Height 7 cm. (3 in.). (Bethnal Green Museum.)

NO. 13.

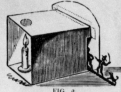

DIALOGUE.

OTHELLO. No 1.
Shakespear's portraits, as drawn from life,
The Moor Othello—but not his Wife,
Whose fate caused many a tear to flow
From those who feel for others woe.

FALSTAFF. No 2.
Fat Falstaff too, so plump and jolly,
Defying grief and melancholly.

WILL OF THE WISP. No 3.
A merry Jack o' lantern chap,
The cause of many a dire mishap,
As soon as in the mud I've stuck'em,
Out goes my light and then I duck'em.

BARDOLPH. No 4.
Talk not to me of cherry lips,
And cheeks more blooming than a rose,
Or ivory teeth, or auburn hair,
I've all those colors on my nose.

HAMLET. No 5.
List, list, Oh list! What can he mean?
Perhaps he wants his tailor,
Or perhaps he wants his son to list
For soldier or for sailor.

GHOST. No 6.
Murder most foul—List, list, Oh list!
To one whose word was ne'er yet doubt-
Your uncle did the deed my boy;   ed.)
Beware of him—or you'll be spouted.

FIG. 2.

Directions for Exhibition.

Paste the Figures on stiff cartridge paper, and when dry, prick the white lin's
smoothly with a pin or needle,—then cut
out the Figures, and fix them on slips of
card or wood for the purpose of passing
them across the Stage.

The candle at the back will give them
a good effect, which may be much improved by your own ingenuity, if you intro-
duce a funny dialogue suitable to the characters introduced.

Published by JAMES MARCH,
24, Webber Street,
Blackfriars Road.   S.

REMARKABLE CHARACTERS.

HARLEQUIN.

Here's Master Motley I declare,
With coal black mask and visage fair,
Whose magic wand transforms with ease,
A full moon into a green cheese,
A post into a postman, or
A broom into a chancellor:
Can raise old nick with horns so funny,
His imps, or any thing, (but money.)

COLUMBINE.

With graceful form and step divine
See the lovely Columbine,
Ever happy, ever gay,
Sport her youthful hours away;
While her partner vainly tries
To guard her from the prying eyes
Of Pantaloon; but in the end
Some goodly genius stands her friend

PUNCH.

What a nose and monstrous hunch
If I mistake not, this is Punch,
They tell me Sir you beat your wife,
And that's disgraceful on my life.
"Well really now the truth to tell
I do not use her very well,
But I'm determined she shall know
I will be master of my show."

JUDY.

'Your show indeed! why Punch you're no man
Thus to beat a helpless woman,
You think to torment and perplex
And take advantage of my sex;
But I'll soon pay you off this score
When you'r asleep and loudly snore,
I'll give you then a belly full
And crack your nose or else your skull.

CLOWN.

Fools we have plenty in the town,
But very few can play the Clown,
To play the Fool, we all agree
A clever fellow he must be,
Should upset gouty pantaloon
Or swallow the vauxhall balloon,
Laugh, joke, and sing, then is a trice
Prig every thing that's sweet and nice.

PANTALOON.

Old Pantaloon does all he can
To baulk the lovers, silly man!
They'll soon convince the artful sage
That youth is quite a match for age,
For Harlequin and Columbine
Will then in hymen's bands entwine
Their hearts, when that will show
Tom Lillywhite his suit's "no go"

TOM LILLYWHITE. 13

'Pon honor Pan its very hard
Your Girl for me has no regard;
I think I look divinely fine,
And much should like to call her mine
Observe my quizing glass and waste,
The girl is surely without taste—
Pray Pantaloon do what you can,
Tell her I'm a nice young man

JIM CROW. 16

"A nice young man" did you say so!
Not half so nice as Jimmy Crow,
I teach America, Spain, and France,
To twirl about and sing and dance,
In England too I make a rout
And teach them all to wheel about;
I may without the least romance
Declare I've taught the world to dance.

SPRITE. No 14.

Sometimes on a table, sometimes in the air,
And at a pantomime you'll sure find me there.

JOHNNY GILPIN. No. 15.

Away went Gilpin, and away went Gilpin's hat and wig;
He lost them sooner than at first: for why?—they were too big.

ROBIN HOOD. No. 17.

Bold Robin Hood was a forester good,
As ever drew bow in a merry green wood.   (old song

RICHARD TURPIN. No. 18.

Richard Turpin was a highway-man &c. who joined King, another
notorious vagabond, and after many depradations, they robbed a rich merchant, and then retired to the Green Man public house, where King being
captured, he called on Richard to shoot the officer, he fired—missed the
officer but shot King; then rode away on his mare benny bess, clearing a
toll'gate in his way, and reaching York (190 miles), in 24 hours, where
he was acquitted on the improbability of him being the same man who
shot King.   Put the horse on wire to jump over the gate.   END

Winkelmann was manufacturing a number of plays in the 1830s and there was also some manufacture in Nuremberg. Walter Rohler discovered that sixteen firms in German-speaking countries produced sheets of figures for the opera *Der Freischütz* alone. Among these perhaps the most attractive set is that produced by Riedel in Nuremberg around 1830, with gloriously coloured devils and mythological creatures in abundance. The toy museum at Nuremberg has several theatres, including a substantial model of the Opera, with a very heavy wooden proscenium to which plaster decoration has been applied. The stage, which is now furnished with a setting made by Schreiber, was provided with a trapdoor and was made by M. Gottschalk of Marienburg in Saxony. Another, much later example was hand-made in 1865 by a Schweinfurt bookbinder with a proscenium decorated with gilt and cut-out paper. Bestelmier, in his catalogues, offered theatres that were especially designed for the glove puppets he sold, as well as for his well-made marionettes, whose limbs could be individually moved. He also sold several shadow settings, and his most unusual piece was a 'Chinese Shadow Play with Chinese Fireworks, behind which a person can hide and direct everything'. The fireworks were simulated optically by two wheels that moved one behind the other.

The English model theatre developed, almost independently of European developments, from the theatrical prints that were published four to a sheet as souvenir items for theatregoers. From around 1810, scenes with a wing attached were added to the plates of characters; each set was based on a particular production of a play, and the names of the actors as well as the characters they represented were given. The sheets were sold 'a penny plain and twopence coloured', and sometimes they are found mounted on card and set out in home-made theatres.

In 1834 J. K. Green claimed to be the original inventor and publisher of 'Juvenile and Theatrical Prints, Established 1808', though it is more likely that William West was the first in the field, as by 1811 he had produced at least a dozen different prints. George Speaight raises the possibility that Green might have worked for West at an early age and therefore felt justified in making the claim. Other early producers included Mrs Hebberd and J. H. Jameson, although their work can hardly be told apart as an almost rigidly uniform style of presentation had been achieved by 1812.

William West's first 'Juvenile' drama was 'Timour the Tartar', published in 1812 with characters, scenes and a wing at either side of the plate. Printed prosceniums of the Theatre Royal were also supplied in the same year, a date which is usually taken as the starting-point of the English model theatre on a really commercial scale. West was an eccentric and muddled character, and there were sometimes delays of years between the issue of a set of characters and the scenes appropriate for the display of them. The notable caricaturist and illustrator George Cruikshank, who once worked for him, remembered how 'Boys used to go into his shop and abuse him like anything for his frequent delays in publishing continuations of his

Opposite A shadow theatre sheet of characters published by James March, 24 Webber Street, Blackfriars Road, London, with information or amusing verses accompanying each figure. The theatre was intended to be candle lit. *Circa* 1860.

plays.' In order to prevent any rival from using his plates, West is thought to have destroyed them before his death in 1845. One of his greatest rivals was Hodgson and Co. of Newgate Street, whose plays were accompanied by a script and, usually, enough sheets for all the characters to appear in the correct situations.

During the 1830s Martin Skelt began to acquire the copper plates of publishers who were closing down, including those of Hodgson and Co. and R. L. Lloyd. Skelt produced so many plays in this way that he was actually able to reduce the price of some sheets to as little as a halfpenny (as did J. K. Green, who produced almost completely original plates between 1832 and 1857). Skelt's name became synonymous with the model theatre, for his plays were sold all over the country from small shops and were thus available to a very wide public. Joseph Myers, who also sold polyoramas and prismatic dioramas, issued a number of plays in 1857 that were published by Trentsensky in Vienna. The plays of J. K. Green were eventually acquired by Redington, who also published plays originally printed by Skelt, by A. Park and by W. A. Webb, although from around 1850 he issued some of his own in addition to these. After Redington's death in 1876, his shop was inherited by a daughter who had married a certain Benjamin Pollock. Pollock took over the running of the firm and at first issued some scenes of his own, though later he followed the common practice of reissuing old plays. One of the more unusual publishers of model theatres at this time was W. G. Webb, an etcher who engraved, drew and printed the plays himself. For the most part, however, the plays were a miscellany of the talents available, and the work of individual artists cannot be identified.

Opposite A scene from Cinderella, lithographed from the copper plates used for the original edition in 1849. Width 54 cm. (21 in.). (Bethnal Green Museum.)

Jumping Jacks, to be pasted onto a card. 'Polichinelle & Arlequin. Imagerie Pellerin. Imagerie d'Epinal No 1351'. Hand-coloured in reds and blues. *Circa* 1900.

The model theatre was very directly aimed at boys, and the scenes are full of drama and colourful incident. The engravers would visit plays equipped with outline figures in the accepted poses and then simply sketch in the appropriate costumes as the characters appeared on stage. The toy theatre was in something of a decline by the 1880s until *A Magazine of Art* published an article by Robert Louis Stevenson, 'A Penny Plain and Twopence Coloured', and it became suddenly fashionable to buy prints from Benjamin Pollock. Great men such as Chesterton and Stevenson himself all enjoyed playing with such models as boys, and Webb remembered Winston Churchill vaulting over his shop counter in his enthusiasm.

America relied heavily on imported toy theatres at first, and in New York and Philadelphia, Turner and Fischer were the agents for plays printed in England. Despite the skill of American printers, the toy theatre was not published on any scale until 1870, when Scott and Co. of New York issued 'Seltz's American Boys' Theatre' with hand-coloured woodcuts. Among the plays known from this series are 'The Fiend of the Rocky Mountain' and 'The Pirates of Florida Keys'. Each play cost 25 cents plain and 50 cents coloured and consisted of sixteen sheets with a twelve-page script. The footlights were also provided, lit either by gas or oil. In Denmark children's theatres were published by firms such as Jakobson and Prior from the 1860s.

After the First World War the standard of the commercially made model theatre declined steadily as the average child became more interested in the cinema, so that the model theatre of today is very much an artistic, cultivated plaything.

Optical toys with moving pictures

The theory of the persistence of vision fascinated both adults and children. Among the toys that exploited the phenomenon, the 'Thaumatrope', introduced in 1826, is one of the earliest that is still sometimes available for the collector. This toy was devised by Dr J. A. Paris and consists of a disc of paper, on either side of which are related images, such as a horse and a rider. When the disc is rotated rapidly by threads, the eye unites the two, so that the man is seen to be riding the horse. The original box has the inscription: 'Thaumatropical Amusement. Seeing an object which is out of sight and to demonstrate the facility of the retina of the eye to retain the impression of an object.'

Plateau invented his 'Phenakistocope' in 1832, a device that was simultaneously invented by the Austrian, Stampfer, who called it a 'Stroboscope'. The importance of this invention lies in the fact that it was the first optical instrument to give an illusion of a moving picture, and thus to embody the principle of the cinema. It consists of a cardboard disc with a series of drawings in slightly different positions to be viewed in a mirror through slots around the edge of the disc while it is rapidly spun. Each drawing has a corresponding slit so that every individual movement can be seen. The eye retains these separate impressions, and the effect of continuous movement is thus achieved. Toys based on this principle were produced in 1833 by Ackermann and Co. of the Strand, London, and labelled 'Fantascope'. Men on bicycles, dancing couples, horsemen and jugglers were all included as appropriate themes. In 1850 Franz Uchatius modified the device: the mirror was abandoned in favour of an arrangement of slots on a separate disc, and this new version was called a 'Leliocinegraphe'.

The zoetrope or 'Wheel of Life', described theoretically by Horner in 1834 but first made by Desvignes in 1860, was made in considerable numbers by the manufacturers of tin toys. Carette sold a zoetrope of Russian iron, that was provided with grooved pulleys so it could be driven by a steam-engine; this example came complete with twelve pictures. The zoetrope was basically a modification of the slotted disc device. The diagrams are here placed in a hollow cylinder that is rotated on a vertical axis, so that they can be viewed through slits in the metal sides. Although large numbers were made, the breakage rate must have been high, as they do not appear in the salerooms as frequently as might be expected.

Some distortion was inevitable in pictures viewed through slots, and in 1877 Reynaud attempted to overcome this with his 'Praxinoscope', in which a band of pictures was placed inside a shallow cylinder at the centre of which was a set of as many mirrors as there were pictures. The images were viewed in the mirrors, and because they were much better lit, they were clearer than had previously been possible. Emil Reynaud later invented a method of projecting scenes onto a screen by a series of pictures on a long roll of paper, a device known as the 'Théâtre Optique'.

At the 1861 Society of Arts Exhibition, William Thomas Shaw showed a 'Stereotrope', in which eight pairs of stereoscopic photographs were mounted on the outside of an octagonal drum, and as it rotated the photographs were viewed through a lenticular stereoscope. A rotating shutter between the viewer and the photographs meant that each pair of photographs could not be seen while in motion.

Cinematic toys

The long exposures needed for photographs before 1880 precluded the continuous photography of moving objects, although movement, of course, could be synthesized, as in the zoetrope. It was first analysed photographically by Eadweard J. Muybridge, who worked as a photographer in California. His long experiments in photographing horses in trotting motion by using a series of separate cameras produced twenty-four consecutive frames of a moving picture in 1879, and these were considered by the press to be particularly suitable for viewing in a zoetrope. Muybridge subsequently designed his own 'Zoogyroscope' to show his animals in motion. Drawings based on the photographs were mounted around a glass disc, while a second disc with slots was placed in front of the first, as in the early card versions, the two revolving in opposite directions. Later, the meeting of Muybridge with the French Professor E. J. Marey resulted in the development of a photographic gun which took

A stereoscopic viewer marked 'Breveté s.g.d.g. vues prises avec le Vérascope Richard'. *Circa* 1905. Width 16 cm. (6½ in.).

twelve exposures on one plate; this was first used in 1882. In 1888 Marey was again working on the development of a moving film, and built what are considered to be the first successful moving-picture cameras. At this stage the film was made of paper, but celluloid was soon substituted. The first public exhibition of moving pictures, with scenes such as a train pulling into a station, took place in London in the spring of 1896. Within a few years simple models purely for the use of children were available.

Bing's cinematographs were made of Russian iron, and their 1912 catalogue suggested that they could be used for all films 'with Edison perforation'. The best versions were claimed to run almost noiselessly. A few were obviously sold for the use of adults and were known as 'Theatre Cinematographs'. Bing offered a good range of black-and-white films, such as 'Comical Street Cleaner', 'Fencer on Horseback' and 'The Amusing Clown'—subjects not far removed from those intended for the zoetrope. Bing's coloured films were much more progressive in theme; one of them, for instance, represented the 'Airship z vii over the Royal Train'. Their 'Kinographone' (a registered name) consisted of a cinematograph show combined with a talking-machine, and was a surprisingly adventurous toy for 1912.

A child's tinplate candle-powered cinematograph with the original metal-boxed film. *Circa* 1920. Height 25 cm. (10 in.).

Other optical amusements

Quite apart from those falling within mainstream development of the moving picture, a very wide variety of interesting optical toys was marketed in the nineteenth century. In the very early years of the century the London Stereoscopic Company sold a toy consisting of a piece of wire bent to form an outline of a figure and set in a hollow spindle; when revolved, the figure appeared whole. The kaleidoscope was patented by Sir David Brewster in 1817 and consisted of an arrangement of mirrors within a tube. When rotated, pieces of coloured glass could be seen in a number of patterns. A few kaleidoscopes, such as those made by Carette which stood on polished wooden revolving stands, contained 'Child Scenes' made up of photographs. The better kaleidoscopes all had turning mechanisms, but by the 1890s there were some cheaper tin types that were simply shaken, rather like those of today.

'Les Anamorphoses' was an amusing toy involving distorted figures, printed on paper, that were viewed in a polished metal cylinder standing in the centre of a circle. When seen reflected in this metal mirror, the figures appeared perfect. The toy museum at Nuremberg has an equally interesting example of an optical toy printed in Stuttgart by Gustav Weiser. Six fairy stories are projected by daylight or lamplight into a picture frame which is being gazed into by a printed lady in medieval dress.

Though the various instruments for the viewing of photographs were adult in origin, and made of walnut or mahogany, they were often enjoyed by children. Carette was selling sliding view-holders in 1911, and providing the best models with plush edgings for the eye-pieces. Some were designed to be rested on a table and were given a folding extra foot. Others held a number of views, so it was not necessary to put down the instrument in mid-showing. At a much lower level of sophistication, tiny stereoscopes made of tin, some given away as advertising material, were made by the producers of tin toys.

The Anorthoscope or Magic Disc. The distorted pictures become clear when spun and viewed through the slots. English, *circa* 1842. Height 48 cm. (19 in.). (Bethnal Green Museum).

A particularly complete kaleidoscopic colour top invented and patented by John Gorham, 18 April, 1856. The various sheets, placed on the revolving table, were viewed through patterned shapes cut in the top card. (Victoria and Albert Museum.)

A lavishly ornamented French Magic Lantern with a lens hood dating to the mid 19th century. (Victoria and Albert Museum.)

A child's tinplate magic lantern with a celluloid zootrope device and the original oil lamp. Made by Fritz Neumeyer of Nuremberg. *Circa* 1905. Height 20 cm. (8 in.).

The magic lantern

To the majority of collectors the toy that is most evocative of the Victorian age is the magic lantern, through which pictures that were slightly yellow and with the paint often scratched would be viewed with alternating horror and laughter by complete families on winter evenings. The lantern had already become a fairly commonplace item by the early nineteenth century, yet country audiences could still be raised to fever-pitch by projections of ghouls and demons in performances such as the 'Phantasmagoria of Robertson'. The finest lanterns, with complex mechanisms and lavish ornamentation in brass, were designed for adults,and the toy versions can be easily distinguished by their economy of construction. Oil was the usual means of illumination but it is thought that some 'Galantee men' worked by candlelight. Long narrow slides, drawn slowly across the lens, were used in the Regency period, a type that continued to be produced alongside square slides until the end of the nineteenth century. Early slides are very finely painted and often have light backgrounds, whereas many of those made late in the century are merely isolated painted figures on plain black backgrounds. As the lantern came within the price range of a greater number of people, the travelling showman disappeared and it was now the men of the family who were expected to provide an exciting show. In this they were helped by the improved lighting provided by such sources as oxy-hydrogen limelight and, later, the electric arc light. Despite these advances, the lanterns and even cinematographs made for children were often lit by candle well into the nineteenth century and even sometimes into the twentieth.

The box cover of a magic lantern indicating how misleading was much Edwardian advertising. It has the 'Opus Coronat Laborem' trade mark of Fritz Neumeyer of Nuremberg who made mechanical and optical toys.

It is thought that the magic lantern as a child's toy was first made by Auguste Lapierre, a Parisian tinsmith, for the amusement of his own children in 1843. Because this toy, which was basically a tin box fitted with a candle-holder, concave mirror and lens, was highly successful, Lapierre decided to produce the toy commercially. Some of his lanterns were very richly and attractively finished with bright metallic colours, and one model, known as the 'Square Lampascope', was so heavily ornamented that it gave the appearance of cast iron. The firm worked from 1850 to 1914 and in addition to its lanterns it also made a cinematograph which would project either slides or films.

Fine lanterns, created with precision, were often supplied by the makers of optical instruments, but those intended for play came from the makers of tin toys such as Ernst Plank, Carette, Bing or Jean Schoenner of Nuremberg. These manufacturers described almost all their lanterns as 'Russian Iron' and provided spare parts, attachments and, of course, a vast number of slides. By 1911 illuminants included petroleum lights, gaslights, acetylene lamps, or high-pressure methylated-spirit gas-lights. One of the finest examples around this time was Carette's 'High Class Lantern',

A fine-quality magic lantern with brass detail of the type used by adults. (Collection Robert Hallmann.)

which in the largest size was supplied with 'brass fittings, brass objective with three lenses', and was packed in a pasteboard box with separate partitions for slides. The effect of movement could be simulated by the clever use of the lantern itself, as well as by moving slides, while for dissolving one view into another a double lantern was often used. When the cinematograph was first introduced, the manufacturers were careful to ensure that it could also be used to project all the regular-sized lantern slides.

Lantern slides

Most toy collectors like to own at least one example of a lantern, but because they are so large there is sometimes more interest in the slides with which they were equipped, especially those involving movement. One of the commonest early forms of the mechanically-moving slide was the 'slipping slide', consisting of a frame with several pieces of movable glass that could be pulled to the sides or passed across each other to imitate simple movements such as a nodding head or a woman's hat flying away. There were also 'lever slides', comprising two glass rectangles, one of which enclosed in a brass ring, was attached to a lever and worked up and

down over the other, so that, for example, a ship could appear to ride on the waves. 'Rackwork slides' were more expensive but produced a smoother movement. Some rackwork slides just showed patterns, to be used in the intervals between stories. A few slides were made of celluloid to avoid duty, but the majority, of course—after the early hand-drawn examples— were printed on glass. After 1860 the designs were transferred to the glass by photographic means and then hand-coloured, although J. Theobald and Co. were using chromolithography for their slides in the 1860s. Some amateurs made their own slides, and from certain firms they could be purchased plain and painted at home with the specially made transparent colours that were sold separately.

The German manufacturers were particularly aware of the importance of the American market and offered sets such as 'Life and Business in the United States' and 'The Discovery of America'. For the home market 'Slides of Airship and Aeroplane Voyages . . . with the well-known views of Zeppelin's voyages'. 'The airship shed at Manzell, the rising, the catastrophe near Echterdingen' were sold in 1912, and illustrated how close the subject matter was coming to some of today's trends in cinema.

A group of slides for a magic lantern including one of the rackwork type in which glass plates rotate in opposite directions when the handle is turned.

Wooden dolls

CARVED wooden dolls with inset iris-less glass eyes are commonly associated with the eighteenth century, although quite a large number were produced until around 1830. There is an almost traditional belief among collectors that those with dark brown eyes belong exclusively to the eighteenth century, and in the case of the more poorly constructed figures this generalization is well-founded; however, finely made examples wearing original Regency costumes are often seen with dark eyes in the earlier style. Much less often, eighteenth-century dolls of good quality are found with blue eyes.

The so-called 'Queen Anne' types (in fact made well into the Regency period) have tremendous primitive appeal, with flat backs and stylized skittle-shaped bodies. The majority appear to have originated in England, as German woodens of the same period are carved with much more character, with an apparent attempt at realistic faces. With the exception of William Higgs, who was involved in a court case over the theft of some of his stock, the makers of Queen Annes are not known. Their manufacture was gradually brought to an end as the market was flooded with much cheaper German dolls of a more fashionable type in the early nineteenth century. The delicately carved breasts, faces and stomachs that were seen in the best early woodens, together with well-made ball-jointed articulation, are not found on the late Queen Annes, which were aimed, it would seem, at a far more general market. In order to produce this cheaper-style figure, even the relatively simple standard eighteenth-century shape was modified and the jointed wooden limbs often replaced by sawdust-filled leather or fabric tubes with the minimum of shaping. The sharply jutting hips of the early dolls had been necessary to help support the shape of the full skirt, but the flowing, body-clinging Regency costume made it possible for doll-makers to dispense with this shaping, and it is more common to find simple pointed torsos with a hole drilled through so the legs could hang from string or wire. The heads of the late dolls were sometimes carved and shaped with such economy that they are referred to as the 'bedpost' type. Though this style of construction is more typical of the Regency period (1811–26), it should be remembered that a few dolls were made in this way in the 1780s, so that precise dating usually depends on the remains of any costume.

The dolls that most perfectly epitomize the Regency period are those of

A typical wooden doll of the Queen Ann type dated by the original costume to 1800. It once belonged to a Quaker family. It has a hair wig sewn to a linen base, leather arms, brown irisless eyes and high colouring on the cheeks. This very stylized colouring is found on the majority of dolls in really good original condition. Height 51 cm. (9 in.). (Collection Betty Harvey-Jones.)

A carved wooden Grödnertal doll with unusual swivel neck. Detail such as the carved ears was only put on larger sizes. *Circa* 1820. Height 60 cm. (23½ in.).

jointed wood described as 'Grödnertals', after the region of Germany where most of them were made. It was customary until quite recently to group all the nineteenth-century woodens together under the category of 'Dutch dolls' (Francis H. Low, writing of Queen Victoria's dolls in 1894, commented on the 'common twopenny Dutch dolls', despite the fact that the figures he was describing were delicately jointed and decorated). The Grödnertals are recognized by their slim high-waisted bodies and black hair that is either upswept and decorated with comb, made of delicately plaited cord that is painted and varnished, or painted to resemble the guillotine cut, with short curls around the face. Flat-heeled painted slippers and the relatively small size of the head are also characteristic features.

Doll-manufacturing developed quickly in the Grödnertal region of Germany, where it was aided by improvements in communication, and before long the agents of Sonneberg, Gröden and Berchtesgaden were all offering what they claimed to be different wares, although from the catalogue illustrations they would appear very similar. The Oberammergau dolls displayed in the town's folk museum are distinctly different from these. Among the exhibits is a particularly large and fine 'shoulder-headed' lady with an unusual deeply curved shoulder, probably intended for attaching to a fabric body although it could possibly have been jointed into wood. The finish is in a natural flesh colour that is quite unlike the yellowish tint found on the Grödnertals, and it is strange that assembled dolls of this very striking type are not encountered. An unusual male wooden doll was also made in Oberammergau, with characteristically painted black whiskers but with a beard treated in an almost abstract, stylized manner that is completely idiosyncratic. A number of these rather fierce male dolls are shown in the museum, and all have bodies that are much thicker than those typical of the basic Grödnertals. As so many of the Oberammergau products were exported eastwards, it might be possible to find examples of these interesting dolls in Eastern Europe or Russia.

The early makers of Grödnertals are believed to have sent them to Oberammergau for decoration, but as the movement of workers became more fluid and skills dispersed, they later began to finish the dolls themselves, with a water-based colour that was protected by a resin and alcohol varnish, giving the warm tone to the faces. The range of sizes produced was considerable, from 2·5 cm. (1 in.) to as much as 110 cm. (43 in.); the more expensive types had an additional joint at the waist and, more rarely, at the neck. There was only the most rudimentary suggestion of ears, and the earrings were often screwed into the head itself. It is difficult to be precise regarding the date at which dolls of this type were first made, as I have examined some occupants of eighteenth-century dolls' houses that are almost identical in form to the Grödnertals, though without combs. The only real difference of construction was in the cutting of the torso, which in the small eighteenth-century examples was not shaped in any way.

Despite the survival of some superb, very large examples that are comparable in quality with the best dolls of any period, there was a general levelling of standards in the early nineteenth century. Dolls comparable in style and quality could now be obtained from a variety of sources as diverse as elegant town-arcades and hiring fairs. In order to create a few dolls that were slightly different, some were given a coating of wax, presumably for added realism, while others were decorated with a painted black spot on the crown. Gwen White mentions a wooden with glass eyes that opened and closed by means of a wire, and occasionally a figure with a moulded surface of brotteig or plaster is found, though this method was mainly used for the more complicated hairstyles. In the 1840s papier mâché was used more frequently over the wooden core of the head.

Early American dolls

American toy-makers, always concerned about durability and possibly dissatisfied with German-produced heads that were liable to chip if dropped, began to manufacture their own dolls on a commercial scale from the mid-nineteenth century onwards. The first American patent for a doll's head was registered in 1858 by Ludwig Greiner of Philadelphia, described in a directory of the time as a 'toy-man'. These are the first truly American dolls and are a cornerstone in any representative collection. The patent specification describes the method of manufacture: white paper was first boiled and then beaten and pressed into a moist consistency. After the addition of whiting, rye flour and glue, the mixture was rolled out and the cut pieces pressed into moulds. Wherever a part projected it was reinforced with linen and muslin. When half-dry, the two parts were again saturated with the glue. At this stage linen or muslin was also pressed into the inside of the head. When completely dry the parts were removed from the moulds and fixed together, the joins being strengthened with further strips of muslin (this is a characteristics by which Greiner can be recognized).

Greiner dolls range in size from just over 30 cm. (1 ft) to 90 cm. (3 ft), and the hair is centre-parted. In the early versions the hair is invariably black, but from 1872, when the patent was extended, an almost equal number of blonde dolls are found. Glass-eyed dolls of this particular type are only rarely found, as the vast majority were painted. They were originally marked with a characteristic black and gold label, though this is now sometimes missing.

There was no American interest in the commercial production of jointed wooden dolls until 1873, when a patent was granted to Joel Ellis of Springfield who in the previous year had established the Co-operative

A turned and carved American wooden doll brightly painted in primary colours and faintly marked 'Mary L' on base. A robust folk-type figure dating to the mid-19th century. Height 27 cm. (11 in.). (Collection Betty Harvey-Jones.)

A pair of American papier mâché dolls. The smaller blue-eyed doll has a Greiner label 'Greiner's Improved Patent Heads. Pat. March 30th '58'. Both have fabric bodies with leather arms. Height of taller doll 58 cm. (23 in.). (Collection Betty Harvey-Jones.)

An unusual doll that skips when the wires are fully extended and the wooden handle turned. It has a composition head with painted features and a wooden body. Marked 'Patent' under the foot. It is wearing the original printed blue pinafore and a cardboard hat. Several firms registered similar patents up to 1900. *Circa* 1885. Height of doll 26 cm. (10 in.).

A Cossack doll with composition head and jointed wood and composition body wearing the original quilted cotton coat and cord hat. Unmarked but probably made for Russian refugee funds. *Circa* 1925.

Manufacturing Company with some sixty employees to make dolls. Ellis was an energetic inventor and improver, and among his other products was a steam-shovel and a child's carriage. The jointing of his wooden dolls enabled them to be positioned at will; they were therefore a great improvement on those imported from Germany that were made with feet on which the figure could not possibly balance. In appearance these dolls were much heavier and less graceful than those of German manufacture, but must have gained considerably by the fact that they could be posed in such a variety of ways. Rock maple was used for the dolls' bodies but the hands and feet were metal. There was a single model for the heads, as the cost of making dies was so great. Even dolls in different sizes have almost identical expressions.

George W. Sanders patented an improved joint in 1880; and Henry Mason and Luke Taylor, both of Springfield, combined to produce dolls with this improvement as well as with heads of moulded composition over a wooden base. The Mason and Taylor dolls again have metal hands and feet. The whole group of dolls made in this area are now often simply grouped together and referred to as 'Springfield' dolls.

Papier mâché dolls

Papier mâché dolls are mentioned before the eighteenth century but actual examples are not known. Those dating from before 1760 are usually of a very crude construction, moulded to waist level in a carton-like substance and then provided with leather thighs and legs. In one example, only the carton torso remains and the limbs are left as mere armatures of wire. Far more attractive are the later dolls of the century with deep-fronted papier mâché 'shoulder heads' mounted on shaped leather bodies. Others with this type of head were given bodies of jointed wood. The faces were decorated in a mannered way and were completely different from those used on the typical early nineteenth-century papier mâchés that originated almost exclusively in Germany.

Regency papier mâchés usually have moulded hair that is arranged into the most complicated styles. Whenever a coiffure defeated the modeller, real hair, heavily stiffened with size, would be used instead; occasionally an application of hair would be used in combination with a moulded shape. In the late 1830s, a rounder-faced type was developed that looked rather more realistic, as the face was painted in natural flesh tones and sometimes left completely unvarnished. Glass eyes were sometimes inserted and the painted hairstyles became much simpler. An unusual papier mâché doll of this period with a painted bonnet is illustrated here, together with a more typical leather-bodied male doll. Hair wigs, that are often found glued over a black spot or even a rudimentary hairstyle, were very beautifully made with realistic centre-partings and the most intricately plaited arrangements, while some heads were even provided with bamboo teeth. When in good condition, the dolls of this period have great charm, but the lack of protective varnish has often resulted in disfigurement.

A papier mâché lady doll with a wooden Grödnertal type body, blue painted eyes and black hair, wearing the original 18th century style brown-sprigged cotton open robe with a pink quilted petticoat. *Circa* 1830. Height 36 cm. (14 in.).

A papier mâché lady with a straight-limbed body of pink kid and painted blue eyes. The hair is set into a slit in the crown and elaborately plaited. *Circa* 1835–1840. Height 33 cm. (13 in.).

Wax dolls

Wax was a traditional material for doll-making and as naturally used as wood, but the first documentary reference to the method occurs in the fourteenth century, when goods at a Venetian fair were said to include dolls of wood, papier mâché and wax. Effigy and mannequin figures for commemorative purposes were made of wax earlier, however; wax models of the deceased were laid out in costly garments and placed on public view, and the first record of a full-sized wax figure being used in England as a substitute for a body in this way dates from the thirteenth century. In Renaissance Italy, Vasari commented on the popularity among the nobles of wax figures that were embellished with stones, tinsel and human hair. These techniques were to continue until the nineteenth century, particularly in the decoration of figures of the Infant Jesus where realism was not as important as the achievement of a lavish, icon-like effect.

Early examples of wax dolls have to be studied in the context of dolls' houses. One of the earliest lady figures is that in the Kress cabinet house, which was built in the second quarter of the seventeenth century and is now in the Germanisches Nationalmuseum in Nuremberg; this doll has a shaped fabric body and the fingers are small rolls of fabric, most beautifully made. In the hall of the same house stands a wax patrician lady with black painted eyes, wooden legs and unusual flocked grey hair. In Margaretha de Ruyter's house at the Rijksmuseum, Amsterdam, dating from the mid-seventeenth century, there are exquisitely made wax dolls modelled with great realism as individual characters, ranging from beautiful women to an old peasant man at work in the attic. All these dolls wear wigs and the hands in almost every instance are modelled with one fist clenched, with a hole running through it, and one open. The clenched hand was useful in that it could carry a stick or have an item sewn to it. The bodies are of silk-bound wire and are very similar in construction to the figures seen in crèche settings, so that a doll found out of context could be easily misdescribed.

A two-roomed cabinet dating from the late seventeenth century, now in the Germanisches Nationalmuseum, contains an unusual adult male doll with wax hands and a face that is apparently wax over a plaster core. Other Nuremberg dolls' houses of the period contain lady dolls with wax heads and tow-bound bodies, including one with intricately plaited hair arranged in several layers around the head. The wax dolls of the German makers were praised by a contemporary, Joachim von Sandrart, who commented that the work of Daniel Neuberger in Augsburg was as hard as stone and so well coloured that the dolls seemed alive.

Jointed lady dolls, known as 'Pandoras', were used in the seventeenth and eighteenth centuries for the display of fashionable garments, so that women in other countries could see exactly how the elegant women of Paris and even London were dressing. Much more unusual wax figures of this intention were displayed at the Stadtmuseum, Munich, in 1976 in a special exhibition whose theme was the various means of communicating fashion designs through the ages. The dolls themselves, cast in wax around 1700 complete with wax ruffs and farthingales, were displayed together with their wooden two-piece moulds, which were intricately carved with a considerable degree of surface detail. The wax was sensitive enough to pick up even the delicate patterns carved on the 'fabric', and the result was suprisingly informative of the look of contemporary costumes.

Ann Sharp's baby house, built between 1691 and 1700, contains an interesting group of wax dolls, among them 'William Rochett ye heir', a title on a label written by Ann herself. This boy doll has a wax 'shoulder head' with an unusual open-closed mouth revealing the tip of the tongue. The very bright light-blue eyes have small black pupils and a wool wig is worn. The feet are moulded with red buckled shoes and the hands from the wrist down are also of wax though the remainder of the body is fabric. In the same house there is also a very small wax child dressed in yellow. Several of the dolls, both in this and in the Nuremberg houses, are modelled only to waist level, the lower part of the body being built up of card (in Ann Sharp's house, playing cards were mainly used for this purpose). This type of construction, using a modelled torso which was sold individually and allowed the doll to be assembled as required, is also seen in the woodens that inhabit Ann Sharp's house, and it would appear that it was an accepted doll-making practice. The pair of very typical dolls illustrated on page 24, dressed to represent Mary and the Infant Jesus, have their skirts supported by a page from a Latin prayer book. All the known wax doll's house figures made in this way have bead-like painted eyes and the hands and faces have obviously been finished with the aid of a carving tool.

German museums exhibit several fine eighteenth-century poured wax ladies and one, dating from 1730, has a strangely modelled mouth in an open position revealing the tongue. Another, believed to have been made in Nuremberg itself, represents a plump, middle-aged woman with an ample bosom and painted brown eyes with highlights. This doll was obviously a prestige piece and the fingers are exquisitely made of fabric wrapped around wire. It wears a dress of pink silk and white muslin with a lace fichu. Another early example has very beautifully shaped wax hands of a standard not often seen on dolls.

Defoe, writing in Paris in 1722, commented that 'The Duchess of Orleans has made a present to the Infant Queen of a wax baby, three foot high, with diamond earrings, a necklace of pearls and a diamond cross, with furniture of plate for a toilet and two indian chests full of linen and several sets of cloaths for the Baby, the whole for that Princess to play with.' Confusingly, 'baby' referred in the eighteenth century to a doll representing an adult, and the term continued in occasional use until the 1830s. The great interest of Defoe's reference lies in the fact that already, in 1722, such a doll was accompanied by lavish trousseaux, even though intended for play.

Various innovations in the construction of dolls occurred in the eighteenth century, one example of which is the 'Wax baby with an invention to make it cry and turn its eyes' that was bought by Dr Claver

An unusually slim-faced, waxed composition doll with mohair wig and fixed blue eyes. It has painted blue boots and is wearing the original red woollen frock with muslin overskirt. *Circa* 1850. Height 34 cm. (13½ in.).

Morris of Wells, Somerset, in 1701. There was also a great increase in the number of toyshops and suppliers where commercially produced dolls could be selected. A wax doll bought in 1797 by George IV for his year-old daughter was supplied by A. Loriot of New Bond Street. Waxed compositions appear in the late eighteenth century, when a papier mâché shell would be dipped in wax to give a more realistic effect. Surviving examples have fabric bodies with leather arms, and unless they retain the original costumes they are frequently misdated to the Regency period when their manufacture became more common.

The study of wax dolls up to the Regency period shows some differences between those of German and English origin, but after 1800 it is virtually impossible to differentiate by nationality, especially in the case of waxed compositions. A few, with coiffured hair in intricate arrangements, are fairly obviously German as they are almost identical in style to the German

A waxed composition lady doll dated by the original faded pink net dress and high-crowned straw hat to *circa* 1795. The arms are of pink leather and the fair hair is pinned to the crown. Height 33 cm. (13 in.).

A waxed composition doll of the 'slit head' type with blonde hair and pale blue eyes, wearing the original 18th century style costume of a red velvet jacket over a white muslin gold and white-trimmed lace frock. The sequin decoration is pinned in place to give a gaudy effect. *Circa* 1825. Height 61 cm. (24 in.).

Opposite A poured wax lady doll with fixed brown eyes wearing a cream silk dress. The head is unusual for the type as it is bald and a wig is glued on. It is usual for poured waxes to have implanted hair. *Circa* 1865. Height 56 cm. (22 in.).

papier mâchés. However, the majority have ringletted hair that is crudely applied through a slit running along the crown of the head, a feature which has given rise to the collectors' term 'slit heads'. Some of these dolls were equipped with wired sleeping eyes, and I discovered a fascinating reference to the invention of this method in a copy of *The British Toymaker*, which contains an interview with a maker of wax dolls, a certain Mr Wheelhouse who was still working in the Waterloo Road in 1910. He was described in the magazine as almost the last craftsman of wax dolls in England, as the industry had been 'ruined by foreigners'. He explained to his interviewer:

> Before the advent of the china dolls of Germany there were over one hundred hands employed here in the Waterloo Road making wax dolls, and even then we couldn't turn these dolls out fast enough. My father, grandfather and great grandfather were all practical doll-makers and it was the last named who invented the first made dolls with movable eyes. In those days the mechanism that controlled this was rather a primitive affair. You pulled a wire that protruded about the middle of dolly's ribs and the eyes shut and opened.

The greatest effort of doll-makers in nineteenth-century England was put into the making of poured wax dolls, and these were regarded as the finest in the world. The most prized examples are those made by the Montanari family, who worked from several addresses in London. At the Great Exhibition of 1851 Madame Montanari showed dolls representing all

ages, from infancy to womanhood, but the jury considered that her figures were too lifelike for a child and also over-expensive. Most Montanaris have rather child-like heads, although the very slender-waisted bodies are definitely those of women. These dolls are also characterized by the almost violet blue that was sometimes used for eyes and the heavy rolls of fat at neck and wrists. The costume was often given a fringed decoration and the inspiration for the clothes is very much that of the mid-nineteenth century. After 1887 members of the Montanari family no longer appear in the London directories as doll-makers, so it is probable that they ceased trading altogether at this time. As their work was only very rarely marked, comparatively few of their dolls can be positively attributed, so that the term 'Montanari type' has to be used. Some of the marked dolls exhibit none of the firm's better characteristics, although they are of great interest. As well as the simple poured wax examples, the Montanaris also made the so-called 'London' or 'English' wax babies that were given a layer of stretched muslin over the faces with the intention of creating a softer and more durable effect. Few have survived in a good state, as the fabric easily discoloured and the mixture of media makes cleaning almost impossible.

Charles Marsh of London was listed as a maker of both poured wax and

A poured wax doll with fixed blue eyes and inset brown hair marked 'Chas Marsh Model Wax Baby Doll Manufacturer, 114 Fulham Road S.W. Dolls cleaned and repaired', wearing the original cream silk and lace dress and well-made purple boots. *Circa* 1880. Height 53 cm. (20½ in.).

waxed composition dolls and continued to produce toys until 1895. After this time his wife worked as a repairer for a few years. Their dolls were stamped with the name of the firm in an oval on the chest, and they supplied both C. Gooch and E. Moody of the Soho Bazaar. Herbert Meech, who also cleaned and repaired, made a few dolls with sound boxes operated by the pulling of a string. Perhaps the best-loved of the English makers, however, are the Pierottis, who came to England in the mid-eighteenth century and ended their production of wax dolls only in 1935. Henri Pierotti, born in 1809, was principally a maker of wax portrait figures but he is thought to have also produced dolls, and a family tradition among his descendants claims that he modelled some of them on his own children. During the nineteenth century hair stuffing was used for the poured waxes but by the early twentieth century a type of kapok-like filling was employed. Like the Montanaris, the Pierottis inserted the hair into the doll's head with heated tools to give a natural effect, although they often grouped the hair in small tufts. Some very interesting portrait dolls were specially created, such as a grey-whiskered Lord Roberts and even some Old Testament figures, while their elegant lady dolls often have rich titian hair. An advertisement for the firm stated that 'Young ladies, by sending

An Edwardian poured wax lady doll with titian hair of a type often used by the Pierotti family, with wax limbs and blue glass eyes, wearing a pale blue silk gown trimmed with pearls and lace. Height 46 cm. (18½ in.).

their own hair, can have it implanted through the composition to form the wig. Likenesses modelled and casts taken.' Lucy Peck, who worked between 1891 and 1921 at the Doll's House, 131 Regent Street, also offered to implant customers' hair and made use of a wired sleeping device for the eyes.

By the end of the nineteenth century, waxed composition was mainly used for very cheap dolls, and only rarely are examples found with implanted hair. Lady dolls with very elegantly shaped faces were made in some number during the Edwardian period, and when in good condition and accompanied by well-made fashionable outfits they can look very striking.

Porcelain and bisque dolls

The traditional doll-making materials—wood, wax, and papier mâché—were all gradually ousted from popularity by the increasingly economical production of porcelain. It is thought that china dolls were first made around 1800 but surviving examples of early types date largely to the 1830s; after 1845 they were made in vast numbers and were within the price range of practically every child. The cold white faces of the porcelains were hardly realistic and were easily broken, but they had one great advantage over the other substances in that they were easily washed. Porcelain was used for the parts of the body that might be seen when the doll was costumed, but the torso and the upper parts of the limbs were made of sawdust-filled cotton. There was some variety in the construction

A pair of pink-tinted porcelain dolls both wearing their original costumes. The boy doll, wearing a grey woollen suit dating from about 1860, is marked on the body in an oval 'Fr H & C Patent'. The shoulder head has one central sew-hole back and front. The black-haired lady is pink-tinted. Height of boy 19·5 cm. (7¾ in.).

A pink-tinted porcelain lady doll with long ringlets and painted blue eyes. Dolls of this colouring are often described as the Berlin type. Height 46 cm. (18½ in.).

A porcelain doll with blonde, crisply modelled hair and painted blue eyes wearing the original maroon silk frock trimmed with lace. Fair-haired porcelains are much rarer than those with black hair. *Circa* 1870. Height 41 cm. (16 in.).

of the heads, ranging from elegant women's heads with hair swept into chignons and decorated with moulded flowers, to others made more realistic by a soft pink tinting. Heads in the latter style are often described as being of the 'Berlin type'. A few porcelains were given bald heads, either with a black spot painted on the crown, or left plain, and sometimes unglazed so that the well-made wigs would adhere more securely. A much plumper-faced type of porcelain had developed by the 1840s, with less interestingly shaped hairstyles, and for some time these were sold alongside the dolls with more delicate heads.

Very few porcelains are marked, though several bodies are stamped on the torso. It was once thought that virtually all the porcelains were of German origin but examples do occur suggesting a French manufacture on a much smaller scale. A few porcelains, especially in doll's house sizes,

A particularly fine porcelain lady doll with moulded flowers in the dark brown hair and slightly modelled breasts. The head is tinted pink and has three sew-holes at the back and front of the shoulder plate. Marked 'Fr H. & Co. Patent' on the body in an oval. Probably of French origin. Height 43 cm. (17 in.). (Collection Betty Harvey-Jones.)

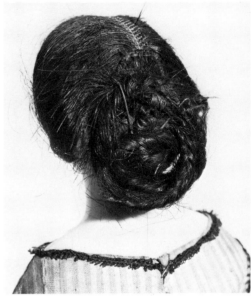

Detail of the plaited hair of the parian-type lady doll.

A parian-type lady doll with a particularly well-made plaited wig wearing the original cotton and silk dress, *circa* 1865, and a pink-tinted male doll with a moulded beard and moustache wearing a red velvet jacket. Height of lady doll 26 cm. (10 in.).

continued to be made until 1930, and the price of these basic types has remained low in consequence of their long-running production.

White bisque was a popular doll-making material between 1855 and 1880, as the substance was particularly suited for the representation of the very complex hairstyles of the period, incorporating beads and flowers. The white bisques, often called 'parians' by collectors, were facially quite different from the porcelains and imitated the features of haughty and elegant women. A few rare parians were given swivel necks and inset glass eyes, sometimes in combination with applied flowers and lace. As with the porcelains, quite considerable numbers of heads were sold loose, to be made up at home, so that fine examples are sometimes found mounted on inappropriate but completely authentic bodies. In order to create a more realistic face, the white bisque was sometimes tinted pink, a colouring that

Left A bonnet doll wearing the original pink and white pinafore and a purple silk frock. The moulded bonnet is decorated in pale pink and blue and the ribbon on the neck has a gold lustre. The sawdust-filled body has bisque limbs. Unmarked but of German origin. Late 19th century. Height 38 cm. (14¾ in.).

Opposite A white bisque lady doll of the type described as 'parian' with unusually stylized shoulders and chestnut coloured hair arranged with a plait and bun at the nape of the neck, brilliant blue painted eyes and flat-heeled black shoes, and wearing the original white and lilac costume trimmed with braid. *Circa* 1865. Height 30·5 cm. (12 in.).

A very delicately-tinted bisque lady with moulded fair hair looped up by a black comb at the nape of the neck and a very well-modelled face with blue painted eyes. No sew-holes to shoulder head. The original lilac silk costume is decorated with lace, jet beads and black velvet ribbon. *Circa* 1865. Height 24 cm. (9½ in.).

became popular after 1865–70. Pink-tinted bisques are rather more frequently found with swivel necks and glass eyes, and they vary much more widely in quality. A more child-like face was becoming popular in the last quarter of the century and there is a noticeable lowering of standards, both in modelling and decoration. Later dolls of the parian type were sometimes given moulded hats and bonnets and more boys were made. Long after this type of head had passed out of general favour, it continued to be used by the makers of doll's house inhabitants as no other material was so effective in reproducing features on a very small scale.

A parian-type lady with a well-modelled face and the unusual addition of gilded, moulded earrings and a cross. This doll has red and blue moulded flowers on the hair, blue painted eyes and is wearing a green shot silk dress. *Circa* 1870. Height 36 cm. (14 in.).

Parisiennes

French involvement in the mass production of dolls does not seem to have begun in earnest until after 1860, although Paris had long been recognized as the centre for their fashionable costuming. It is thought that the French imported papier mâché heads from Germany in the first half of the nineteenth century and mounted them on French leather bodies. This theory is difficult either to prove or refute. My own view is that it is often over-stressed and that the majority of Sonneberg-type heads have bodies that also originate in Germany. Equally, the manufacture of papier mâché heads could have presented few problems to the French toy-makers.

The earliest *Parisiennes*, the term given by the makers of the period to the elegant French lady dolls, are generally considered to be those with glazed porcelain heads and gusseted kid bodies. It was once thought that these were all of German origin, but as they are not discovered in German museums or mentioned in catalogues it seems more probable that they were of French manufacture. These early heads are immediately recognizable by their plump cheeks and often child-like features. The painting of the nostrils, with two red spots, giving a rather pug-like effect, is particularly idiosyncratic and is unlikely to have been suddenly introduced by the Germans. Early *Parisiennes* in this style are often referred to by collectors as being of the 'Rohmer type', since this factory produced the majority of attributable pink-tinted examples.

Rohmer was granted patents for dolls as early as 1857, though none that can be positively dated to the 1850s are recorded. The necks of their dolls are unusual in that instead of the usual curved socket they have a flat swivel, with what is known as a 'cup and saucer' joint. Marked Rohmers bear the name 'Mme Rohmer. Breveté. s.g.d.g. Paris' (s.g.d.g. means 'without government guarantee'). Marked Hurets with glazed porcelain heads are also sometimes found in original 1860s costume, so it is obvious that firms other than Rohmer experimented with similar heads. Jointed gutta percha bodies as well as the more usual gusseted kid are known on such examples.

Bisque was used for the heads of *Parisiennes* from about 1860. The early bisque dolls usually have rigid necks and plump faces and are similar in features to those of porcelain. Glass eyes were usual, but sometimes the eyes were skilfully painted so that even from a short distance the effect of glass was given. The wigs were almost invariably of sheepskin and the bodies were gusseted leather firmly packed with sawdust, hair or even cork. More interesting body constructions include those with a fabric-over-metal armature (known as the 'Gesland' type), and others in which fine leather was stretched over turned and carved wood. Some bodies were made entirely of wood painted to look like flesh. Sometimes a combination of several methods was used. Display stands were sold by toyshops, but so fine was the balancing and jointing achieved by some of the makers that some of their figures could stand unsupported.

The costumes of dolls made in the 1860s, such as that illustrated here with its trousseau, are of fine quality. Although the sewing machine was

A *Parisienne* doll in particularly fine condition marked on the shoulder 'F G' for Fernand Gaultier, with bisque lower arms, stuffed leather legs with a wooden hip section, wearing the complete original costume in maroon and cream. Height 46 cm. (18 in.). (Collection Betty-Harvey-Jones.).

A swivel-headed *Parisienne* with blue eyes and a gusseted leather body wearing the original pale blue woollen silk-trimmed dress. *Circa* 1875. 33 cm. (13 in.). (Collection Betty Harvey-Jones.)

An unmarked *Parisienne* doll of very pale colour with a two-tone mouth, light blue eyes and a swivel neck, a gusseted kid body, wearing the original pale grey walking dress and straw hat. *Circa* 1875. Height 41 cm. (16 in.).

A selection of the clothes contained in the trunk of a marked Simonne doll. Other items can be seen in colour illustration on page 165. *Circa* 1868. Height of doll 45 cm. (18 in.).

available at this time, delicate garments such as these were more often hand-stitched, cheaply and skilfully, by the seamstresses of Paris. Small, specialist companies supplied the gloves, hats, shoes and fans with which the trunks were equipped, and consequently the number of these accessories was sometimes surprisingly large for the size of the doll. Fournier describes a mother *Parisienne* with a baby that needed a layette of some ten different items. Exclusive shops often stamped their name on dolls, so that a mark sometimes refers to the retailer rather than the maker. Gaultier, among others, provided heads to several assemblers, and their products are found on bodies marked both by Jumeau and Simonne.

The firm of Huret spent a great deal of time on sales ploys for the promotion of their dolls; for example, balls and garden parties were organized. They also introduced several improvements, such as a doll's head that could turn or tilt in its socket.

Although the work of Bru, who were in business in the Rue St Denis from 1866, is the most coveted, very few *Parisiennes* made by this firm can be positively attributed. A Bru catalogue of 1872 offered a range of dolls with the clothes sewn in place at a cheaper rate than those that could be

'The History and Adventures of Little Henry Exemplified in a Series of Figures' printed by D. N. Shury, Berwick Street, Soho, and published by S. & J. Fuller at the Temple of Fancy, Rathbone Place, in 1810. One head is slotted into seven figures illustrating Henry's adventures. Height figures 11 cm. ($4\frac{1}{4}$ in.).

Delicately coloured cut-out figures printed on card and representing Crown Prince Friedrich Wilhelm and Crown Princess Cecilie. *Circa* 1911. Unmarked.

Opposite An Edwardian bisque-headed lady in the original cream coloured lace and silk dress with a spare white lace dress in the trunk. Marked '792.7' and with indecipherable green numbers. The cut-away head with cardboard pate has fixed blue eyes. The body is a cheap cotton type with composition limbs and low, modelled shoulder plate with suggested breasts and no sew-holes. Height 28 cm. (11 in.).

redressed. The cheapest material for costumes was wool. Bru's least expensive dolls were given painted eyes, while their dearest were those with glass eyes and wooden bodies. The quality of their *bébés* is usually good, but that of their attributed *Parisiennes* varies considerably. Heads marked with the initials 'B.S.' are thought to originate at this factory, although the quality of these is often very poor. One example with a very plump face wearing its original cheap blue-and-white-striped muslin frock is marked 'B Jne et Cie' on the back of the shoulder and 'E. Déposé' on the front. A few others are authenticated by their original boxes but in judging *Parisiennes* the collector generally relies more on the appearance of the doll than on the presence of a mark.

Jumeau *Parisiennes* also vary in quality, some being of poor bisque while others are superb, with huge eyes and effective painting. The Jumeau company was established in 1842 when a partnership existed with a certain Belton. Early heads appear to have been obtained from other companies and the firm did not begin to make their own at the Montreuil-sous-Bois factory until the 1860s. One rare type was given moulded breasts and moulded bisque high-heeled shoes (an unmarked version of this doll was sold at Christie's in 1976). Jumeau staged exhibitions of their dolls in miniature furnished rooms, and specially constructed settings were staged in many towns in Europe and America to publicize the company's name among all the trade buyers.

Large numbers of firms produced *Parisiennes* and they still exist in reasonable quantity, although fully costumed examples are found only occasionally. As these dolls gradually passed out of fashion, their level of workmanship and presentation declined, and by 1885 most of those produced were of the type with basic gusseted kid bodies. Other, cheaper lady dolls were made in the late nineteenth and very early twentieth centuries by firms such as Lanternier. S.F.B.J.'s dolls of this type were particularly economical, with unjointed composition legs and arms in combination with the marked '60' heads used mainly on their child dolls—a pathetic reminder of the fine dolls of the earlier years.

Lady dolls were also made in the early twentieth century by a few German makers. There is a range of bisque ladies in various sizes that was probably made by Gebrüder Heubach, since the marks found on the shoulder plates are similar to those used by that firm and the combination of a fine-quality head with a poor body is also a Heubach characteristic. An example of this type, with a spare dress in a trunk, is illustrated here. Later, slim-jointed women were made by Simon and Halbig; the open-mouthed versions, however, are more in the manner of young girls than of elegant ladies.

Child-like dolls

A poured wax girl doll with inset bone teeth and fixed, dark, irisless eyes wearing the original green silk dress and bonnet. The hair is inserted in groups. *Circa* 1840. Probably German. Height 74 cm. (29 in.).

Early child dolls

ALTHOUGH the bent-limbed baby doll with a bisque head was an early twentieth-century concept, many dolls, particularly those of wax, were made to resemble babies in the preceding centuries. Plaster moulds for casting crèche-type figures and images of the Infant Jesus (the latter were often given as baptismal gifts) can be seen at Oberammergau. One very complicated figure, made in that town in the late eighteenth century represented an infant lying on a cushion with its legs crossed and each arm in a different position—a posture which must have created a very difficult casting problem. Despite the skilful moulding of the figure, the hair is simply a crude application of threads of wool dipped in wax. The Infant Jesuses that were made in this area are particularly distinctive, as the features are heavy and the heads look sharply to the side, so that when the figures are lying in a case the faces can be seen in detail, even down to the inset bone teeth. Simpler figures of this type (later made of wax over composition) were often contained in oval matchwood boxes as gifts. In these smaller versions, the body was a simple tapered cylindrical shape wrapped around with ribbon, tinsel or lace. Other figures, obviously intended for much rougher play, were made of brightly painted carved wood.

Probably the earliest known wax baby is that contained in the Stromer cabinet house built in 1637 (now in Nuremberg) where it is the sole occupant and lies in a filigree cradle. It has painted black spot-like eyes and is similar in appearance to the doll's house figures particularly associated with the eighteenth century. In the Kress house, in the same museum, is a wax bent-limbed baby with painted black hair carried in the arms of a lady doll. The baby dolls seen in late eighteenth-century baby houses are much simpler in construction and are sometimes just a roughly carved length of wood wrapped in a shawl, like the example in Ann Sharp's house discussed in the previous chapter. Many of the exquisitely made wax figures of babies, often protected under a shade, were made to commemorate a dead child or, sometimes, simply to record a period of a child's life in portrait form. In the late nineteenth century, the Pierotti family made a rather unsatisfactorily shaped baby doll with bent limbs, mounted on the usual type of stuffed fabric body. Few examples of this doll are known and it was presumably not popular.

A bisque-headed, jointed girl made in Germany and marked 'My Cherub'. Made by Arthur Schoenau. Trade-mark registered 1912. Height 58 cm. (23 in.).

Bébés

In the work of both the wax and the china doll-makers there was a development in the second half of the nineteenth century towards a more child-like image. The finest child dolls were made by French craftsmen, who developed a peculiarly idealized form of child in the last quarter of the century, with huge, fine-quality glass eyes, heads of delicate bisque, and bodies made of composition and wood, enabling the doll to stand. Such dolls, known as *bébés*, are very popular with collectors as they combine the appeal of antique objects of acceptable quality with expressive and often very beautiful faces.

It is difficult to establish precisely which of the many French companies introduced the *bébé*. Steiner was among the first to claim the credit for their invention, a claim that was countered by Bébé Bijou, who stated that Grandjean was the true innovator. These well-made dolls were displayed in prestige showrooms in Paris; the costuming was carried out in the city, although the factories themselves were in the suburbs, the potteries in particular being located in the Montreuil area. Children were encouraged to demand the new type of doll, together with appropriate accessories, at parties that were organized by the manufacturers. Each child would take along her own lavishly equipped bébé, and an atmosphere of rivalry was encouraged. The Jumeau company was particularly advertisement-conscious, and their sales literature frequently referred to 'beautiful French faces', the makers probably finding it in their own interests to accentuate the facial differences between their products and those of the cheaper German makers.

Many *bébés* were originally purchased costumed only in a simple muslin dress and chemise, although the shoes were generally supplied with the doll and in some cases it was only these that had a lasting manufacturer's mark. Muffs, umbrellas, hand-sewn gloves and writing cases were all provided separately in appropriate scale. Very small dolls sometimes lay in a trunk surrounded by clothes, hair-brushes and combs, while others were sold with wardrobes of clothes and ribbon-tied linen. Not only white but also negro, mulatto and oriental style *bébés* were made, to appeal to children not just in France, England and America but also those in the colonies. *Bébés* were produced by many small firms, such as Blampoix, Denameur and Petit et Dumontier, some of whom registered patents and labelled their dolls 'Bébé Breveté'—'patented doll'. Although many collectors today prefer the earlier leather-bodied dolls, the makers were originally very proud of the wood and composition bodies that enabled the doll to sit, stand and move each limb independently.

The evolution of the leather body, derived from the existing method for lady dolls, is seen particularly in the work of the Bru company, which made the most exquisitely constructed *bébés* with gusseted leather bodies, bisque lower arms, and heads that swivelled in the shoulder plate as in *Parisiennes*. Bru's dolls were intended to represent a child somewhere between the ages of eight and eleven, the Brus with shoulder plates, having delicately shaped

A French bisque-headed doll with fixed brown eyes and a closed mouth marked 'R.D', probably for Rabery & Delphieu, dressed in blue and cream silk. Dolls made by this firm are often characterized by their sturdy bodies and a very thick type of bisque. Height 63 cm. (25 in.).

adolescent breasts with tinted nipples, a touch of realism not often seen in dolls of this period. The degree of colouring in the faces is sometimes quite high and would be considered unattractive in a German doll of the same period, but here it is compensated for by the extremely high quality of the bisque and the skill of the colourist. Another Bru characteristic is the modelling of the hands, the fingers drooping in a rather lifeless way that helps in the creation of an idealized figure. Similar hands are seen on dolls made with poorer quality heads marked simply 'Breveté'. Early Brus, with a sheepskin wig, mouth modelled in a slightly open position and a crouching stance, often seem far from beautiful to non-collectors, despite their high value.

The firm supplied dolls to an extravagant public that enjoyed

A bisque-headed French doll with closed mouth, marked 'Bébé Breveté', with a gusseted kid body and a head that swivels in a shoulder plate. The doll has pierced ears and a sheepskin wig and is wearing a red silk dress and a velvet cape. *Circa* 1885. Height 32 cm. (12½ in.). (Collection Betty Harvey-Jones.)

innovations, and some pieces were produced almost purely for their novelty value. For example, there is a Bru whose chest moves as though it were breathing. 'Bébé le Téteur' appears to drink from a feeding bottle: milk can be sucked in and returned to the bottle through the mouth by turning a key at the back of the head. In 1880 a jointed all-rubber *bébé* was patented in an attempt to create an indestructible doll. Bru's leather *bébés* with carved wooden lower legs and bisque lower arms were made for some time alongside the earlier gusseted leather dolls, and it is only if the original costume is worn that a relatively precise date can be given. Because the firm was working for a fashion-conscious clientèle, the costume followed current trends quite closely, although of course it was specially adapted to doll form. The majority of the leather-bodied dolls still wearing original costumes seem to date to the 1880s, after which they were superseded by jointed bodies in composition and wood.

Jules Steiner made high-quality *bébés* that were offered for sale in the trade catalogues with the doubtful attribute of 'real human eyes'. The Steiner Company was established in 1855 and from 1860 onwards patents were continually registered, including many relating to mechanical improvements. In 1880 Steiner introduced an interesting mechanism which moved the eyes by the action of a lever protruding from a point just above the ears. When Steiners appeared in the same catalogues as Jumeaux they were more expensive, presumably because they were not produced in such vast numbers. In an American catalogue of the 1890s, fourteen-inch (35·5 cm.) Steiners were offered at sixty dollars a dozen and eighteen-inch (45·7 cm.) at ninety dollars. The open-mouthed doll, though now much less desirable, was originally hailed as an important advance as it was thought to be more realistic. One of Steiner's mechanical *bébés*, when key-wound, lifts its arms, kicks its legs and cries 'mama' while rolling its head. A wide range of standards is found among the heads used for this model, even though all come from the same basic mould: some have the finest decoration combined with delicate bisque, while others are crudely finished and have imperfections in the paste. Steiner *bébés* are characterized by their gentle faces and heavy brows, and some have a purple wash under the flesh-coloured paint of the bodies. The majority of the medals won by this firm were achieved when it was under the management of Jules Steiner, the original founder. Like Bru, he experimented with the manufacture of a rubber *bébé,* and in 1872 the firm claimed to produce five different kinds. Steiner dolls are usually marked 'Steiner Paris' and sometimes have the 's.G.D.G.' mark. At other times, for example on the walking dolls, the brand-name is found on the mechanism rather than the figure itself.

Most new collectors aspire to possess a marked Jumeau, as the very name of this firm, to many people, epitomizes the French doll industry. Good Jumeaux have very distinctively modelled features of a slightly scowling appearance and particularly large and lustrous eyes, specially made by the firm. An interesting sleeping mechanism was introduced in 1887 whereby the lids came down over the eyes by the manipulation of a

An all-bisque doll with an unusual large lower tooth as well as the usual upper, with sleeping violet eyes, blue painted socks, and wearing original red ribbed-silk frock and hat. Probably made by Simon and Halbig. *Circa* 1900. Height 18 cm. (7 in.).

lever at the back of the head. The 'Médaille d'or' stamp often found on bodies is an indication of the pride felt in the achievement of a gold medal at the Paris Exposition Universelle of 1878, where it was won in the face of the fierce competition of the other leading firms. The stamp is of little help in dating, as it was used for some years after the event. Jumeau was eventually amalgamated with several other firms and after this time, although the Jumeau mark was retained, some work was contracted out to German factories; French marked bodies are therefore found with their original marked Simon and Halbig heads. There is controversy among collectors regarding the heads marked simply 'D.E.P.' that are sometimes found on marked Jumeau bodies. Some are particularly French in feature, but others bear much more resemblance to the work of Simon and Halbig and are sometimes attributed to that firm.

Belton was a doll-maker who was in partnership with Jumeau in the middle years of the nineteenth century, and although his name disappears from the doll-making scene after 1855 it has been used to provide a term for unmarked French dolls with full domed heads. Two or three holes are often cut in the top of these heads and one suggestion is that they were used as a means of attaching a wig by a length of ribbon; it seems more likely that they were a stringing aid, however, as several are found with heavy springs protruding at the crown and linking the head to the body-stringing.

As a result of the vast production of child-like dolls in Germany, the French were forced to make slightly more economical dolls in order to be competitive. Even this was not sufficient and in 1899 several French doll-makers amalgamated to form the Société de Fabrication des Bébés et Jouets (S.F.B.J.), with a membership that included both Bru and Jumeau, as well as Rabery et Delphieu and Danel et Cie. It was hoped that further economies both in marketing and production could be effected by this alliance. Early S.F.B.J. products were characterized by the large number of heads obviously taken from Jumeau moulds, though often marked with the initials of the new group. A *Toy Trader* report of January 1909 commented on the crisis among the French toy firms: by then it had practically reached breaking-point with the 'manufacturers nearly at the end of their wits'. The report went on to say 'one must not think that the French market is to be blamed ... the export trade is greatly hampered by the heavy and prohibitive duties placed upon French goods by other countries'. In fact, however, there were difficulties in the home market as well as in the export field. Despite the retaliatory duties imposed by the French on German goods, the German toys were still considerably cheaper in France than the home product.

In 1909 S.F.B.J. advertised themselves as the 'sole makers of Jumeau dolls' and claimed to employ some 2,500 workers. Their dolls for export were costumed appropriately for their countries of destination. After the play *Chantecler* had created a stir in the theatrical world and given rise to a new fashion in ladies' hats, as well as influencing dolls' costumes, S.F.B.J. were sold the sole rights in France and abroad for making dressed dolls, and cartonage and paste toys, of all the characters in the play. A special display was held in their London showrooms at 8 and 9 Chiswell Street, and among the exhibits were a cock and hen pheasant 'in every way exact copies of the original dress of the play'. The dolls themselves appear from photographs to have been made from basic '60' mould, but with the amusing addition of huge bunches of real feathers protruding from their bottoms. Such sales ploys were necessary to a firm that produced 5,000,000 dolls a year (in the later years, unfortunately, often of the most economical type).

German child dolls
The dolls that dominated the French market, undercutting the prices of the Jumeaux, were made mainly in the Thuringia area of Germany, and it is

Opposite A bisque-headed French doll with a full domed head with two holes in the slightly flattened crown, fixed blue eyes, a closed mouth and pierced ears. It has carved wooden limbs with fixed wrists and is wearing a turquoise, lace-trimmed frock. Height 37 cm. (14½ in.).

these that are most frequently purchased by new collectors, particularly the work of Armand Marseille, who made so many pretty and delicately coloured examples. Some of the German companies, such as Dressel, had a long history of doll-making in other media before they began to make bisque heads, but others seem suddenly to have come upon the scene as producers of bisque dolls in the late nineteenth century. The earliest German examples were given leather or fabric bodies, often of a rather grotesque shape, although some of the better-quality German bodies were so well made as to rival the French. Eventually a purely German type with bisque or composition lower arms and fabric or composition lower legs was evolved, a type that was in turn superseded by jointed bodies of wood and composition.

A jointed girl doll with 'googly' eyes and closed mouth, marked 'Armand Marseille Germany 323 A 6 M', wearing the original navy blue serge suit with a lace blouse and pleated, feather-stitched skirt. Height 30 cm. (12 in.).

A jointed girl with well-defined features and made of a pale tinted bisque, with pierced ears, open mouth and brown sleeping eyes, wearing a two-tone brown velvet dress. Marked 'Max Handwerck'. Height 66 cm. (26 in.).

A large character baby with an open-closed mouth and brown sleeping eyes, marked '14' and made by Kestner. Height of doll 57 cm. (22½ in.).

It has been estimated that about half the world's total output of dolls in the early twentieth century was created in Germany, in particular in Thuringia. The tariff laws of 1890, which made it compulsory for all items to be marked with their country of origin, makes attribution much easier as the manufacturers often added their own names as well. Even so, many marks that are still completely unattributable are found on the heads of German dolls. The development of the doll trade in Germany at this time, however, can be understood from the work of a few market leaders whose output is typical.

One of the more progressive firms was Kämmer and Reinhardt, K. & R., established in Walterhausen in 1886. As with the majority of firms the main

Opposite A bisque-headed German doll with sleeping brown eyes and closed mouth, marked '12' on the shoulder plate, with the original extremely long, commercially made body. Height 78 cm. (31 in.).

Opposite A bisque shoulder-headed German doll with sleeping blue eyes, open mouth and well-defined features, wearing the original green wool braid-trimmed coat and hat. It has composition lower legs and arms and a leather body, and is marked '309 0'. With the doll are pressed cardboard flock-covered dogs. Height 56 cm. (22 in.).

Below right A bisque-headed German character doll marked 'C P 220 38' for Catterfelder Puppenfabrik. It has blue sleeping eyes and the original mohair wig plaited into earphones over the ears. The mouth is of the open-closed type. The original outfit consists of a pink silk frock trimmed with maroon velvet with a hat also of velvet. Height 41 cm. (16 in.).

Below A closed mouth character boy with brown painted eyes, a jointed French type body and wearing a black velvet suit. Marked '1'. Height 51 cm. (20 in.).

production was of sweet-faced girls, but in 1909 a new type of bisque-headed doll was introduced, modelled as a realistic likeness of a baby. This doll, which was given the model number '100', was the fore-runner of a whole series of character babies and jointed dolls that are now amongst the most collectable of German products. In this field the Germans were soon copied by the French. In one of the trade magazines of July 1910 there is an advertisement, accompanied by a picture of a smiling boy with a jointed body, for s.f.b.j.'s range of 'Character dolls with glass eyes, representing babies and children's faces. The pleasant expressions of these character dolls are greatly enhanced by the glass eyes which have a very bright effect on the face.' This brilliance of eye is one of the most noticeable differences between the French and German character dolls, although the German dolls have the softer features.

The interest in realistic dolls developed from an increasing German awareness of the importance of 'art in the life of the child', a key phrase of the period that was enthusiastically responded to by Germany's leading artists and sculptors. An exhibition of old dolls was held in Germany in 1908, to show that no matter how simple the general construction of a toy, it should be made from the best materials available. In September of the same year there were two other important exhibitions, to which well-known artists contributed, showing the most modern examples of dolls and their accessories. *The Toy Trader* commented at this time: 'The public taste is slowly altering and it seems that the blank doll's face is becoming a thing of the past, more interest being taken in characteristic and realistic heads and dress . . ..' In December 1909 Marian Kaulitz staged a display of her dolls in the window of Aug. Polich of Leipzig. She had helped initiate the new movement by an earlier exhibition of dolls that 'show the life-like characteristics of human faces and reflect in their artistically selected wearing apparel the customs of different countries they represent'. There were some three hundred of her dolls on display and they 'seemed to express in their features all the emotions of human life'.

Many of the heads used by Kämmer and Reinhardt were made for them by Simon and Halbig, who also produced many attractive dolls under their own name. The greatest mass-producer, however, was Armand Marseille, established in Koppelsdorf in 1865. This firm made a vast range of dolls that vary considerably both in interest and quality. Their most frequently found mould is the '390', although dolls marked in this way can range from the very beautiful, with huge eyes and fine bisque, to others that are so

Opposite A bisque-headed German doll with jointed body and brown, sleeping eyes, marked 'Simon and Halbig. K star R 76', with pierced ears and an open mouth, wearing a contemporary child's cream silk frock and a blue straw bonnet. Height 76 cm. (30 in.).

Below left A jointed child doll with bisque head, marked 'K & R Simon & Halbig 121 for Kämmer and Reinhardt', with sleeping brown eyes and an open mouth, wearing its original woollen coat. Height 76 cm. (30 in.).

Below An unusually realistic, poured wax baby doll with the hair skilfully laid in place on the head and blue fixed eyes with implanted lashes. The modelling of the shoulders is unusually strong. The whole of the original costume is embroidered by hand and dates to the 1840s. Height 56 cm. (22 in.).

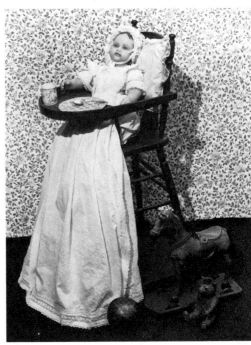

The nun wears very correctly made miniature costume consisting of some fourteen separate garments and is an Armand Marseille '390', made in Germany. The bisque shoulder-headed boy in a blue silk suit with an open-closed mouth revealing the tongue is marked with the Heubach sunburst mark and '5/0 7590'. There are no sew-holes to shoulder plate. The eyes are blue intaglio. Height boy 28 cm. (11 in.).

A pair of unmarked, tinted bisque, shoulder-headed boys wearing their original Scottish costumes. The doll with the black moulded hair is the more unusual. *Circa* 1880. Height 26 cm. (10 in.).

badly decorated and finished that it is difficult to believe they are of the same origin. Some of their closed-mouthed coloured and oriental baby dolls are extremely appealing, as the tinting was usually delicate. Their open-mouthed black babies, however, are sometimes too heavily coloured and the effect of the bisque is killed. Among Armand Marseille's more amusing products is the 'Googly' girl doll illustrated here. A few of their character dolls were made with painted instead of glass eyes.

Gebrüder Heubach, who traded from Sonneberg, made a surprisingly large selection of character-type heads in addition to the basic pretty child

A small Oriental baby in original costume, marked '4/0 Germany'. A brown-tinted boy with a closed mouth, marked 'A.M. 341 2½ K'. A scowling character baby with wig and open-closed mouth, marked '1428 6'. Height 34 cm. (13½ in.).

dolls. The quality of the bodies on which some of their heads were mounted is often surprisingly poor, but is more than compensated for in the eyes of the collector by the attractiveness of the heads themselves. Some of them are pink-tinted, instead of being simply of white paste with a surface colouring, as was more usual. The 'Googly' dolls produced by Heubach, some with eyes moved by a lever, are at present among the most sought-after examples of their work.

Character dolls in Britain and America

American doll-makers quickly moved into the field of character dolls. In 1909 the Horsman company of New York, established in 1865, registered the first known copyright for a complete doll. 'Billikin' had a composition 'Can't Break Em' head and by October 1909 it was on sale in England in celluloid form. 'Baby Bumps', rather similar to K. & R.'s 'Baby' was introduced by Horsman in 1910 and by June was on offer in England from William E. Peck and Co.'s warehouse in London. Horsman described 'Baby Bumps' as 'the sensation of the doll trade . . . the merriest little fellow in toyland. Sells at sight. Can't Break Em art head and jointed pink or white velvet bodies'. 'Billikin' was advertised at the same time as '12 inches of sunshine for 5/–. 300,000 sold in four months. A combination of the character doll and the teddy bear'. The advert was accompanied by an excruciating rhyme typical of the doll trade at this period:

I'm Billikin whose lucky grin
Makes gloom fly out and joy run in
I'm fond of little boys and girls
I love to nestle 'gainst their curls

K. & R.'s 'Baby' was described in a Whyte Ridsdale and Co. advertisement for October 1909 as 'The jointed Boo Boo doll. The only natural shaped baby doll made. Although only produced a few months ago thousands have been sold. 45/– or 36/– a dozen'.

The new character dolls caused consternation among some *Toy Trader* reporters who felt that they were not aesthetically pleasing. Others were enthusiastic, however, while there were many too who could not decide

A group of early 20th-century character babies. From left to right: Kämmer and Reinhardt '100', Gebrüder Heubach, Kestner '142', Kämmer and Reinhardt '116'. Height of largest 28 cm. (11 in.).

either way. The following opinion, published in March 1909, is one of the more open-minded:

> As was only to be expected, the great movement in Germany to replace the uninteresting monotonous doll's face by one with a certain amount of characteristic realism has been adopted by the trade, and a well-known firm in Walterhausen whose motto is 'Realism united with Beauty' has brought out a series of highly interesting 'Character' dolls and baby heads. There is no doubt, with regard to the wars waged in the trade papers and the daily press, as to the value of the innovation. It is very difficult to declare oneself for or against the new movement as, what is most important, we have not had any experience of how the new dolls will be received by children. I certainly think that the tiny babies, depicted only a few weeks old, are hardly likely to find favour with a child, and it would undoubtedly be a matter for regret should the artists and firms interested in the new movement allow their enthusiasm to be carried to such an extreme of realism that the dolls themselves would have to be declared quite the contrary of beautiful.

All those who had felt cautious about the new character dolls later turned out to have been justified in their reservations, for the craze was short-lived. Although a few examples appeared after the First World War, the impetus by this time was gone, while the traditional pretty-faced girl dolls remained overwhelmingly popular. Since the character dolls were never made in very large numbers, they are obviously very collectable, all the more so because the portrait quality of the faces often appeals to a modern adult taste. Those produced by s.f.b.j. and k. & r. are among the most desirable, especially those made as jointed children rather than babies, and those k. & r. models, with names such as Hans or Gretchen, which were modelled on actual children.

As a result of the cessation of imports during the First World War, firms both in England and America were compelled to create bisque-headed dolls, so that the complete dependence upon imported toys would not be too suddenly evident to the public. In comparison with European work, the heads modelled in both America and England at this time seem poor. Nevertheless, these dolls are of some interest to collectors as they were produced for such a short time. Once the war was ended. German imports soon re-established themselves, though European sources could now no longer be called upon to supply new and adventurous lines of bisque-headed figures: both French and German doll-makers seeming resolved

A metal-headed closed-mouth boy with blue painted eyes and metal lower legs and arms, and American cloth body. Unmarked but probably of German origin. Height 33 cm. (13 in.).

probably because of the difficult economic conditions, to continue to create dolls in the old proven styles. From this time onwards doll-making innovations were very much connected with the use of unbreakable substances. Unfortunately, dolls made of such materials are often so discoloured and cracked that they have little appeal to the antique collector.

'Unbreakable' dolls

One of the earliest materials used in the manufacture of a doll that would not smash if dropped was gutta percha, to which there are references in the 1820s, although it did not come into regular use until the 1840s. Huret was among the leading French makers to have utilized gutta percha for the heads and bodies of *Parisiennes* and *bébés*; few examples have survived, however, as they eventually hardened and cracked. Rubber (similar to gutta percha) was also popular, especially in America from around 1840 also, where shoulder-headed figures, very similar to the porcelain lady dolls of the period, were made, in particular by Charles Goodyear. European makers, especially the French, made complete dolls of rubber; the firm of Bru described their jointed hard rubber dolls as 'new' in 1879. Bathtime toys were particularly suitable for this medium, and these were often provided with a squeaker, like the plastic bathroom toys that are popular today. Some of the 'bather dolls' made by the New York Rubber Company differed from the usual moulded figures of this type and were dressed in knitted outfits. The bent-limbed babies of the early twentieth century, with their relatively simple basic shapes, lent themselves well to manufacture in rubber, and among the best known of this type is the 'Dydee Baby', which effectively utilized the possibilities of the medium. This American-made doll, designed by a school-teacher, 'drank' from a bottle and appeared to wet its nappy when a rubber stopper was removed from the buttock. Rubberized composition was used for the heads of 'Dydee Babies' and these have usually survived in acceptable condition; the bodies, however, have often shrivelled most unpleasantly. 'Betsy Wetsy' was introduced in 1937 by Uneeda but never became as popular. Interest in rubber was less great in Germany, although in 1932 Kämmer and Reinhardt were registering patents for rubber heads with strengthening supports around the eyes, nose and neck.

Metal dolls, including some of silver, had been made since the Middle Ages but there was no manufacture in quantity until the last quarter of the nineteenth century, and then mainly in a manner that imitated china. Brass and zinc were occasionally used but the collector is more likely to find examples in tin or aluminium, with bodies made of leather, leathercloth or rag. Socket heads were mounted on the conventional jointed bodies. Although tin-headed dolls did not shatter if dropped, the paint was easily damaged, and so examples in absolutely perfect condition are worthwhile purchases. Those marked 'Minerva' and made by A. Vischer in Germany are the most commonly found, and it was claimed that these were coated with a 'new process combination celluloid washable enamel'. Tin-headed

The Americans turned to the manufacture of wooden dolls after the Europeans had tired of the material. This advertisement dating to the 1920s illustrates Schoenhut's All-Wood Perfection dolls that were supplied with a metal base into which the feet could be pegged so that any realistic pose could be assumed.

A group of composition-headed figures with cleverly jointed metal bodies marked 'Made in Switzerland. Patent applied for A. Bücherer', wearing the original felt and cotton costumes. All the joints snap apart so that parts and heads can be interchanged. Height 20 cm. (8 in.).

An advertisement from the March 1926 edition of the *Ladies Home Journal,* published in America, showing the George Borgfeldt Copyrighted Bye-Lo Baby that was popularly known as the 'Million Dollar' baby because of its popularity. 'Sole Licensee and Distributor of the Genuine ᴋ and ᴋ "Bye-Lo Baby"'.

dolls were manufactured in some quantity in America by firms such as the Metal Doll Company, whose products were given snap-on interchangeable wigs, and the Amor Metal Toy Stamping Company based in New Jersey, whose range included some walking dolls. In France Paën Frères was alone in using metal heads for a few dolls in the 1880s, although several companies utilized the strength of the material for dolls' hands.

Wood, one of the most basic of doll-making materials, was revived in America in the early twentieth century because of its virtual indestructibility. In 1911 Albert Schoenhut of Philadelphia was advertising his 'All-Wood Perfection Art Dolls' that were painted in washable enamel colours and dressed in fashionably simple contemporary children's clothes. The heads were roughly carved to shape and were then pressure-moulded to represent chubby children, some with moulded hair and others with mohair wigs. As many boy as girl dolls were made by this progressive firm, as well as an interesting baby with bent limbs jointed both at knee and elbow. The dolls were jointed by a very ingenious system of wire springs that were extremely strong and could hold a doll in any realistic pose. The feet were pegged into place on a metal stand so that the dolls could even balance on one foot with their arms held above the head—a feat of which no German-made doll was capable. Early dolls were provided with fixed eyes but in 1921 Harry Schoenhut also patented movable eyes. The firm made great efforts to stay in front of their German competitors, but the low cost of the imported dolls were their eventual defeat and production ceased around 1930. When in good condition the Schoenhut dolls have considerable appeal to collectors, but unfortunately the paint used for the heads was often soon damaged, and repainted dolls are spoiled from a collector's point of view.

Another, rather more adventurous material, celluloid, was invented in England in the middle of the nineteenth century but was first seen as a possible doll-making material in the 1860s by an American company, Hyatt Brothers of New Jersey, who worked under the trade-name of the 'Celluloid Novelty Company'. The disadvantages of celluloid heads were fairly quickly revealed: they discoloured if left in a strong light, some becoming very pale while others assumed an unnatural brown shade. Continual experiments were made in an effort to overcome these problems

but never with any great success. Only individual examples that have been kept in ideal conditions are found in an acceptable state.

Best known of the celluloids of good quality are those made by the Rheinische Gummi und Celluloid Fabrik, which was established in the 1870s and branded its products with an easily recognizable trade-mark in the form of a turtle. This firm provided heads for several well-known doll-makers, among them Kämmer and Reinhardt, and worked from designs used for various ranges of bisque head. Thus a few celluloid 'Baby' model 100s were made, but marked '700' in this material. Although celluloids are not at present highly popular, they were widely applauded when they first appeared and cost far more than the bisque-headed dolls we now consider so much more beautiful.

A material known as Biskoline, introduced by the American doll-making firm Parsons Jackson, was described as being similar to celluloid except that it would 'never break, crack, surface chip or peel'. The use of Biskoline was typical of the manufacturers' efforts to find a substance that would withstand the much more energetic play of children who were no longer carefully supervised. In 1892 Solomon Hoffmann claimed to be the sole maker in America of composition dolls; his products were marked 'Can't Break Em' and were hand-painted. The Ideal Novelty Company, also of the U.S.A., claimed that their dolls could be dropped on a stone floor without fracturing, a feature that was regularly demonstrated by their salesmen. Adtocolite, a composition that has usually cracked very badly, was employed by many makers in the U.S.A. Most of these composition mixtures were based on various combinations of fibres, plaster, glue, whiting and even in one case stone! One of the most collectable composition dolls is 'Shirley Temple', made by the Ideal Toy Corporation in the 1930s and supplied with a fascimile signed photograph. 'EFFANBEE' made 'W. C. Fields', with a jaw that was moved by a wire protruding from the back of the neck, and the Alexander Doll Company even made the 'Dionne Quins'. Deans, of Rye, a firm that made very progressive rag dolls, did not produce compositions until the 1930s when they announced their 'Bye-Bye Baby' with sleeping eyes and a cloth body. Deans relied more on the good costuming of their dolls than on exciting, innovatory ideas such as those that prompted the Americans. One effective doll they produced, named 'Stormy Weather', wore a correctly made mackintosh, a sou'wester and Wellington boots.

Early compositions can be recognized by their similarity of construction to the basic china-headed dolls, as the heads were often used as an alternative on double-jointed bodies. They are very undervalued in Europe, where collectors search for a conventionally beautiful antique item, but are popular in the U.S.A., where there is more interest in recent trends in doll manufacture. Many designers were also creating interesting and inventive soft fabric and velvet dolls and toys, and it is these, together with the compositions, that most accurately reflect doll-making trends in the early twentieth century.

A celluloid schoolgirl in original costume and original hair wig, with brown sleeping eyes and American cloth jointed body. Marked with a helmet for Buschow & Beck. German origin. *Circa* 1920. Height 66 cm. (26 in.).

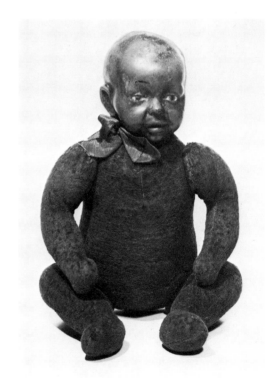

An American baby doll with a plush body stuffed with cork, a 'Can't Break Em' composition head and painted eyes. Produced by Horsmann in 1910. Height 33 cm. (13 in.). (Collection Betty Harvey-Jones.)

THE creation of a simple child's plaything from waste materials found in the home is one of the most ancient of toy-making methods, and dolls of coarse fabric are found even in the tombs of Egyptian and Roman children. Examples of fabric dolls dating to the seventeenth and eighteenth centuries have survived, but strangely there are no animals (except for a few miniatures in baby houses and some fabric-covered toys on wheels), and neither do they appear in paintings or prints. It is likely therefore that the full potential of a soft toy that could be cuddled was not fully realized until the nineteenth century, when very young children began to be shown playing with such obviously appropriate toys as woolly lambs and plush-covered elephants.

Golliwogs and bears

That half-human, half-imaginary figure known as the golliwog was not introduced until the 1890s and very little is known of its development, apart from the fact that it appeared on the market shortly after Florence Upton published *The Adventures of Two Dutch Dolls and a Golliwog* in 1895.

A leather-covered squeak toy of a pug on a press base. The lower jaw moves up and down. *Circa* 1855. Height 15 cm. (6 in.). (Collection Betty Harvey-Jones.)

'Golliwogg—A round game', published by Thomas De La Rue & Co. Ltd. 110 Bunhill Row, London by kind permission of Messrs Longmans Green & Co, publishers of works by Florence K. and Bertha Upton. The series of 48 pictorial cards taken from Florence Upton's original designs. Note the shaped nose of the golliwog. *Circa* 1900. (Collection Betty Harvey-Jones.)

As the author is known to have made some toys herself, it is often thought possible that she was the inventor. Very early versions have properly formed noses and are much more human-looking than the later examples, which assumed an almost abstract effect and were made in considerable number by British toy-makers in particular.

Of all soft toys, it is the teddy bear which maintains the strongest appeal, not only in childhood but often into adult life, as this is the one toy that many elderly people are found to have retained. The origin of the teddy is debatable as it is claimed by both the Americans and the Germans. Current thinking tends to ascribe this delightful toy to the U.S.A., where it is said to have originated from a political caricature appearing in the *Washington Post* in 1903, drawn by Clifford Berryman and showing President Theodore ('Teddy') Roosevelt with a small brown bear cub that he had refused to shoot lying at his feet—a political allegory. Morris Michtom, who was later to found the Ideal Toy Corporation of America, saw this cartoon and made a series of plush toys with button eyes for his toyshop after obtaining permission to call them 'Teddy's Bear'. In Germany Margarethe Steiff also produced teddy bears in the same year, though the precise date is not known. These early versions were jointed at the top of the arms and legs and were deliberately made to resemble a standing doll rather than a four-legged bear. Hump backs and very long noses also characterize early bears and it is through study of the gradual evolution of this design to the present simplified form that individual examples can be approximately dated.

The toy trade eagerly welcomed teddy bears and they were produced in thousands, not only in the traditional form but also as finger or glove puppets, containers for musical boxes, Kelly-like figures, and mechanical and even cut-out toys. In 1908 Wertheims, a large Berlin store, displayed a tall climbing-pole in the centre of their toy department and this was

Below left An Edwardian postcard illustrating a black fur-covered cat and an unusual light-faced golliwog with a hair wig and a shaped nose.

Below Detail of a postcard postmarked 1907 showing the popularity of toy mascots among Edwardian ladies. Few actual golliwogs have survived but the long nose of the early versions can be seen here.

"Playtime"

supplied not only with bears but also—apparently a new arrival in the world of animal toys—with monkeys; one of these monkeys was mechanical and after being wound up reached into a basket of nuts, stole one and then cracked it in his mouth. Teddy bears were the focus of attention in a window display in William Whiteley's store on Queensway, London, in the same year. Whiteley's sold a number of clockwork bears that performed gymnastic feats, turned somersaults and caused endless amusement. Many of the bears sold in England were made by Steiff but there were British makers too. An advertisement of 1909 suggested: 'Before placing your orders for bears elsewhere, sample those bred at the "Bear Pit" 3, St Peters Road, London N.E.'

The demand for bears was so great that many shops were unable to obtain stock and more and more native manufacturers began to create the new toy in a variety of grades. William J. Terry of Kingsland, London, claimed to be the largest manufacturer of soft and fur toys in Great Britain and sold bears in some quantity. At around the same time Samuel Finsberg and Co. produced a cotton flannelette printed sheet of a 'Lifelike Teddy Bear', consisting of a large bear accompanied by a miniature. In 1909 it was claimed that the teddy had a rival in the form of a china—or bisque-headed doll with the body of a bear, so despite its obvious popularity the soft teddy bear was not yet fully accepted as an essential feature of the nursery. 'The passing of our old and honoured friend, the Teddy Bear' was announced in the same year by an American correspondent to *The Toy Trader* who claimed that Teddy had been supplanted by 'Billy Possum'. His letter

A pair of Edwardian mechanical bears. The dark bear with a ring in the nose walks on all fours while the key-wound standing bear rocks from side to side. Height 36 cm. (14 in.). (Collection Betty Harvey-Jones.)

described a visit paid by Mr Taft, the President elect, to Atlanta where he tasted 'the typical dish of the South, roast Possum, and was so infatuated with it that he declared that he was "for Possum first, last and all the time". This short speech was the death-knell of the Teddy Bear. His tottering throne collapsed, his reign is over!' The *New York Herald* stated that a factory in Atlanta had begun to manufacture opossums in the same sizes and same variety of forms as the teddy bear and added: 'It is not without regret that we part from our old friend whose mission has been accomplished.'

The American correspondent afterwards realized that he reacted to a false alarm. A few months later he wrote: 'We notice that several of the wholesalers are showing examples of the Possums but the Teddy Bear is still all the rage. Possum is not wanted.' After this early attempted overthrow, the popularity of the teddy was steadily maintained and an amusing variety of uses was found for this engaging figure. It was commented from a fashionable South Coast resort in England in 1909 that nearly all the young women,

> like lovely fashion plates in all their bravery of embroidered white and silken gowns and frilly seaside hats were carrying immense brown, buff or pale yellow teddy bears, tucked tidily under their pretty sunburnt arms. It is not chic, should you be a fashionable August girl, to be seen on the sands or on the sea wall without your Teddy Bear! It is part of the holiday outfit of the season and the big London toyshops are selling a particular grown up sea-side brand of this particular toy—the last amazing folly of amazingly foolish fashion!

In the same year Peak Frean, the biscuit-makers, fixed teddies to the top of each of their delivery vans to promote 'Teddy Bear' biscuits. These bears, measuring some 90 cm. (36 in.), were made by Ralph Dunn and Co. of the Barbican, London, and by October three hundred of them were to be seen on the firm's vans around town. The teddy was also quickly adopted as a motorist's mascot and cyclists even fixed teddies to their handlebars. Very small versions were also made as charms. In March 1910 a white 'Barbara Bear' was introduced, named after the polar bear in London Zoo, and was initially claimed as Teddy's successor although it failed to gain a permanent foothold.

The toy trade found it difficult to believe that children would continue to want bears indefinitely and thought it would be necessary to stimulate interest by incorporating various novelties. One such refinement was that registered by E. Decamps of 10 rue Parc Royal, Paris, on 12 October 1910: 'A mechanical toy in the form of a bear etc. which is constructed to fall about and turn somersaults. The front limbs . . . are rotated continually by a spring motor enclosed in the toy [which] causes it to rise and fall over. One of the remaining limbs is pliable and allows the figure to fall sideways when it rises.' Similar mechanical bears were made by Steiff, while swinging trapeze bears, sometimes suspended from chains, were made by several English companies.

A very large Teddy Bear illustrated on a postcard that is dated 1913. The humped back and the long pointed nose can be clearly seen.

BEAR THIS IN MIND.

Chad Valley in particular made a wide assortment of bears and their 1921 catalogue describes 'The most lifelike toys ever produced. Made throughout from British materials. Teddy Bears in six qualities and thirteen sizes. Upright golden fur, Long golden fur, Thick nigger brown woolly fur, Long Beaver brown fur, Long white fur, and Best long golden fur'. Growlers were fitted to all bears over 43 cm. (17 in.) high, with best-quality sleigh bells on the smaller versions. The very largest sizes, however, were fitted with 'Patent Chad Valley grunters'.

Another rival for the teddy bear was suggested even as late as 1925, when

Dean's Rag Book Company of London offered in their catalogue 'Bendigo the Australian bear ... with the advantage of being of British origin and design and manufacture. Apart from these sentimental associations Bendigo is every bit as pleasing and cuddlesome as Teddy. Is evripose-jointed and is moderate in price!' After this date there seems to have been no major effort to supplant the teddy bear, and it has remained highly popular to the present day.

German soft toys

The largest producer of soft toys in the late Victorian and Edwardian period was the firm of Steiff, founded by Margarethe Steiff, (1877–1909), who began to make toys from a local factory's waste felt, while she ran a small dress-making business with her sister. She initially made the toys for the children of her friends in her home-town of Giengen-am-Brenz, where she was affectionately known as 'Gretel Steiff'. Her work was greatly appreciated and her fame spread, so that one building after another had to be erected to keep pace with the increasing demand. After her death in 1909 her nephews Paul and Richard took over the firm and in the same year it was made a limited company. The Steiff dolls, with pressed felt heads, were made in 1894 and at the Leipzig Fair of 1903 there was a display of Steiff teddy bears, of which 3,000 were ordered for America alone. Children quickly became familiar with the firm's work through the 'Knopf im Ohr' (Button in the Ear) trade-mark, and so hugely successful were the bears in particular that the years 1903–1908 are known in the history of the firm as the 'Bärenjahre' (Bear Years). During this period Steiff expanded prodigiously, and for one year the total production of toy animals of all kinds reached 7,000,000.

A great deal of Steiff's impact depended on the strikingly large display pieces that were created for the various fairs and exhibitions. At the 1909 Leipzig Fair their exhibition was considered to be the finest and most pleasing; a whole room was filled with large magnificent set pieces 'ingeniously set out and beautifully made':

> The most effective setting displayed part of a zoo, complete with houses lit by electricity, water chutes, gardens and other accessories. Included in the majority of her sets were many stuffed dolls and animals making the entire production both representative and effective ... In another part of the room was to be found a model of a village school; here were desks with a class of children in various amusing attitudes, while the usual paraphernalia associated with this tableau was to be seen, including the stern old pedagogue with cane, easel, etc. To show off the Polar bears and dolls dressed in winter sports attire was a snow scene, and visitors could wind up the mechanical tumbling bears and watch their antics. (*The Toy Trader*, March 1909)

There was also a bear-pit and a rabbit-hutch, with the animals displayed in all sorts and sizes. It was customary for exhibitors at the Leipzig Fair to publicize themselves by wheeling large toys around the streets. The Steiff

A realistic chicken of feather-covered white felt with a wooden beak and feet. The body contains wooden eggs and when it is depressed a coloured egg is laid. *Circa* 1900. Height 28 cm. (11 in.). (Collection Betty Harvey-Jones.)

Shock-Headed Peter.

A felt-headed Struwwelpeter illustrated on a pre-First World War postcard. The seam down the front of the face suggests that it was made by Steiff.

mobile display in 1909 was said to have been 'almost a parade trundled around by means of huge elephants on wheels with voices that proclaimed Steiff's whereabouts'.

Among the newest lines were dolls that said 'mama' and 'papa' on being turned over, and various animals with voices, included growling bears, mooing cows and grunting pigs. The new toys for 1909 were a chimpanzee, tumbling elephants and a kangaroo. It was claimed at this time that the firm had been making amusing animals for eight years and that they now employed 3,000 workers. Shortly after the fair, Margarethe Steiff died; her achievement at this trade event can be seen as the culmination of her efforts to produce interesting and amusing toys. *The Toy Trader* commented: 'The beauty of Steiff's productions lies in the fact that, in every instance, they get as near the real living object as it is possible and where the living object is parodied this is done in a clever and amusing yet dignified manner.'

Steiff dolls are characterized by the seam that runs down the centre of the face, giving them a completely idiosyncratic appearance. The general finish of the toys is invariably good and the costumes are well made. Many of the figures are caricatures made with humorous intention, although they are sometimes misunderstood by English and American collectors who imagine some menace in the military figures. One of Steiff's more amusing dolls for 1907 was a 'Struwwelpeter' with large feet and a shock of hair.

Steiff's wares were advertised in 1910 as 'indestructible toys, dolls, animals, grotesque figures, etc. Perfect models in felt, plush, velvet cloth'. Among the dolls were a Kelly-like figure with a small head and huge hands, a boy doll in a sailor suit, and a clown. The most up-to-date toy was the

'Krackjack', which had a grinning mouth and large ears and distinctly resembled the American doll 'Billikin'. At the 1910 fair a complete parade ground was displayed, with soldiers of different ranks placed in the background, with battlements behind them, while in the foreground, before the barracks, were other soldiers in various attitudes and groupings; the show-piece gave an excellent indication of the variety of soldier dolls produced by the firm. The 1910 range concentrated particularly on Dutch dolls, and a display of these sitting at a table in a garden surrounded by dogs and other soft toys was specially made for the fair. In the same year it was claimed that

> Many new designs in stuffed animals have been included this season, amongst which may be mentioned foxes, seals and lion cubs. The newest line and one only ready just in time for this messe is the 'Marionetten', a series of figures and animals in various costumes which make life-like movements. The effect is produced by strings attached to various limbs and parts of the body. By pulling these strings, the figures assume grotesque attitudes. (*The Toy Trader*, March 1910)

Fur fabric monkeys were among the most popular toys made by Steiff. This example has stitch-moulded felt hands and feet and glass eyes. *Circa* 1930. Height 34 cm. (13½ in.).

In December 1910 Steiff registered a patent for a 'mechanical toy of the type by which clockwork is wound by means of the limbs . . . so constructed that the limbs connected to the driving-shaft can be turned an unlimited number of times in either direction without damaging the clockwork'.

Saint Bernard dogs, pigs, horses, cows, polar bears, dachshunds and swans were also available from Steiff, the larger sizes being mounted on spoked wheels. At an extra cost the horses could be put on 'dismountable' rockers. In 1913 the favourite toy of the range was 'Alfons and Gaston', a pair of polite Frenchmen who bowed to one another. Other pairs of grotesque figures were also made, such as the very fat and ugly 'Captain and Mrs Captain', a spindly-legged postman with his mail bag, and a 'Highlander'—all of them basically the same doll but in different costumes. Other characters made in the same year included a 'Red Riding Hood', a 'Hunter Hubertus' and an 'Esquimaux', as well as the ever popular Dutch

Below right A child doll in entirely original costume with brown painted eyes, made entirely of fabric by Käthe Kruse and with her special number '40415' on the foot. Height 43 cm. (17 in.). (Collection Betty Harvey-Jones.)

Below 'Bill Stickers', an Argentine cowboy of moulded felt with glass bead eyes made by Margarethe Steiff and marked with a button in the ear. German, *Circa* 1920. Height 35 cm. (14 in.). (Bethnal Green Museum.)

dolls. It was claimed that 'Steiff's stuffed character dolls, the best in the world, will stand without support, their clothes take off, are fully jointed, do not break, have individual fascinating features and their hair will not come out.'

Push-along toys of fur fabric standing on metal spoked wheels are particularly associated with Steiff, and Edwardian shop catalogues show a wide variety of these, as well as dogs in all the popular breeds.

One of the most respected producers of soft toys before the First World War was Bertha Caspar of Berlin who created dogs that barked, hopped and ran, as well as the more traditional fur and velvet animals.

Several companies best-known for their dolls also made fabric toys, among them s.f.b.j. and Fleischmann and Bloedel of Berlin and Paris, who showed a new collection of toys and stuffed felt animals in 1912. Bing, renowned everywhere for tin toys, also made a number of soft dolls and animals. A group of exhibits at the toy museum at Nuremberg includes a spaniel type wheeled dog called 'Bello', covered in plush fur and made in 1920, and a few dolls of the same date with painted fabric faces, cloth arms and legs, and mohair wigs. Lili Bing recounted that much of the costuming of these dolls was done by out-workers. In the same group is a felt-faced doll with separately applied ears made by the Floresta Plüschwerk in around 1925.

American soft toys

In America a few patents for rag dolls were issued in the 1860s and 1870s but there was no significant production of soft toys until Thomas Mast designed a Santa Claus, which was patented by E. S. Peck in 1886 specifically for a paper version, although a few printed muslin dolls of this type are also known. On 5 July 1892 a patent was granted to Celia M. Smith of New York that was eventually assigned to the Arnold Print Works. This Massachusetts company, established in 1876, was one of America's largest manufacturers of prints and dress fabrics. Customers were warned that their dolls were genuine only if they carried the firm's trade-mark on the sheet of cloth, alongside the printed figures. Among the firm's most popular toys were the 'Palmer Cox Brownies':

> These funny little fellows have been produced in the most attractive colourings on cloth under special arrangement with the noted artist. They are twelve in number and all come in one yard of cloth. Easily cut out, sewed together in accordance with directions and accurate lines and stuffed with cotton, bran or sawdust. When completed they are about seven inches [17.8 cm.] in length and can be bent or twisted into all sorts of funny positions without injury.

The 'Brownies' represented small characters who always did good things and never sought praise, and their popularity is reflected by the fact that they were available in paper and china as well as rag. Among the other toys made by the Arnold Print Works were 'Our Soldier Boys' (patented in 1892), 'Little Red Riding Hood' and 'Piccaninny', and a jointed doll that

Paper King and Irishman from a set of Palmer Cox Brownies that were originally printed on fabric by the Art Fabric Mills. The heads fit the bodies by long tabs so they could be interchanged. These were made as an advertisement for Lion Coffee and are marked 'Patented and copyrighted 1892 by Palmer Cox. The Thomas & Wylie Litho. Co. N.Y. By permission Arnold Print Works. North Adams. Mass'. Height 14 cm. (5½ in.).

was patented in 1893. The firm's very attractively coloured range of animal toys included 'Tabby Cat' and 'Little Tabbies', various dogs (with names like 'Tatters and Little Tatters', 'Bow-wow', 'Jocko' and Floss), an owl, and a hen with chicks. The figures were enabled to stand by a sheet of thick card that was cut to fit the bases. The printed fabric was sold either by the yard or the half-yard.

Printed toys were also made in America by the Art Fabric Mills of New York (1899–1910), who produced a 76 cm. (30 in.) doll on heavy sateen as well as 'Buster Brown', a Negro doll and 'Foxy Grandpa'. A 'Buster Brown' was also made by the Knickerbocker Speciality Company, who accompanied him with his dog 'Tige', a toy that was designed by R. Outcault who had created the original comic strip character. In America great use was also made of printed rag toys for advertising purposes. 'Aunt Jemima' advertised Pancake flour from 1900 and was at one time accompanied by 'Uncle Mose', 'Little Diana' and 'Little Wade', all printed on muslin and given away in exchange for box tops. 'Sunny Jim', printed by the Niagra Lithographing Company of New York, advertised the cereal Force, and Dolly Dimple Flour was also promoted by a cut-out doll. Spence Wildey designed a rag doll named 'Kookie' to boost sales of a type of kitchen range. Kelloggs' cereals created 'Goldilocks and the Three Bears', with the bears much more effectively printed than the girl.

Traditional fabric dolls were produced by several American makers, such as the Beecher family, who made them from silk underwear in aid of missionary funds between 1885 and 1909, and Martha Chase who made them much more professionally from 1893. The earliest recorded maker, however, is Izannah F. Walker of Rhode Island, who patented her work in 1873 but is considered to have produced her first dolls in the 1850s. Her fabric dolls with stiffened faces are characterized by the curls painted in front of each ear, and it is these dolls that are said to have later inspired Martha Chase to become a doll-maker.

The urge to develop unusual and interesting toys led manufacturers to create some very elegant and long-legged lady dolls, now known as 'boudoir figures', early in the twentieth century. 'Dolls are now used as fashion plates,' a toy trade report humorously stated in 1909: 'At one of these large shops in New York, these figures, unlike ordinary dolls, are dressed with as much care as a lady of society would be.' Boudoir dolls are often found with faces of pressed felt, or of silk stretched over a shaped card mask, while a few were made with moulded and painted composition masks and the bodies are almost invariably stuffed fabric, with plaster or composition lower arms and legs. Harlequin characters were often portrayed in fabric; for example there was a series of 'Carnival Dolls' issued by Chad Valley in 1933–4, costumed in silk Pierrot-type outfits. Similar dolls were made by a number of firms in France, Germany and England, with the result that unless they are marked they are very difficult to attribute unless the costume can be matched against an illustration in a catalogue.

A typical Lenci felt doll wearing a magenta frock trimmed with royal blue flowers and piping and with the original shoes. Marked on the thigh with a metal button marked 'Lenci'. Painted eyes with highlights. Height 25.5 cm. (10 in.).

British soft toys

In Britain, as in Europe, much of the energy that in the nineteenth century was put into the creation of dolls seems to have been transferred in the twentieth to soft toys. Although the making of these in Britain is principally associated with Dean's Rag Book Company and Chad Valley, there were many other, smaller producers. One of these was Henry H. Hughes of the Tottenham Court Road, who described himself as a maker of 'Model Rag Dolls' and introduced a new series just before the First World War that included 'Miss Hook of Holland', 'Our Little Dutch Boy', 'Territorial Boy and Girl' and 'Dreadnought Boy and Girl'. The 'Territorial Girl' wore a soldier's jacket in combination with a very full and feminine skirt. A contemporary opinion stated that 'Mr Hughes' products have a character all their own; they are natural and British in appearance and are well made and indestructible. In addition to this, each could be described as a character doll, everthing in connection with it having been carefully thought out and produced to represent exactly the character the doll is meant to portray.' The new series of dolls which had hair-stuffed bodies and washable faces that were unaffected by heat or cold, was considered particularly suitable for export. In July 1910 the firm introduced 'Picture Rag Dolls' printed on fabric in bright colours and illustrating nursery rhymes. Printed dolls were also made by Bell and Francis of Bread Street in the E.C. district of London who sold a series with characters such as 'Tabby Cat', 'Chantecler Hen', 'Bunny Rabbit', and a spaniel and a duck.

Fur-covered finger puppets were made by Whyte and Ridsdale of Houndsditch, while several organizations, such as the Lord Robert's workshops and the Sir William Treloar Centre for crippled children, produced soft toys commercially. (It is interesting to note that the Treloar Centre was making lead soldiers in 1909.) Hamley Brothers produced 'Bolo', a representation of the famous Drury Lane dog 'splendidly and strongly made in plush with jointed limbs and movable head'. The interest in moving toys was much stronger at this time, and there were jumping rabbits and dogs, activated by squeezing a rubber ball at the end of a tube. 'Trippel Trappel' toys mimicked the natural movements of animals as diverse as lambs and lions without using clockwork. The 1913 catalogue of Gamage's department store offered key-wound walk-about animals, such as elephants with a slow and stately tread, fast and furious lions, trotting horses and convincing cats ('Pussies gentle tread is natural to a degree').

Soft toys were produced by Dean's Rag Book Company before Samuel Dean put his rag books on the market in 1903. In this year printed toys began to be in sheet form, although they were not made in great numbers until 1906 when a range of cut-out dolls was issued, lithographed in bright colours on sheets that also included their clothes. The 'Rag Knock-about Toy Sheets' of 1912–13 included a set of 'Punch and Judy' glove puppets, a 'Profile' cat and dog, and 'Mama bear, Teddy and Susie', all printed on soft woolly cloth. The 'Knockabout' series was continued after the war and

An advertisement for cloth dolls and toys made by Bell and Francis of 29 Bread Street, London as advertised in the *Toy and Fancy Goods Trader*, April 1910. (By courtesy of *The Toy Trader*.)

A page from the *Toy and Fancy Goods Trader* for
October 1909 showing the toys available from
Whyte, Ridsdale & Co. including a fabric Billikin
doll with a celluloid head, finger kittens and fur
covered clockwork tumbling bears from 8/6d a
dozen. (By courtesy of *The Toy Trader*.)

WHYTE, RIDSDALE & CO., 73, 74, 75, Houndsditch,
— LONDON, E.
Telephone—833 CENTRAL (Two Lines). Telegrams—" WHYTSDALE, LONDON."

**Call and see our Show of FANCY GOODS, TOYS,
GAMES, BEARS.**
XMAS LIST POST FREE.

Hand Motion Finger Kittens. Very
Comical. R 3369. **8/-** doz.

R 3368. **Soft 'Billikin' Doll,**
with Celluloid Head. Price **7/11**
per doz.

**Fine Quality Miniature
Jointed Doll.** On Stand.
Each in a Box. L 2117. Price
12/6 per doz.

Clockwork Motor Bus. fitted with Strong
Coil Spring. Very Large Value. F 5960. Price
7/9 per doz.

**The Jointed Boo-Boo
Doll.** Only natural-shaped
Baby Doll made. Although
only produced a few months
ago, thousands have been
sold. Delivery in November.
L 2102. Price **45/-** per doz.
Smaller size, price **36/-** per
doz.

**Fur-Covered Clockwork
Tumbling Bears.** F 5991.
8/6, 12/6, 22/6 doz.

Lehmann's Latest Success. **Clockwork Quack,
Quack.** F 6021. Price **4/6** doz.

Celluloid Aeroplane. A Wonderful Flyer.
Flies in a circle when suspended. Strong Clock-
work Movement. Size, 8 ins. long by 5 ins. wide.
R 3309. Price **7/9** per doz.

When writing Advertisers please mention "THE TOY & FANCY GOODS TRADER."

Below A felt-faced doll with a velvet body dressed in
orange felt trousers and with a white label sewn on
under foot reading 'Made in England by Nora
Wellings'. The doll has painted brown eyes with
highlights and separately applied ears, dark blonde
hair, and legs cut in four sections for better shaping.
All original. Height 30·5 cm. (12 in.).

included the 'Three Bears'. Dean's also made a wide range of ready-stuffed
toys, some of which were mounted on wheels and advertised with the
remark: 'It follows like a well trained living pet—all you have to do is pull
the string.' In 1920 scooters were very popular, so Dean's mounted their
bears on scooters to maximize sales. 'Evripose' joints, that were widely
acclaimed on their dolls, were also used for the soft toys, such as the 'Peter
Rabbit' and 'Bobby Whitetail' (after Beatrix Potter) offered in 1920. 'Dickie
Blob', made of inky velvet, was made in 1927, based on a series of
gramophone records on which his exploits were recorded. As children in
all English-speaking countries became quickly familiar with the new
entertainment characters, the toy-makers produced appropriate toys.
Dean's, for instance, were making 'Mickey and Minnie Mouse' with
Evripose joints in 1933 and frog toys representing 'Vicompte de Maudit's
Mimie and Shah' in 1935. Other toys of stage and screen characters
included 'Will Hayes', 'Popeye', 'Lupino Lane' and 'Felix the Cat', the
latter appearing in the 1923 catalogue. In 1926 'Dismal Desmond' was
added to the range.

Among Dean's more amusing toys was 'Ole Bill', a walrus with

Left Pooh Bear being rescued by Eeyore, Soft toys made to represent the characters of A. A. Milne, both with swivel heads. *Circa* 1926. Height of bear 36 cm. (14 in.). (Collection Betty Harvey-Jones.)

Below left A kind-faced monkey made of soft plush fabric with printed detail of red jacket and blue trousers. The eyes are glass. On the right foot is a label 'British Manufacture. Hygenic Stuffing. Tru-to-life. Patent No. 25131/12 U.S.A. Patent April 13. 1915'. On the left foot is the Dean's trade mark of two fighting dogs. This is of interest as so few toys were made in the war years. Height 30 cm. (12 in.).

Below A fabric doll with needle modelled hands dressed in a black and white woollen suit and black velvet shoes with a green Dean's Rag Book Company label. Around the torso is a sewn-on label of white fabric reading 'Lupino Lane in "The Lambeth Walk" Specially made by Dean's Rag Book Co. Ltd London. Reg. Design 830106'. Height 30 cm. (14 in.).

The Royal Dolls.

We have pleasure in announcing that the Princess Elizabeth and Princess Margaret Rose Dolls have been approved by THEIR MAJESTIES the KING and QUEEN, and the Prince Edward Doll by H.R.H. THE DUKE OF KENT. The Dolls are made in Velveteen, fully jointed. Chad Valley Heads, specially modelled from likenesses of the originals, fitted with curly hand woven Wigs, and dressed in clothes as worn at the present time by the Royal children themselves. The Princesses are supplied either in Blue or Pink colour schemes.

Above 'The Royal Dolls' made in velveteen and representing Princess Elizabeth, Princess Margaret Rose and Prince Edward of Kent. A page from the 1938 Chad Valley catalogue. (By courtesy of Chad Valley Ltd, Birmingham.)

Right The figure of Bonzo enjoyed great popularity during the 1920s and it was made in bisque, fabric and rubber as in this example marked 'No 1352 38'. The book is dated 1925 and was published by Partridge of London. (Collection Betty Harvey-Jones.)

'Bonzo', from the 1929 Chad Valley Catalogue, ranging in size from four inches to twelve and a half, and made of a plush fabric. (By courtesy of Chad Valley Ltd, Birmingham.)

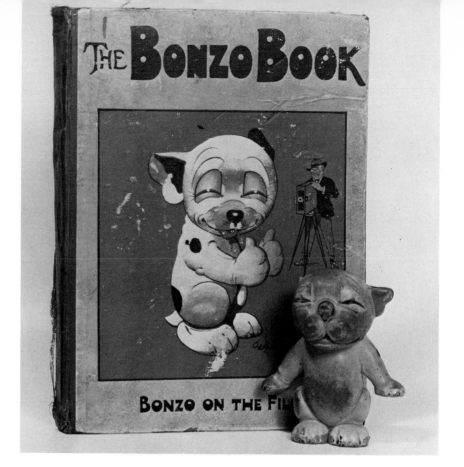

overtones of the First World War cartoon character; 'Popski', a wild and whiskery dog in yellow plush; and 'Wabbly Walley', made in 1928 as a British Legion mascot, intended to be danced from a string. 'Thirsty' was a flop-eared, untidy hound; 'among his other features is a tongue which is pink under normal conditions but turns blue if the weather is likely to be fine'. 'Tatters the Hospital Pup' was issued in 1928 by arrangement with the Stock Exchange Dramatic Society, while 'Peter Pan and Wendy' were used to raise funds for the Great Ormond Street Hospital for Sick Children.

The other great British producer of soft toys was Chad Valley, though it was not until 1920 that the Wellington factory introduced a range of fabric toys, including 'Bobby Penguin' wearing a policeman's helmet and 'Dr Quack' with an umbrella under his wing. Their very early toys appear very poorly made, but the quality soon improved, and in 1921 stuffed clockwork pull-alongs were sold with pressed metal wheels. Elephants, tigers, lions and grisly bears were all made in natural coloured velveteen. 'Bonzo', the famous 'Studdy' dog, was made both in sitting and standing positions in 1929, together with an amusing matching puppy known as 'Baby' 16.5 cm. (5½ in.) long, with a permanent dummy in its mouth. The largest 'Bonzo' was 32 cm. (12½ in.) high. In 1930 A.A. and R.A.C. Scout mascots were advertised, as well as 'Buster Bunny' in art silk plush.

A great deal of the impetus passed from the soft toy makers in the 1930s, possibly because the depressing economic situation meant that parents were less inclined to spend money on novelties. This field of toy-making now became almost boringly traditional, with only occasional flashes of inventiveness, such as the 'Gonks' of the 1960s and some exquisite and accurate soft animals designed as adult mascots and made by Aux Nations.

160

A group of interesting, early 20th-century Teddy Bears. The largest, known as Jo Codham to the original owner, has a head which is manipulated into any position and tilted by the lever action of the tail. The long-haired bear has a squeeze musical box in the stomach. The Kelly-like bear with the very long nose, indicative of an early date, contains a rattle. The other bear wears an original felt and serge soldier outfit; only the head, paws and feet are made of fur fabric and the remainder is cotton. Height of largest bear 49 cm. (19½ in.). (Collection Betty Harvey-Jones.)

A papier mâché lady with painted features and a leather body wearing the original silk brocade court dress, indicating that the doll dates back to 1780, two calf-length linen petticoats, silk stockings and black silk shoes with buckles. The doll is also wearing rings and earrings made from small beads. The feather-decorated hairstyle is interesting. Height 47 cm. (18½ in.).

Opposite A tabby cat and her kittens. A rare uncut length of Arnold Print Works fabric with a dog made by the same firm in the foreground. The attractive soft colours are seen to best advantage when in an unmade-up state. (Collection Betty Harvey-Jones.)

Papier mâché dolls with glass eyes. The man has a pink leather body and the woman has papier mâché lower arms and a cloth body. The woman is unusual, as the dark brown bonnet is painted. She is *circa* 1835, the man *circa* 1840. Both are of German origin. Height of man 45 cm. (18 in.).

Bisque-headed Parisiennes a dating back to the late 1860s. The doll in lilac silk is marked 'Simonne, 1 à 13 Passage Délorme, Rue de Rivoli, Paris', and on the shoulder is an impressed 'F.G.' for Fernand Gaultier. The body is of leather-covered wood. The other lady with a fixed neck has a gusseted leather body and bisque lower arms with fabric above the elbows. The muslin dress is part of the trousseau of the former. Both dolls have fixed glass eyes and wear their original sheepskin wigs. Height of Simonne 45 cm. (18 in.).

The pedlar doll was primarily an ornamental item to be kept under a dome in a parlour. In this example, a papier mâché doll with a Grödnertal-type wooden body is dressed in Welsh costume with a red silk-lined pedlar's cape. Items on the tray include books, scent bottles and playing cards. *Circa* 1840. Height of doll 27 cm. (11 in.).

A typical early type Bru in its original costume dating back to the 1880s, with a gusseted leather body and wearing Bru marked shoes. The doll has pierced ears, an open-closed mouth with suggested teeth, a swivel neck marked with a crescent, circle and dot, and bisque lower arms. Height 44 cm. (17½ in.).

An open-mouthed Jumeau of very pale colour with fixed eyes, pierced ears and original wig. It is marked on the head with an impressed '10' and on the body with an oval cream label reading 'Bébé Jumeau Diplôme d' Honneur'. Height 61 cm. (24 in.).

Opposite The bébé in cream is a closed-mouth Jumeau with red and black tick marks on the head. The very heavy brows and large eyes are typical of this firm's best work. It wears marked Jumeau shoes and the original costume. Height 50 cm. (20 in.). The doll in the original grey velvet costume is marked 'Eden Bébé' and 'Paris 9 Depose,' and has an open mouth and pierced ears. The body is well-shaped with a suggested bosom. Both dolls have fixed eyes. Height 54 cm. (21½ in.).

The introduction of colour lithography meant that very lavishly-decorated puzzles could be made cheaply. This box of puzzles contains six different trades, including a shoe repairer and a carpenter. Unmarked, *circa* 1885. Size of box 20 × 14 cm. (8 × 5¾ in.).

'Zooloo', published by C. W. Faulkner & Co., 41, Jewin Street, London E.C., and printed in Germany. From the 'C. W. F. One Shilling Round Games'. It was played with counters from a pool of not less than forty.

Opposite 'The Game of Magnetic Fish Pond', with its colourfully lithographed aquarium and original fishing rods with magnet hooks. Marked on box 'J.W.S & S. Bavaria' for J. W. Spear and Sons. The metal-ringed fish show the points won in a circle, but dead cats and old boots were on the outside. The doll in white was made by Kestner and the one in pink by Bergman. Both German. Height of aquarium 27 cm. (11 in.).

Above Late 19th-century Bavarian farm with animals which are also found in Noah's arks. Size 103 sq. cm. (16 sq. in.).

Opposite A typically Bavarian ark containing some one hundred and eighty animals and birds. The decoration on the ark is stencilled and one side slides away. Mid-19th century. Length 45 cm. (18 in.).

173

A Bavarian fort whose design is reminiscent of actual castles in the area. It is made of printed paper on wood. Each section can be dismantled and packed away into the base that opens like a box. Dated by original owner to 1898. Height 38 cm. (15 in.).

The child was expected to spend hours polishing the kitchen range and its equipment as in this well-preserved example made by Märklin and heated by methylated spirit. Height 38 cm. (15 in.). (Collection Betty Harvey-Jones.)

A good and unusual 'Frog and Snake' money bank, the tinplate bank depicting a frog which opens its mouth to receive a coin from a snake when the lever at one side is depressed. German, *circa* 1925. Width 16·5 cm. (6½ in.). (Courtesy of Sotheby's.)

The miniature world

IN both the eighteenth and nineteenth centuries, the majority of toys were considered as a preparation for adult life, and although some children doubtless enjoyed hours of idle amusement, the intention was almost invariably practical. The girl playing with her baby house or the small boy drilling his armies of model soldiers was approved of by adults, who saw in this play aspects of their own world in miniature.

Dolls' houses

The splendid cabinet-type dolls' houses of the seventeenth and eighteenth centuries are very rarely encountered after 1800, although there are individual examples of correctly made display pieces that have been dressed perhaps by a mother and her elder daughters. The complex stately home made for Queen Mary and now at Windsor Castle is the most memorable cabinet house of this type in Britain; while in the United States, Coleen Moore's display castle, with its working organ and drawing-room with a jade and rose quartz floor, enchants visitors to the Museum of Science and Industry at Chicago. A few particularly well-made houses constructed in the early years of the nineteenth century are purely Georgian in appearance, although the interiors are not as fine as those of the previous century.

Prints and paintings of the early nineteenth century show children playing with houses of a fairly simple construction that were available from toyshops. However, as they were not so immediately impressive, they were often discarded, and comparatively few examples of this much simpler type still exist. In those that survive it is soon discovered that the simple façade often masks very fine carpentry, and door frames, skirting-boards and windows are usually very correctly made. One interesting house, dating from 1838, was provided with a rudimentary stone-walled bathroom, with a large and splendid cold-water tap; this is at present the earliest-recorded British house with this refinement. Queen Victoria's dolls' house is a very simple two-roomed and completely practical house with a large kitchen downstairs and a papered drawing-room on the first floor. It is a pleasant toy, but surprisingly simple for such an important child, and indicates the way in which dolls' houses were now intended for play rather than exhibition.

The mid-nineteenth century is characterized by much more substantial

Opposite The interior of a late 19th-century doll's house, showing how such toys reflect the lifestyle of the period. The music room contains printed paper-covered furniture, including an ornate piano. In the drawing-room is a metal cat with kittens that can all be removed from their basket. See also the illustration page 179. Height 120 cm. (47½ in.).

Interior of the Blessley house showing the original
bathroom with it primitive tap and original papers
on walls.

A heavy and well-made house of Irish origin with
'Dollette 1838' on plaque above door and 'Blessley'
on brass plate in centre of door. The central panel is
held in place by a brass peg that runs through the
pediment. Width 85 cm. (33½ in.).

The exterior of the late 19th-century doll's house that is illustrated in colour on page 176 has brick-papered sides and the façade is painted grey and white. It is British and made by G & J Lines who used the same component parts on many of their designs. Height 124·5 cm. (49 in.).

A charming lithographed house with a characteristic blue painted roof and an opening front door. Unmarked. Late 19th century. Height 48 cm. (19 in.). (Collection Betty Harvey-Jones.)

houses, often made of inch-thick timber and obviously intended to withstand several generations. Their lavish furnishings exactly convey the atmosphere of actual houses of the time, with beaded foot-stools, china pug dogs and silk upholstered fringed furniture. Houses of this type were usually made in the country of sale, as they were too heavy and bulky to be viable exports. They are very rarely marked in any way, though firms such as Lines Brothers made a large number that can sometimes be identified by comparison of designs with those in reprinted trade catalogues, such as those of Gamages, who appear to have been one of the main outlets for Lines toys.

In America, the most collectable commercially made houses are those

An effective American cast-iron stove with 'Rival' on the oven door and 's' on the side 'Pat July 1895'. This toy once belonged to the Vellacott family. Height 36 cm. (14 in.). (Collection Betty Harvey-Jones.)

covered with attractive lithographed paper and produced from 1895 by the R. Bliss Manufacturing Company of Rhode Island, a firm that obligingly marked the majority of its products. As some of the Bliss houses measured less than a foot, they are of obvious attraction to most collectors, as they can be easily accommodated even in a small apartment. The architecture is highly fanciful and is often described as 'gingerbread', as it has little relationship to real life, despite Bliss's claim that the houses were designed by architects. Bliss houses usually have isinglass windows and lace curtains, but many of the smaller sizes were made with printed curtained windows. Access was given to the fairly simple rooms by hinged fronts or sides. It is not known whether the lithographed papers were made in America or were European imports, although they were obviously specially made. Shops, skyscrapers, folding rooms and warehouses were produced, all characterized by similar decoration. The Bliss catalogue of 1911 featured folding dolls' houses made of heavy board strongly hinged with cloth. These folding houses were thought especially suitable for people living in 'close quarters', as they could be taken apart in less than one minute. The interiors of Bliss houses were at first lithographed but eventually, and rather disappointingly as the effect is less idiosyncratic, normal wallpapers were substituted. The firm claimed to make stronger houses than any that were imported, stating that they would not warp or crack. They were 'American designs to suit the tastes of American children'. In 1909 the company became associated with the Hardware and Woodenware Manufacturing

Company of New York City, a co-operative sales organization in which Bliss had the highest sales record in that year.

Few dolls' houses were sold fully furnished, and much of the child's enjoyment was derived from the careful selection of appropriate pieces. A large variety of tin kitchenware was exported from Germany to both Britain and America in designs that hardly changed as the century progressed, so that similar pieces can be seen in houses assembled in Regency and Edwardian periods. The wooden furniture in a single house can be seen to originate in several countries, such as Germany and France, while in the United States Bliss was unusual among makers of dolls' houses in constructing their own special brightly decorated pieces. Attributable furniture is rare, as it was often marked only on the box that contained it, or with a label. However, the products of a few makers, such as Schneegass of Walterhausen (later the United Toy Factories), are recognizable by their complicated and very idiosyncratic designs. The German makers were particularly skilled in the manufacture of both strong and attractive pieces, some being given marble tops and correctly opening drawers with minute knobs. Fully equipped dolls' houses are now only occasionally found as many, reaching the hands of dealers, have been stripped of their contents, which have been sold separately giving a much greater financial return.

Kitchens and kitchenware

The history of the model kitchen is almost as old as that of the doll's house. Those made in Germany, with their characteristic fireplaces incorporating arched storage space at floor-level for dry wood, were made from the late seventeenth century. Even in the very early examples there is considerable

A typical Nuremberg Kitchen dating from the 18th century with brass and tin utensils. On the left is a hen coop for fattening of table birds. Width 66 cm. (26 in.). (Bethnal Green Museum.)

A print showing the variety of toys available in the very early 19th century. Of particular interest is the model fireplace with meat roasting on a spit and plates on a shelf above.

variation in quality, some being almost perfect miniatures equipped with craftsman-made pewter and silver, while others with cheap tin fittings have obviously been made very economically as toys for the very young. Pieces were often added to such kitchens over the years, so that it is rare, outside German museums, to find any with fully datable equipment. The end of the eighteenth century saw a considerable commercial production of such rooms, and the Bestelmeier catalogues show simple settings with the characteristic metal round-paned Nuremberg windows. They were supplied with a stove on the back wall, a simple table and several chairs. By the early nineteenth century there were various different grades of this model, one of them even having running water worked from a pump on an outside wall, as well as a resident cook. In the same catalogue a fully-equipped laundry was shown. Very early kitchens often contained a hen coop where the fowls were specially fattened for the table by the cook or housewife, while others contain well-constructed working model spits. The wide variety of commercially made kitchens continued to be sold throughout the nineteenth century; thus, even in a single catalogue one example might have only a fireplace and shelf, while the most expensive would be fully equipped with tools, storage jars, skimmers and ladles and even a sweeping-brush. Frequently the basic construction was common to all types, and the different grades were created simply by adding more furniture and equipment. Some of the early American kitchens were made completely of tin and were provided, like the German kitchens, with working pumps.

The German firm that is particularly associated with kitchenware is that of Märklin, whose toy production began in 1859. The variety of their 'furniture for children's kitchens' makes the collector fully aware of the vast selection of dolls' house equipment that was available to the Victorian child: that offered to the children of today is, by comparison, laughable. Their early catalogue shows a range of wood-grain-finished tin buckets as well as fully equipped kitchen ranges. Märklin also sold a wide assortment of model pumps that could be fitted in dolls' house kitchens or stood over a small model bath. Dozens of different moulds and cutters in copper and tin were included, as well as serving spoons and cutlery both in 'German silver' and 'Britannia metal', with handles of bone, ebony, nickel or wood; some of the cutlery was enclosed in presentation boxes, some in knife boxes with carrying handles. The cheapest was sold in sets fixed to cards. Round brass hot-water bottles, 'tin-founded' oval bottles, japanned bread boxes, iron 'flesh forks', a wide assortment of brass, silver and tin ladles and skimmers, japanned storage tins, and even butter syringes were all separately listed and sometimes made in several sizes. There were different types of flat-iron, including special versions for charcoal with accompanying stands and boards. Working coffee percolators with a nickelled finish were provided complete with spirit lamps, and to serve tea or coffee there were also several different types of pots with matching cups and saucers. Coffee strainers, mills and roasters gave complete realism to the game, so that a child learned in play some of the necessary domestic arts before leaving the nursery. Some of the items in a comprehensive set of kitchen equipment would have been found only in the most thoroughly provided full-size kitchen of the time—for instance a vermicelli board, almond mill, or potato cutters. Although Märklin was mainly a seller of tin toys, some wooden pieces such as egg-stands and chopping-boards were also included.

Cards to which were sewn an assortment of cleaning tools such as carpet-beaters, dustpans and sweeping-brushes must have provided cheap gifts. In a different price range altogether were the complete tin kitchens that Märklin also made. These were basically rectangular, without a roof or front, and their price depended on the amount of equipment. The best was complete with a fireplace, table, bench and chairs, as well as the working tap. Their painted wooden kitchens with straight or oblique cut sides, which were even more expensive, were quite literally packed with furnishings, so that the moving of even a single piece must thave caused many others to fall. These so-called 'Nuremberg kitchens', when still complete, are extremely attractive because of this cluttered appearance: the toy-makers obviously felt that any bare section of wall was a sign of failure!

Model kitchens of a similar type were still made just before the First World War in surprisingly anachronistic designs, as were model cooking ranges. Long after the full-sized versions had disappeared from the home, firms such as Chad Valley were still selling tin ranges with a copper and silver finish that were made by Gwenda Toys and look completely Edwardian. The last catalogue in which these metal ranges appeared is dated as recently as 1956.

Caring for a doll's clothes was an essential part of nursery life. The wardrobe is complete with its coathangers and ribbon-tied linen. The mangle is marked 'Gem' and has seen much wear. Height of mangle 23 cm. (9 in.).

A particularly well-made miniature washstand and china that carries the sellers label 'E. C. Spurin, Fancy Repository and Juvenile Library, 37 Bond Street, London'. It is made of inlaid rosewood and has a marble top. Width 33 cm. (13 in.). (Christie's, South Kensington.)

Housekeeping in Miniature

Several makers, such as Bing, made equipment for children that was claimed to be perfectly suitable for adult use, such as mincing machines. Among these gadgets (to be powered by a stationary engine) were dairy implements. In the 1911 Carette catalogue a complete butter manufactory was advertised, 'all mounted on a tile-faced wood base with shafting and a hot air engine on a cast iron bed.' This was sold with a cream separator, churn and kneading machine.

Learning to deal with the vast amount of washing that was inevitable in looking after a large household was also an essential part of nursery practice, and most of the German companies offered an assortment of baths, tubs, clothes-horses, scrubbing-brushes and scrubbing-boards; the latter became an almost traditional toy, and although few women still used these corrugated metal and wood boards in the late 1940s, they were still sold as toys in quite substantial numbers. Chad Valley, in 1932, sold 'Dolly's Washing Day' as a boxed set containing a metal and wood 'Lion Mangle' with a wash tub, pegs, clothes-line, blue bag and soap-shaker. Small mangles were a really vital part of every girl's equipment, and have survived in some number, especially those marked 'Holdfast' on the cast-iron bases. This was the trade-name of Cartwright, whose toys were sold in boxes marked 'Gwenda Toys'.

The thrifty housewife made many of her own clothes, and firms such as Blackmore, and Moden und Schnittmuster-Industrie of Leipzig, mentioned patterns for dolls' clothes in their lists of fashionable adult garments. A child thus learned how to set out the paper shapes at an early age. Judging by the very large numbers that have survived, all but the poorest children must have owned a toy sewing-machine; many of these were highly decorative with gold-printed designs and rococo-inspired bases. The majority were manufactured in Germany by companies such as F. W. Müller of Berlin. Twenty different models were on sale before the First World War. The cheapest of the sewing machines available in 1910 were those that worked a chain stitch, but the higher-priced models sewed between two and four running stitches at each turn of the wheel. Small adult machines sold for delicate work and others made specifically for leather-workers are sometimes sold as toys in antique shops though the genuine toys can usually be distinguished by their lighter weight. Müller also sold fret-sawing and drilling machines for young carpenters.

A child's sewing machine marked 'Made in Germany. 177/600'. It sews in a chain stitch. *Circa* 1900. Height 20 cm. (8 in.).

Shops

Going to market and playing shop are an essential part of each generation's educational make-believe, teaching in a pleasant guise how to count and weigh. Though model shops are mentioned in eighteenth-century catalogues, few seem to have survived. The Germanisches National-museum at Nuremberg has two very small box-like shops, measuring only some 15 cm. (6 in.) across, that date to this early period. In each stands a plaster shopkeeper, male in one and female in the other, with roughly made shelves behind them displaying equally poorly made wares. In the same museum is an impressive milliner's shop, dating to the second quarter of the nineteenth century, that contains a wide range of very exactly and correctly made miniatures. Regency-style dresses hang in glass-fronted cases at the rear, while on the counter are boxes of artificial flowers. Large hat-boxes on which are shown fine bonnets decorated with lace and feathers are piled on the floor, while a few very expensive and stylish hats are displayed on tall wooden stands. Sample cards show ranges of fabrics, pins and threads, and also on the counter lies a miniature yardstick and pieces of toy money. In the foreground are displayed beautifully embroidered bags. The lady shopkeeper has a well-carved head, with the hair arranged in ringlets at the front and drawn to a large bun at the crown. The range of items that a woman of the period expected to buy from her draper can be seen in the well-made windows: they include tiny candles, tapers, hat-boxes and prayer books. Such exquisitely made models, providing useful information about the everyday life of the period, are found infrequently, and there is often a question as to whether they were made as adult amusements or for display in the window of an actual shop, rather than as a toy.

There is no question about the intention of a commercially made haberdasher's shop also at the Germanishes Nationalmuseum in Nuremberg; this is typically German and obviously a toy; it contains a tiny figure with its hair dressed in the 'Queen Adelaide' style. The interior is well-planned. On pillars at the front, bags hang from small hooks. At the back of the shop are two fitted mirrors, while on a shelf between them there is a miniature papier mâché head for the display of a bonnet. From a chain hangs a wooden pattern board, similar to the boards seen in the Nuremberg cabinet houses on which the housewife would mark various items for the illiterate servants. In this case the board is filled with simply drawn rows of socks, aprons and other garments. Cupboards are filled with rolls of fabric, boxes and small newspaper-wrapped parcels.

Most of the surviving shops dating to before 1850 are of German origin, although they were obviously made elsewhere. In a list of the Dauphin's possessions in 1696, nine market-place shops are mentioned, 'filled with little figures of enamel'. The makers of lead flats also made several market-day scenes at the end of the eighteenth century, and in these the wares available can be seen in some detail. The Historical Museum at Basle has several interesting shops, such as a combined draper's and grocer's, in the eighteenth-century style, with wooden shutters that are locked horizontally; when the shop was open the upper shutter, lifted, formed a shelter, while the lower, supported by simple legs, formed the counter. The grocer's has neatly labelled drawers, while the draper's shows mainly rolls of fabric. This museum also has a grocer's with sugar cones standing on the shelves and wooden boxes containing items such as juniper berries. On the floor stand casks of vinegar. This very basic shop, made in the Erzgebirge, is a simple box with fronts that open like a dolls' house, and with red and green painted windows on the sides.

The range of shops available in the early nineteenth century is suggested by the Bestelmeier catalogues, which include one with thirty paintings and several figures. There were also wooden market settings contained in matchwood boxes: these could be purchased in small groups until a really large arrangement was owned. At the stalls were plump market women with baskets of goods, while one Christmas fair even showed a toy stall. These models were made in one piece and the goods could not be moved about, sold, or rearranged; they must therefore have made much less satisfactory toys than the shops that were stocked with miniatures. A few contain figures made of gum tragacanth as well as the more usual carved wood. The simple canopied bazaar stall (now at the Bethnal Green

A mid 19th-century German doll's shop with labelled drawers in three languages. Width 53 cm. (21 in.). (Christie's, South Kensington.)

A shop made by 'Mr Pells, Woodcarver, Felix Street, Hackney' and said to be modelled on a shop called Titchbourne. The meat is made of papier mâché as is the butcher, while the dog is china. English, *circa* 1880. Width 30 cm. (12 in.). (Bethnal Green Museum.)

Museum, London), supplied with many hand-sewn and -knitted items as well as several Grödnertal assistants, was a much more satisfactory toy as the pieces are not fixed in position.

A very correctly made model shop with 'Spratt, Grocer to Her Majesty' written on the fascia board was owned by Queen Victoria's children and can be seen at Osborne House on the Isle of Wight. This was a double-fronted shop with glazed windows, hinged at the sides. Shops of all types, from tobacconist's to chemist's, were made in great numbers in the second half of the nineteenth century, although the standard gradually declined. Printed paper shops, to be pasted to cardboard and then cut out, were made by firms such as Pellerin, established in Epinal in 1790. Some of these are so complex that they would have taxed even the most dextrous of adults. Charles Morell's catalogue for 1896 illustrates some of the very ornate shops the French were so skilled in creating, such as a 'Parfumerie Régence', much of whose elegance depended on the lithographed decoration. The French shops are immediately recognizable because of their colourfully stocked shelves and the very light weight of the complete toy, resulting in irreparable damage to many.

In 1913 Gamage's of London offered grocers' shops with the usual arrangement of neatly labelled shelves at the back and a counter bearing a large scale at the front. Shops of a similar kind were made in most European countries and in America, and unless there are clues in the surviving wares it is often difficult to be sure of the origin. Although the

A model made by a butcher called Mr Fernley and possibly a model of a shop in Swaton Road, Bow, London. A particularly bloody model with a bull being slaughtered in the background and a partly skinned sheep. Carcasses are made mainly of plaster-soaked fabric over wire netting. *Circa* 1880. Width 91 cm. (36 in.). (Bethnal Green Museum.)

butcher's shop is often claimed as a particularly British toy, it appeared in the Bestelmeier catalogues from 1800. A few were made as display models in the nineteenth century and enclosed in glass cases, but others were made as toys with removable joints of meat, rabbits and fowls. Occasionally a particularly fine model was made, such as those in the Bethnal Green or London Museum—precise even to the splashes of blood on the sawdust-covered floor.

Shops, which were often large and bulky, were frequently made in the country of sale but their stock was sometimes obtained from several sources, which add to the difficulty of attribution. J. J. Landmann of Nuremberg, a firm that mainly sold clockwork and mechanical toys, also offered a wide range of shop fittings, including many pieces for the English-

An Edwardian grocer's shop with large hanging scale and a wide assortment of goods on display, though from several different periods of the 20th century. The small labelled drawers are almost invariably found at the back. Width 81 cm. (32 in.). (Christie's, South Kensington.)

speaking market such as jars, bottles and tins, all in absolutely correct miniature shapes. Among them were 'Liebig Companies Oxo Fluid Beef Made in South America' and neat oval tins of 'Lobster, Crown Brand' complete with a key. One of the main German producers of complete shops was Louis Lindner and Sons of Sonneberg, while Kindler and Briel of Boblingen, Württemberg, made a few large enough for a child to stand inside. Many of the shops and cafés were made in the Hesse Cassel region and it was reported that some were made by prisoners in the jails.

The 'Our Pets' series of games and toys made by Ralph Dunn and Co. of the Barbican, London, included a very wide selection of shop-type boxed toys. These ranged from 'Pets Post Office', with a grid-like screen to be erected on a table, together with telegraph forms and note paper, to 'Pets Stores', with edible contents. In 1909 'Pets Emporium' was introduced, described as 'the first time little children have had a draper's shop exactly like the real one. In this box there is a counter with drawers to pull out, real cloth to unfold and measure out, also handkerchiefs, hooks and eyes, lace, cotton, etc.' In 'Pets Bonnet Box' there were 'real dolls' hats with materials for trimming them: pretty flowers, ribbon and even cotton'. It was this company that manufactured the often found Peak Frean miniature biscuit tins for model shops, also many of the tin cash boxes and scales. 'Pets Shopping' included lists, money and a bag. Gages of Liverpool similarly made 'Cash Stores', as well as 'Come to Tea' sets and boxed schools.

'The Children's Game of Model Shops' was made by Chad Valley. The basic shop consisted of a three-sided arrangement with a tiled floor, across which ran a large mouse. The slogan 'Home Stores for Best Value in Everything', painted on a board over the top, was surmounted by a printed clock. A prominent notice stated 'No Credit Given!' On the shelves were packages containing 'Quaker Wheat Berrie' and 'Fry's Cocoa'. These shops, as well as the 'Home Post' and 'Home Tea Shop', were all made at the company's Harbourne works. Peacock's of Islington, established in 1853 and more commonly associated with jigsaw puzzles, sold shops in the

A well-made mahogany money-box with a brass plate inscribed 'Percy 23 June 1877' with leather guards inside the slot to prevent money being removed with a knife. Also a bronzed iron 'Post Office Savings Bank. G.R' with stamped number 128703. *Circa* 1912. The Post Offices held keys for these boxes. Width of wooden box 17 cm. (6¾ in.).

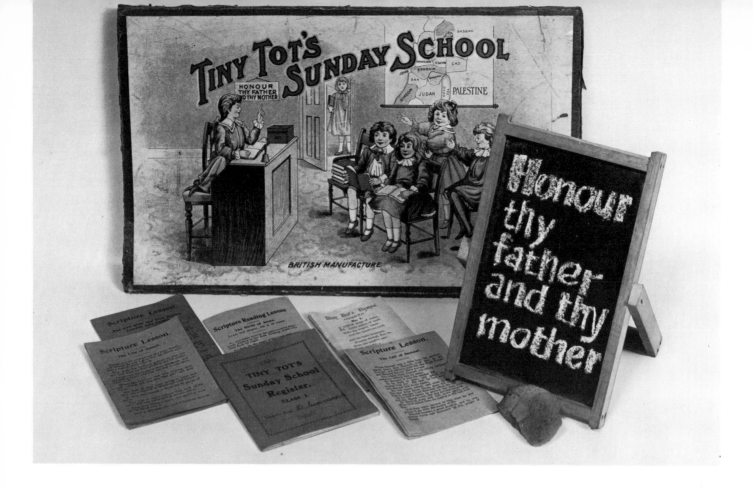

'Tiny Tots Sunday School' of British manufacture with its original price of 1/2d., complete with sponge, School register, Scripture lessons and Hymn sheets. The attractive box is extremely misleading. *Circa* 1910. Width of box 36 cm. (14 in.).

1920s, such as a child-size market stall with a striped canopy. Their 'Model Provision Stores' in the same scale was highly effective with its flower-printed panels and a wealth of drawers and display cabinets. The largest size was 141 cm. (4 ft 8 in.) high. This firm also made small sweet, butcher's and fish shops, all in a very outdated manner that looks more Victorian than 1920s. The Glevum Works in Gloucestershire made shops in the thirties; these were mostly of the cheapest kind—a partitioned box with well-shaped glass jars containing 'Jubes' and 'London Mixture'. Their white enamelled shop with a polished mahogany counter was of better quality. Some shops were produced purely as advertisements, such as the sweet shops made by Pascall's.

Tea-sets

The making of toy china intended purely for the amusement of children did not become generally established until the late eighteenth century, though simple miniature sets of Whieldon ware, with the characteristic cream and brown mottled decoration, were made before this date. A few of the fine miniature Oriental sets that were probably intended as adult 'toys' were bought for wealthy children. A certain Captain Randall in Canton was instructed in 1779 to buy a 'child's set for my daughter'. And a Mrs Delaney's grand-niece Mary, aged seven in 1779, 'made me follow her into the parlour to behold a complete set of young Nankeen china which she had just received from the Duchess of Portland: not quite so small as for baby things nor large enough for grown ladies, there are twelve tea cups and saucers, six coffee cups and teapot, sugar dish, milk mug, two bread

Toy china marked 'Nankin' with a mock seal and 'Davenport', transfer-printed and hand-coloured in red, yellow and purple. Impressed Davenport anchor and date mark for 1852.

A toy dinner service transfer printed in blue and white with the pattern known as Monopteris that is thought to have been made only by Rogers. *Circa 1830.*

and butter plates.' The fact that Mrs Delaney should have found it necessary to explain the composition of the set suggests that such services were still uncommon.

The vastly increased mechanization of the nineteenth century, as well as the demand among the large families of middle-class children, encouraged many factories to produce toy china in quantity. The toy tea-set could be used to instruct girls in the elements of social behaviour and the number of surviving sets suggests their play was often supervised.

Great quantities of largely unmarked German sets were imported during the second half of the nineteenth century, and the porcelain is frequently of a high quality and is well decorated, sometimes by hand. Most of the British factories, including firms as diverse as Davenport and the Old Hall Earthenware Company, made toy sets, sometimes with especially engraved nursery designs illustrating stories like Cinderella or Punch and Judy. Production of these very well-made sets appears to have declined in the early twentieth century, possibly because unsupervised play was becoming more common. Examples of more recent date are almost invariably of very cheap quality.

Mothercraft and handicraft toys

Whether or not she enjoyed the process, the lot of the Victorian woman was one of almost continual child-bearing and nursing. A girl's training in mothercraft began at an early age when she was provided with dolls' feeding bottles, cradles, prams and pushchairs, often made in miniature by firms which also made full-sized equipment. Correctly made dolls' cradles and beds in cast iron with brass decoration were made by such companies as William E. Peck of Bartholomew Close, London, while many mahogany half-tester beds made in the mid-nineteenth century are so beautifully constructed and equipped as to be almost in the class of fine miniatures rather than toys. Hugo Roithner and Company of Schweidnitz were particularly well known in the toy trade for their assortment of high chairs, swings and slides, all made in dolls' sizes. Many of the stained wooden high chairs that fold down (as did full-sized versions) to chairs and tables are found with the Lines Brothers trade-marks, although in comparison with the vast number made they have not survived in great quantity, presumably because their size made storage a problem. Toy prams often met the same fate and were at an even greater disadvantage, since no child wished to be seen pushing a very outdated model.

Prams were usually manufactured in the country of sale. In Britain a surprising number of firms were engaged in their production. One of them was Simmons and Company of Bermondsey Street, London, a firm that supplied a particularly wide range. This firm charged extra for prams painted in light art colours, pure white, cream or pale blue, while leather-hung springs added to the price. Their range included 'The Popular', a pushchair-like pram with an apron and brass-jointed hood. This stood on two very large wheels and was pushed by shafts, so that it also resembled a

Opposite A wrought iron dolls' cradle dating from the late 19th century. Height 90 cm. (35½ in.).

A cane dolls' pushchair in Art Nouveau style with its original label on base 'A. W. Gamage Ltd. High Holborn London w.c.' *Circa* 1895. Height 81 cm. (32 in.).

A late 19th-century doll's pram with metal spoked wheels, a china handle and brass detail. The blue body of the pram is made of corrugated tin. The baby doll was made by Catterfelder Puppenfabrik and has a bisque head. Height of pram 74 cm. (29 in.).

An American advertisement for Lloyd Loom prams, dated December, 1922. The fashion for providing a miniature version for a child was common in Britain also. These prams were made of woven continuous cane.

mail-cart. Simmons' most expensive pram in 1910 was 'The West End', with an upholstered interior, waist strap, detachable cushions and apron, beaded body-work, coach-painted 'steam bent ash shafts and patented bed'. The wheels were of the eleven-inch size (28 cm.) and the tilt wheels were rubber-tyred (until this date wheels were frequently of metal without any cushioning). Patterson Edwards, Bottomley of Leeds, and G. W. Schramm of Birmingham were all among the main producers. The Star Manufacturing Company of London made dolls' carriages with the frame-work of the bodies supplied in 'cane, glossy cane, American reed or wood'. Many of the caned pushchairs, such as that illustrated, were extremely attractive and were popular with manufacturers as they were light in weight and made in a relatively short time by a basket-worker. Patterson Edwards made similar caned pushchairs, and others of the wooden folding type with fabric or carpet seats.

A very strange material, resembling chicken wire, was used in the manufacture of prams and pushchairs by Topliff and Ely Co. of Elyria, Ohio; it was fixed to steel or iron shapes. These prams were known as 'Wire Prams' and the firm also produced 'Go Carts', which must have been extremely hazardous as toys. The Toledo Metal Wheel Company of Ohio also made dolls' prams and claimed to be the 'largest manufacturers in the world devoted to the production of children's vehicles'. The making of dolls' prams of the coach-built type was an extremely lengthy process and involved carpenters, upholsterers, blacksmiths, wheel-fitters and painters, yet it was possible to sell very well-made models very cheaply before the First World War.

In the nineteenth century manufacturers promoted toys as exercises

A tin model typewriter made in Germany, probably by Günthermann, and bought at the Empire Exhibition in 1907. Letters are selected on the wheel and the carriage is brought forward to strike the wheel by pressing the lever on left. Case marked 'Junior'. Width 23 cm. (9 in.).

designed to improve vital skills. The 'Bread Basket Maker', 'Flower Making at Home' and the 'Little Architect', all in boxed sets, were aimed at the creation of a more competent child. Fashionable people at the end of the nineteenth century were aware of the importance of design by the work of the Arts and Crafts Movement, and a number of toys were specifically made for the children of more aesthetic parents, such as Spears' 'Art Needlework'. This, despite its pretentious claims, included simple cross-

Needlework pictures made *circa* 1910 with coloured wools and sheets of designs. It is doubtful whether such imitative work could ever have encouraged any latent artistic ability but this virtue was always claimed by the manufacturers.

stitch designs such as a swan on a wave or 'God is love', all very stolidly worked. In 1908 Gamage's offered 'Pyrography or Poker Work', enamel-painting on pottery, pottery-making with a wheel, and cloth-weaving among their creative toys. As a charming occupation for girls, 'Artistic Pea and Bean Work' was suggested!

Many of the interesting construction sets were aimed purely at boys and there was a considerable emphasis upon carpentry and engineering skills Printed thin card shapes, to be linked together by metal tabs, were made by a variety of firms and sold in attractively boxed sets, such as 'The Bridge Builders' or 'Model Schools'. A similar constructional bridge toy, made by Chad Valley, was claimed to be strong enough to support model trains and carts. Card construction sets were frequently given away as advertising material, while various firms such as Raphael Tuck and Epinal made

'Relief Model L. The Pleasure Steamer. Royal Art Novelty Series 154. Designed at the London Studios of Raphael Tuck and printed at the Fine Art Works in Germany'. Eleven other models were published in this series. It is brightly printed on embossed card. Late 19th century.

printed scenes, vehicles and buildings expressly for cutting out and assembling. Some of the Epinal sheets were very complex, although Tuck's were sometimes helpful and supplied the pieces ready-cut and kept together with narrow joining-tabs, as in the ship illustrated here. It is doubtful whether many children were capable of following the assembly instructions for very small-scale paper towns with tiny pieces, though no doubt many parents felt a righteous glow at having given their child such a taxing occupation.

R. Journet of London made some very intricate 'Kindergarten Occupations', such as 'The Little Clock-Maker' that contained all the working pieces needed to make a correct wall clock. This firm also made gilt metal dolls' house furniture that a girl could assemble herself, as well as the usual craft-type sets such as basket-making. Tools were popularly sold fixed to cards, and trowels, garden forks, hammers and pick-axes could all be obtained from firms such as Chamberlain and Hill at Walsall. Early in the twentieth century Dover Toys sold model blacksmith's shops with anvil, hammer and nails as well as potters' wheels and their accessories. Not even the Royal children were allowed to avoid learning practical skills, and when at Osborne House they worked in the gardens with well-made garden tools and waggonettes marked with their own initials. In the Swiss Cottage there was also a well-equipped model kitchen where the Princesses could make simple meals.

Construction kits and steam toys

Few British schoolboys in the twentieth century were without at least a few pieces of the Meccano sets, patented by Frank Hornby in 1901. As a child Hornby was happiest when playing in his own simple workshop where the lives of great inventors were a continual source of inspiration in his experiments. His own difficulties in obtaining sufficient tools at this early age gave him the idea of interchangeable parts, capable of various uses. Many years later, when helping his own sons in their workshop, he again began to think, in his own words, 'of parts that could be applied in different ways to many different models and that could be adjusted to give a variety of movements by alterations of position etc. In order to do this, it was necessary to devise some standard method of fitting one part to any other; and gradually there came to me the conception of parts all perforated with a series of holes of the same size and the same distance apart.' These pieces could be bolted together in an endless variety of positions and later undone and used for another model. Several basic strips in sizes of $2\frac{1}{2}$ inches, $5\frac{1}{2}$ inches and up to $12\frac{1}{2}$ inches were made with the holes all at half-inch intervals. Wheels were fixed to rods with a simple key, which is a means of identifying early sets. As this model was such a great success, Frank Hornby decided to patent the design to protect it from copyists, such as an American firm that attempted to sell the 'American Model Builder', a fairly obvious imitation. At first the Meccano system was know as 'Mechanics Made Easy' and the original factory in Duke Street, Liverpool, consisted of

Pieces from a large Meccano set dating from the 1930s giving some idea of the wide range of parts available.

a single room. The trade name 'Meccano' was registered in 1907, and on the earlier boxes the 'o' was always printed slightly to the side, a form considered very artistic by the company, while the letter 'c' was also of an unusual form.

Early strips were of tin with turned over edges, but after the firm moved to larger premises they were made of rolled steel with heavy nickel plating; a set screw replaced the early simple key for the attachment of wheels. In the formative years of the company, Frank Hornby himself designed all the models in the Meccano Construction Manuals, but later others helped to create exciting structures that encouraged boys and their fathers to buy additional pieces. In 1926 Meccano in colour was introduced, as it was the twenty-fifth anniversary of the firm. From this time plates and pulley wheels were enamelled in red, and strips, girders and brackets in green. A boy began his construction kit with a simple basic outfit and bought more sections as needed, the maker's intention, the whole time, being to train the boy in good engineering principles whether he was constructing 'The Famous Wright Aeroplane', a complex model loom, or the Tower Bridge with raising and lowering bascules (a model that was eventually worked by electricity). As the hobby gained more followers, the Meccano Guild was set up, and the *Meccano Magazine* was first published in 1916.

Many construction kits resembled 'Meccano' in some way. For instance there was a set of wooden bars that were perforated and fastened by metal parts, as well as a set in metal made by Firma Falk and another by Märklin, an example of which can be seen at the Toy Museum in Nuremberg. 'Burlington Building Bricks', sold in the early twentieth century, consisted of hardwood slabs with small holes in them so they could be fastened together with pegs. 'Kliptiko' was a series of interlocking bricks with notches or slots and was marketed by Gamage's.

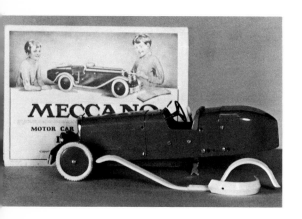

A Meccano Motor Car Construction Outfit, metal with rubber tyres. *Circa* 1935. Size of car 27 cm. (11 in.). (Bethnal Green Museum.)

The depression of the 1930s affected the Danish building industry very badly and a bankrupt carpenter named Ole Kirk Christiansen began to carve yo-yos in his cottage. Eventually a toy workshop was set up and a system of plastic interlocking bricks was evolved. The firm was so poor at first that they could not afford a stand at the Nuremberg Fair in 1954, so they showed the new system in a hotel room. From this beginning, very similar to that of Meccano, the very popular 'Lego' system emerged. Certainly it is the ultimate in a lightweight coloured constructional toy, though without the sculptural complexities of the more adventurous metal creations.

Parents of today enjoy seeing their children playing with construction sets, but few would now countenance many of the highly dangerous toys with which boys of the late nineteenth century were familiar. Toys are now so heavily controlled by safety regulations and government controls that few can provide any excitement for the child of over nine years. Many of the working tin toys were driven by steam-engines which could power a complete model factory, force water into the air higher than a house, or even be used to ventilate a room. These larger steam toys could be

'Skaymo' Junior bricks made by Skaymo toys of Altrincham with an English copyright by Phillip Cundall. 'Makes recognizable Architectural Scale models such as an architect makes'. The blocks, well made from polished and painted wood, were all mulitples of one unit so that boxes could be combined. *Circa* 1920.

extremely dangerous if misused, and even when all the directions were carefully followed scalds and burns were almost inevitable. Georges Carette in 1911 supplied a complete electric light plant consisting of a dynamo and a steam-engine. The engine could also be used to drive any model required, and a large variety of shaftings and pulleys was provided for attaching to models as well as steam-cylinders and water-gauges. One of the toys thought suitable for attachment was a printing-press with a self-inking arrangement, as well as agricultural machines such as a chaff-cutter, threshing-machine and a grain-dresser.

Carette's working models for power-drilling were 'near as possible exact facsimiles of the large machines and must therefore be looked upon not merely as toys but as Educational Models. They are constructed from massive iron castings, the various parts being either highly nickelled or handsomely japanned.' The company also sold wood-polishing machines, power fret-saws, grindstones and cold saws, while their large six-inch (15·2 cm.) lathe was a fine piece of machinery.

'School for Little Builders D.R.P. No 37494. Made in Germany. 3187. Berlin' with a monogrammed 'A. S. Luxus Paper Fabrik. Berlin'. It has Brightly-coloured sections linked by metal tags. *Circa* 1890. Size of box 30 cm. (12 in.).

Electricity and chemistry sets
Carette catered for the obvious interest of boys at the end of the nineteenth century in electricity: 'The growing acquisition of knowledge in the department of electricity for which we are indebted to the acumen in conjunction with information derived from experiments of eminent men, induces the rising generation to work, study and experiment with great eagerness in electricity.' Weak and strong current motors, electric railways and toys with simple electrical movement were marketed by Carette, as well as cases of 'Experimental Apparatus', for use with 'influence machines'. The cases of X-ray experimental apparatus and sets for the study of galvanic electricity sound highly alarming. 'The Little Electroplater' enabled nickel-plating to be efficiently carried out by boys, and the firm also sold an apparatus for 'Wireless Telegraphy' in 1911.

Electric cranes for four-volt current were available from 1912 and described as instructive toys, with a switch and electro-magnets for lifting metal objects of up to two pounds (907 gms.) in weight. In the 1930s every boy could be his own electrician if he owned a Kay 'Electrical Outfit', that was complete with bells, induction coils, motors, tappers, buzzers and dynamos. A telephone set with wires and instructions was also available from this London firm. Among its other products were miniature laboratories.

Chemistry sets were among the most popular of toys as they perfectly mixed inventiveness and danger. The fact that they are now rarely seen in general toy shops in another sign of the safety-consciousness of current manufacturers. Some of the finest chemistry sets, enclosed in handsome presentation cases of mahogany, were made by W. E. Statham and Son, from the simplest type to those suitable for serious students. Unfortunately the cabinets, when found, are usually without their contents, which shows how successful these toys were.

Motor cars
Children of both sexes enjoyed imitating adult behaviour by riding in the new and exciting motor cars that were available from 1905, and mainly produced at this early stage by the makers of velocipede horses and tricycles. Early cars were of wood on a wood or a metal chassis, and the wheels were moved by pedals connected by a chain to toothed gears. From around 1918 the chain was replaced by levers, one for each pedal, and was connected to the rear axle. 'Joiboy Toys', made by Wallis Brothers and Wickstead, described their 1909 car as the most exact replica of a real car yet made: 'The body is low between the wheels and the driver sits back in the seat in the approved fashion: the treads are also placed out of sight inside the bonnet and have a horizontal movement. The wheel steering is an exact replica of the principle employed in real cars.' Joiboy also made a sand yacht that could also be used on the ice. In 1909 the firm stated rather indignantly that their car was 'not a cross between a perambulator and a tricycle', a criticism that must have been frequently voiced.

Right A well-made fretwork bus mounted on a metal chassis with ratchet steering. *Circa* 1920. Length 53 cm. (21 in.).

Give the children a *Gendron*

for **Christmas**

IT'S a present that will keep them healthy and happy all year. Gendrons are made to last many seasons of hard play—the play of active boys and girls.

Examine the features in any "Pioneer" vehicle. Velocipedes with tubular truss frames, padded, coil spring saddles, adjustable handlebars—coaster wagons with roller bearing artillery or double disc wheels—juvenile automobiles with windshields, airflex extenders, speedometers, clocks, motometers—facsimile play reproductions of real autos.

Since 1872, when the first vehicle of the "Pioneer" line was sold, there have been in constant use more Gendron juvenile automobiles, hand cars, velocipedes, coaster wagons, doll carriages than any other make.

Gendron vehicles have all the latest improvements, design and finish, together with the quality acquired from fifty years' experience. They have been developed to perfection for your child.

Gendron vehicles are for sale by the best dealers everywhere.

Free
An interesting book on outdoor games. Write for it.

The Gendron Wheel Co.
615 Superior Street
Toledo, Ohio

An advertisement for a child-size car issued by the Gendron Wheel Company, 615 Superior Street, Toledo, Ohio, in 1925.

A few of the child-size cars could carry as many as four children, such as an example made by Brassington and Cooke of Manchester that was complete right down to a fine horn fixed to the steering-wheel and bicycle-type carbide lamps. Other English makers of wood and metal cars included the Star Manufacturing Company of Davis Street, Manchester, whose cars were given fine upholstered seats and coach-lined sides, and J. Green and C. of Nottingham. All these cars were artistic presentations of motors rather than accurate models.

One of the earliest cars with any attempt at correctness was a fine Italian Redal car made in 1925 with a wooden body and metal chassis, spoked wheels, and tyres with inner tubes; the car was modelled on a Fiat. In 1927 a correct model of a 52-type Bugatti was made. It was created to the special order of that firm and driven by electricity from a battery situated behind the driving seat. The car, with the exception of aluminium wheel-rims, was made entirely of steel and the opening bonnet was strapped with leather. The imitation radiator was fitted with a grill. This car was first revealed at the 1927 Milan Car Show, and because of its obvious correctness was immediately popular.

Child-size cars were also made by Citröen as part of their promotion of full-sized vehicles. The first was made for the son of André Citröen and was so successful that it was made commercially. It represented the Citröen C6

Cabriolet of 1928, a sports car of the period with simple lines. The model was made completely of metal and battery-driven in forward and reverse gears, with variable speeds obtained by an accelerator pedal. Even the lights worked, and the child could check the state of his battery by a voltmeter on the dashboard. Though rarely attaining this degree of detail, similar cars were made after 1930 by a large number of firms, including Lines Brothers (Triang) in England and Eureka in France, a firm that also made a box truck.

A child-size pedal car with a dicky seat for an extra passenger, made of wood and metal and marked with the Triang Mark for Lines Brothers. *Circa* 1935. (Bethnal Green Museum.)

Uniforms and soldiers

Dressing up was a game enjoyed equally by the sexes, but the range of commercially made outfits for boys was much larger than that for girls, presumably because girls could more easily wear cast-off adult finery. Toy uniforms were sold in very great variety, well-displayed on large cards. Uniforms of lancers, policemen, firemen, highlanders, boy scouts, dragoons, guardsmen, and Royal Horse Artillery and Territorial Army officers were all well-made, and often accompanied by metal helmets and nickelled metal breastplates.

The popularity of army uniforms among the dressing-up outfits indicates how fine the soldier's profession was considered by parents in nineteenth-century England, who saw little of the reality of war and were happy to encourage their children in military games. However, soldiers were equally popular in countries that had been ravaged by conflict, and war games here must have engendered more intensity of feeling than in the more romantic British nurseries.

The Hilpert figures, including Prussian, Russian and Turkish 'flats', were widely exported in the early nineteenth century when the Napoleonic wars provided exciting subject matter. 'Napoleon', 'Blücher' and 'Wellington' were all made by this firm, as well as lower-ranking troops. Similar regiments were mass-produced by other Nuremberg and Fürth makers, such as Johann Gottlob Lorenz of Fürth and Johann Wolfgang Ammon, who made soldiers of this Napoleonic period and was succeeded in business by his sons. Ernst Heinrichsen began work as a pewterer in Ammon's workshop but in 1839 set up his own factory; this was to become one of the greatest producers of models, for he was not only a fine craftsman but also a very efficient businessman. His Russian guards were ordered by Tsar Nicholas, and he also made 'Frederick the Great' and 'Voltaire at Sans Souci', as well as 'Washington at Valley Forge'. One of his most effective armies was Hannibal and his troops marching on Rome. Heinrichsen made his 'flats' in a variety of sizes, and it was not until 1843 that he used the 30 mm. ($1\frac{3}{16}$ in.) size, eventually to be generally accepted as the standard size for all historical tin figures, and known as the Nuremberg or Heinrichsen scale. Berlin and Hanover scale pieces are 40 mm. ($\frac{9}{16}$ in.)

Group of early 19th century Nuremberg type flats mainly from a military band. Great detail was always given to the painting of these small figures.

high. Thousands of figures of genre as well as military subjects were designed by several generations of Heinrichsens.

The early 'flats' were sold by the pound weight. Because engravers and designers moved between factories it is difficult to attribute unmarked sets. Many of the individual figures are very fine objects with detail and character, and even in those of the smallest scale the painting is often lively and explicit. Despite the limitations of the flat surface, the impression of movement is very skilfully achieved, with many of the rearing horses finely balanced on their delicate back legs. The figures of classical themes, such as Vulcan forging a helmet or a rather underfed Bacchus holding aloft a cup, are very reminiscent of the primitive style of British Staffordshire figures, even down to the way in which the characters' names are impressed on the bases.

There was a great increase in the production of soldiers after 1830, as news of wars in other countries was now spread more quickly, and there were frequent conflicts to provide a continual supply of subject matter. Heinrichsen even wrote a book telling children how to play war games. As well as battles, all sorts of incidental war scenes were made, such as the Heinrichsen encampment at the toy museum in Nuremberg, with some soldiers standing about in groups, their rifles piled into stacks and others busy lighting fires. The sets of retrospective knights made by Carl Ludwig Besold of Nuremberg between 1830 and 1840 are quite ravishing, with delicate soft colouring and moving arms. Other beautifully constructed foot soldiers were marked 'L', probably by Johann Gottlob Lorenz of Fürth. A group of knights on horseback, made by C. Ammon of Nuremberg around 1840, are possibly even finer: each figure has two pivoted arms and even the visors on the helmets move. Such soldiers have a very lively effect because of their lavish gold and red decoration. Other groups represented tournaments, with figures in dramatic postures reminiscent of theatrical prints. Scenes of the Roman Empire were also popular, such as those made by I. E. Dubois of Hanover in the 1870s.

Figures in the round, or 'solids' as they are termed, were made in France as early as the sixteenth century, although they were first made on a commercial scale in the nineteenth century, probably by Lucotte in France. These figures were made of a mixture of lead and antimony and were usually 5 or 6 cm. (2–2½ in.) in height. These solid models gained only slowly in popularity, as they were more expensive; their greater strength, though, was a special attraction. The two major French makers are Mignot and Lucotte, both of whom made riders that could be removed from the saddle. J. Garrat mentions one figure marked 'JOSE CBG Paris' from which the figure, saddle-bag and cloth can all be taken off. Mignot made a very wide range of soldiers and historical figures. This caused the German makers to try to make their traditional 'flats' stronger by adding more lead, but as their general quality and decoration were deteriorating, they began to look old-fashioned and sales dropped. German production of 'solids' was never as great as that of 'flats', but the work of Johann Haffner of Fürth

Opposite Paper cut-out soldiers 'Musique
d'Infanterie', with original colouring. Epinal prints
published by Pellerin & Co. 'No 62.' *Circa* 1875.

was fine enough to win him a Gold Medal at the Paris Exposition of 1867. Georg Heyde of Dresden produced boxed sets of historical and classical scenes, as well as the more obvious soldiers.

Although the majority of collectors favour metal soldiers, many were made of other materials, especially wood. Regency prints show children playing with mounted soldiers of this type, and at the Luton Museum in Bedfordshire is a set of some twenty-four figures with trees and a cannon, owned by a child in the 1860s. Wooden figures, marching in full company, were made particularly in Bavaria. Some big scenic pieces were produced here, showing model fortresses under siege, sometimes with mechanisms for moving the figures. In 1816 Alois Lechner, a carpenter of Oberammergau, was reported to have 'endeavoured to represent the capture of several fortresses, triumphal marches and battles. The ensemble is about the size of an ordinary table and many hundreds of figures of every variety are set in motion at a stroke: detachments of soldiers parade on foot and on horseback . . . . one can hear the drums, the bugles and the cannons.' A similar very complex arrangement can still be seen at the Oberammergau Folk Museum.

Composition figures were also made, but because they were so fragile it is hard to estimate the quantity manufactured from surviving examples. One amusing variety consisted of horses supported on small springs so that the effect of trotting was given when the toy was set in motion. The most frequently found composition figures are those manufactured by O. and K. Hausser and marketed as 'Elastolin'. These figures, though clumsy in comparison with the metal soldiers, are both lively and colourful, but complete sets are found only rarely as the substance was affected by damp and broke easily if dropped. This firm was founded in 1836, but most surviving pieces date after 1880.

Paper soldiers were printed in some quantity in Germany as well as more particularly in France. Hand-coloured examples were made after 1845 by Silbermann. The earliest-known American soldiers of this type relate to the Spanish-American war and represent 'Rough Riders'.

British toy sellers throughout the nineteenth century completely accepted the dominance of the German and French manufacturers of military figures, and the monopoly was not broken until William Britain, who had made clockwork toys since 1850, entered the field in 1893 with his hollow cast soldiers. Britain decided that lead soldiers like those imported from Germany would be too heavy and expensive to attempt to mass-produce in England. Helped by his family, he created his first hollow casts by using a thin alloy casting instead of solid lead. From the beginning the decoration of these figures was of paramount importance, as Britains were worried that the light weight of their models would not be popular. Great attention was paid to meticulously correct costumes, as this was another aspect that the German makers were considered to be careless about. Among the early models were the 'Life Guards', the 'Grenadiers' and the 'Black Watch.' These early examples, distinguished by the fact that the

An employee of William Britain's lavishes care on the decoration of model soldiers. The firm has a traditional interest in the importance of accurately rendered uniforms. (By courtesy of William Britain's Ltd.)

sword or rifle was separately made and plugged into the cuff of the right arm, were consequently known as 'Plug-handed Highlanders' by collectors. From 1900 lettering was put under the bodies of horses, and the labels on foot-soldiers were replaced by embossing in 1905. By 1902 the factory was making 104 different lines. At first all the models had fixed arms, but after 1896 movable ones were provided, except on shooting and charging infantry. Foot models were usually made with round or oval stands up to 1906, but after this the characteristic oblong bases were used.

In order to help the enthusiast in setting out large armies, in 1930 Britain's introduced a series of cards into which the figures could be slotted. The great success of the company depended not only on the fine painting but also on the vast number of accessories such as guns, armoured cars, range-finders, lorries, ambulances and stretchers. In the firm's 1938 catalogue is 'an exceptionally fine working model searchlight lit by a torch battery and a Sound Locator, complete with operator and a correct model of the type used in detecting enemy aircraft'. The 'Predictor' was the latest type of instrument used in anti-aircraft defence, and there was also a 'Barrage Balloon' unit. All these products indicate how quickly the firm incorporated new ideas into its range. Sadly, plastic began to be used in 1957. All metal figures in good condition are now collectable, though many are still very cheap. Similar figures were also made by John Hill and Co. and by Reka Ltd, but these are not so popular as Britain's among collectors.

American children were at first reliant upon imported soldiers, but in 1904 the American Soldier Company of Glendale produced crude models. Soldiers were later made by McLoughlin Brothers of New York. A number of companies produced them for short periods between 1910 and 1930, and the Gray Cast Iron Casting Company, founded in 1904, produced iron military figures until 1939. It is strange that no figure comparable to William Britain appeared in America. Nowadays, because of the current interest in military models, there are a number of American companies producing fine quality work purely for enthusiasts.

A group of Arab horsemen by William Britain showing the palm trees that were supplied with the set.

Board games and jigsaw puzzles

THE staging of mock battle scenes and naval engagements, while girls played at wash-day or pastry-making, was often both noisy and messy. Parents and governesses were thus eager to find pursuits that could occupy the child's time in a much quieter manner. The manufacturers of board and table games were very aware of this need, especially with regard to the very large families of the nineteenth century. Infant mortality had steadily decreased as the century progressed, and the problems involved in keeping ten or more children quiet, especially on Sundays, must have taxed the ingenuity of even the most inventive adults. The variety of games that were introduced therefore increased steadily each year, and by the end of the century the tastes of children of all ages and inclinations were catered for. The purely educational aims that had so characterized toy-making in the eighteenth century were gradually dispensed with, so that by the Edwardian period some occupations for children were designed purely for enjoyment. This enjoyment was often shared by adults, and the covers of many games show the whole family playing around the parlour table.

Games played in the parlour were traditionally considered in quite a different light from those played in the much feared gaming houses. In the first half of the seventeenth century the distinction was made between parlour games, games of chance and games purely for exercise. The games of chance and exercise were described in Sorel's *Maison des jeux* as being 'as easy for the vulgar and the ignorant as for the clever and the learned'; while parlour games of 'wit and conversation appeal only to persons of quality bred on civility and gallantry, quick at repartee and speeches and full of knowledge and judgement'. The high regard for parlour games was to continue throughout the eighteenth and nineteenth centuries, and at the 1851 Exhibition in London a complete section was given over to them.

The majority of early nineteenth-century board games were printed from engraved copper or steel plates. Coloured versions are obviously lively in effect but were more costly to produce. Simple stencils were sometimes used to speed decoration, but the majority of games were hand-painted: even when designs were lithographed rather than engraved, much of the detailed colouring was still brushed in by hand. Copies of the same game often exhibit considerable variations in colour depending on the whims of the painter, and it is therefore the hand-finished specimens that

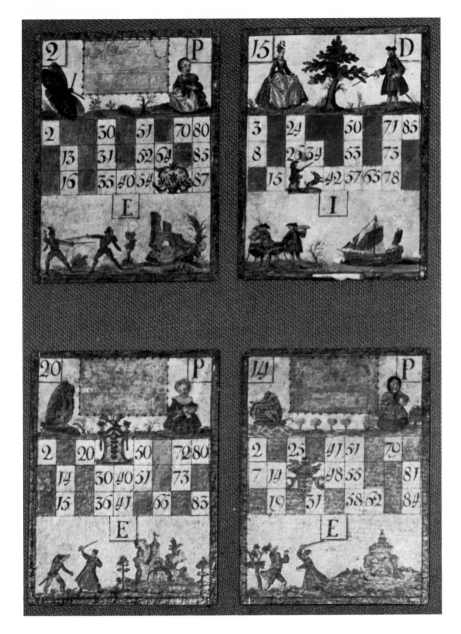

The game of Lotto originated in Genoa in the 17th century. Italian hand-coloured engravings, *circa* 1750. Size of Cards 19 × 14·5 cm. (7½ × 5¾ in.). (Bethnal Green Museum.)

are most favoured by collectors. Lithography began to be used for dissected puzzles and table games around 1839, but firms continued to produce a number by the old methods and hand-coloured examples are found as late as the 1870s. The hand-painting of children's toys remained common long after the technique had been replaced with lithography in purely adult games, possibly because so many junior types were sold in virtually unchanged form over a very long period. Colour-printing was used in the manufacture of playing cards from 1832, when Thomas de la Rue was granted Royal Letters Patent for 'improvements in making and ornamenting playing cards'. A similar invention was used in America by 1835, the printer having previously worked in London and presumably exported the new technique. In 1836 George Baxter registered an invention that gave his prints their attractive and characteristic matt surface. These

'Peter Pan. The new Artistic and Amusing game.
Published by authority of Mr J. M. Barrie and
consisting of characters from the well-known play.
Beautifully printed in colour from original drawings
by Mr. Chas. A. Buchel. The International Card
Company, 96–98 Leadenhall St., London E.C. With
the original price of 2/-. Notice Wendy's fashionable
Art Nouveau type dress. There are 52 cards in the
pack.

A group of very colourful alphabet scraps that could
be used for word building and later glued in an
album. *Circa* 1898.

developments in colour-printing meant that decoration could now be used much more extravagantly, and De la Rue employed established artists to design the backs of his cards. Among them was Owen Jones, the architect and designer who supervised the decorations at the Great Exhibition.

These new techniques meant that children's games could also become more colourful. The manufacturers were increasingly aware of the importance of presentation, so that a most effectively gaudy box will often contain some extremely boring word or spelling game. Many early table games were enclosed only in a simple marbled slip-case, bearing purely factual labels. The continual folding of the paper games often caused them to tear, and so a backing of thin fabric became commonplace. The cases were soon dispensed with, and a section of the backing cloth would be covered with linen or leathercloth over cardboard to act as a strong cover, a method that is still occasionally used today. These leathercloth covers were attractively gold-blocked and sometimes further embellished with a bright label. This protection was much more suitable for games in regular use and has ensured that many have survived in acceptable condition. Sometimes the protected game was further guarded by a leathercloth box, as in the extremely well-produced 'European Tourist' illustrated here, published by Joseph Myers and Co. of London, who supplied a japanned container for the counters and leathercloth-covered passport cases. The lead figures are particularly indicative of the period. The Englishman has to pay 'double stakes and fines into the pool, receiving a double share therefrom, as the winner during the progress of the game. The German workman has only to

'The European Tourist', a well-presented game, contained in a leathercloth box and accompanied by metal flats representing travellers from various countries. Published by Joseph Myers & Co. of 144, Leadenhall Street, London, and printed by Thomson and Vincent of Great St Helens. *Circa* 1861.

pay half stakes.' The German was in the form of a 'travelling journeyman', a character that was very familiar to the toy warehousemen of all European countries. The instruction, that is the main aim here, seems very heavy meat for a child: 'Corinth is situated on the Greek peninsula called the Morea. Our traveller, out of respect for the antiquity of Corinth, forgoes a move, and then visits Cape Matapan, the most southern rock in Europe.' Eventually the traveller arrives at the most northerly point of Europe and the rewards accorded him are obviously German in inspiration, as he is made 'an honorary fellow of the Geographical Society of Berlin and Doctor of the University of Padua'. Heavenly bliss and redemption was now, in the nineteenth century, fast giving place to the more practical achievements of academic life.

'The Mansion of Bliss', a hand-coloured etching with medallions representing good and bad characters. Published by William Darton, 1822. Size 56 × 43 cm. (22¼ × 17¼ in.). (Bethnal Green Museum.)

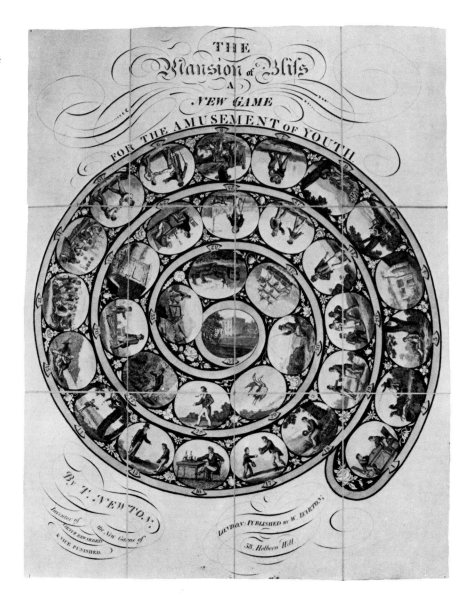

The manufacture of board and table games was not the province of the toy-man but was more usually a side-line of a map-maker or publisher, and this possibly accounts for the lack of understanding of a child's interests. Many items, such as the expensive dissected puzzles, were purchased by adults as gifts rather than by the child himself from a small shop or pedlar's basket, as was the case with cheap wooden or tin toys. Few of the ponderous games would have survived long if dependent on direct sales to children. Adults, however, felt an urge to improve young minds and supplied them most lavishly with instructive games such as 'The New Game of Virtue Rewarded and Vice Punished, for the Amusement of the Youth of both Sexes', invented by T. Newton and published by William Darton of London in 1810, with several later editions. The engraving was hand-coloured and was mounted in twelve sections on linen, the whole game being contained in a slip-case. The player progressed from the 'House of Correction' to 'Virtue'. The aims of the exercise are forbiddingly set out in the book of rules: 'It is designed with a view to promoting progressive improvements of the Juvenile Mind and to deter them from pursuing the dangerous Paths of Vice.' The 'Mansion of Bliss' was also produced by Darton, though in a slightly lighter mood, while Laurie and Whittle issued the 'New Moral and Entertaining Game of Mansion of Happiness, invented by George Fox, W. M., author of "The Cottagers" and various poetical pieces'. This last piece of information was obviously provided to make parents feel that their children were under instruction from a great mind. The game was run as a race and the panels illustrated the familiar virtues of honesty and piety. Further respectability was claimed by the proud inscription: 'To Her Royal Highness the Duchess of York, this plate is with PERMISSION most respectfully dedicated by her devoted and most obedient servants LAURIE AND WHITTLE.'

The nineteenth-century thirst for knowledge, often acquired with little understanding and in a repetitive fashion, spread even to the rather less repressive nurseries of America. F. and R. Lockwood, a New York manufacturer, offered 'a large assortment of Juvenile Pastimes, all of which are calculated to improve as well as to amuse the youthful mind'.

The majority of games in America in the first half of the nineteenth century were still imported, as they had been in the eighteenth century, and they were often adapted, so that 'The European Tourist' becomes 'The Traveller's tour through the United States', with no less tedious comments. A set of vernacular playing cards taught the 'prominent parts of the history, government and commerce of the United States'.

In London many games are found to have been sold in or near St Paul's Churchyard, where most of the booksellers worked. Games often still carry the labels of the retailers, such as The Noah's Ark Toy Warehouse, Bath, which opened in 1852, or the Essex Bazaar in Soho Square. Early in the nineteenth century such games were also sold by chapmen, together with broadsheets.

The Wallis family of London had supplied eighteenth-century children

'Criss Cross Spelling Slips. Set One. Published by Mc Loughlin Brothers, New York. Entered in the office of the Librarian of Congress in the year 1879'. The game had three uses, as a puzzle, for word building and to play 'The marvellously lively and instructive game entitled the Cobhouse Spelling Game'. Width 25 cm. (10 in.).

with games and puzzles, but there were many competitors in the early nineteeth century, so a label was issued with the following words: 'J. Wallis, the original Manufacturer of Dissected Maps and Puzzles, having dedicated full 30 years to that particular line of business, requests the public to OBSERVE that all his dissected puzzles are superior both in correctness and workmanship to any in London and that none are genuine but what are signed on the label John Wallis, No. 42 Skinner Street, Snow Hill.' This claim was, of course, incorrect, as J. Spilsbury had made dissections in the 1760s. In 1813 John Wallis issued a catalogue of his 'Amusing publications for the Improvement of Youth', sold from his Dissected Map Manufactory and Instructive Repository; among the games listed were 'A Geographical Pastime, Tours of Europe, Asia, Scotland and the County of Somerset', and 'The Royal Genealogical Pastime of the Sovereigns of England from the Dissolution of the Saxon Heptarchy to the reign of King George III, with Apparatus for Playing'. Juvenile books and games were sold exclusively by the Wallises at the emporium which they were running by 1815, when the firm was known as J. and E. Wallis. In 1818 E. Wallis was alone at the Skinner Street address, with a branch at 12, Islington High Street. An interesting Wallis teaching toy was published around 1820, which consisted of a picture of a man with a child at his knee. The man points to a circular mirror on the wall, and when a knob at the back of this picture is turned, the letters of the alphabet appear. In 1837 Wallis and J. Harris and Son combined to produce 'Historical Pastime', which showed the new Queen, Victoria.

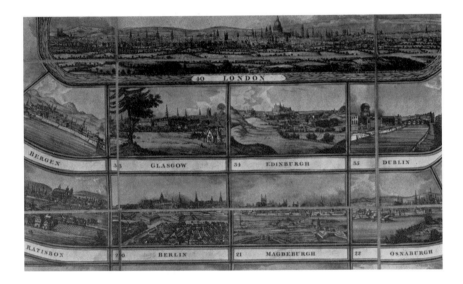

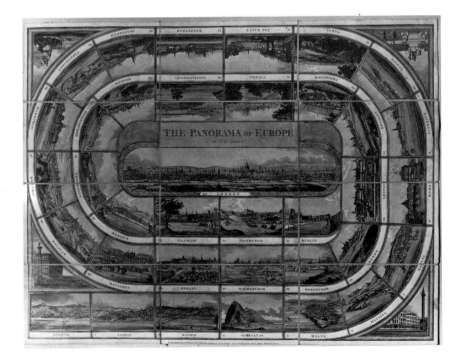

'The Kings of England'. A dissected puzzle with woodcut portraits of monarchs ending with Victoria, 'Began to reign 1837. Born 1819. Whom God Preserve'. Published by N. Carpenter, 29 Goswell Terrace, London, whose name in earlier versions appears on the piece occupied by Victoria. (Collection Victoria and Albert Museum.)

'The Panorama of Europe' (with detail), a hand-coloured engraving mounted on linen and published by J. & E. Wallis of London, November 1815. Size 63 × 48 cm. (25 × 19 in.).

A dissected map of England and Wales, published by W. Peacock and contained in a cream painted box that is typical of this firm.

A jigsaw puzzle issued as a 'commemorative piece by Raphael Tuck, 'Art Publishers to their Majesties the King and Queen and to His Royal Highness the Prince of Wales', in 1935. (Bethnal Green Museum.)

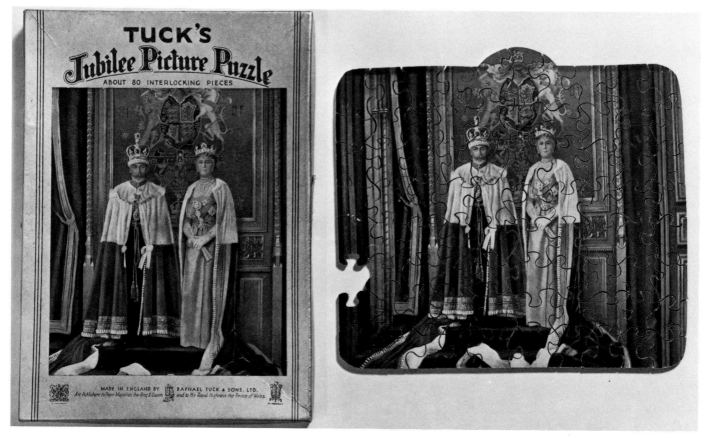

Trains had formed a subject for toys and games since their introduction in the 1840s. Wallis published 'The London, Birmingham and Manchester Railway' as a dissection, while 'Railway Scenes' were also produced by J. W. Barfoot in 1850.

William Spooner, first recorded in Regent Street in 1831, replaced the majority of his earlier games with lithographed versions around 1835. It is for lithographed items that the firm is famed, especially in the field of the transparencies known as 'Transformations' or 'Protean Views'. Spooner's first dissected puzzle was issued in the early 1840s. Although his dissections are usually attractively boxed, they are nothing like as amusing as his table games.

Dissected puzzles became much less severe as the century progressed, so that by the 1870s many were published purely for amusement. Mahogany and cedar were the most popular woods for backing until the nineteenth century, but the cheaper softwoods soon became generally used, although this type of wood needed a heavier quality of paper to help lessen warping and to aid cutting. Although the pieces were originally contained in quality mahogany boxes, softwood boxes became almost universal after 1820; they are characterized by the large pasted-on labels that virtually cover the sliding tops. These dissected puzzles were frequently used in the schoolroom and must have provided hours of quiet, if not particularly educational, toil for the young.

The sharply curved pieces that are associated with modern puzzles were not made until the jig-type saw for cutting appeared in 1872.

Many toy collectors possess a puzzle published by William Peacock, contained in a characteristic colourfully labelled and cream-painted box. The firm is recorded in 1868, when it was based at City Road, though it is probable that their establishment dates to 1853. Peacock's maps were published by G. F. Cruchley, Phillip and Son, or Gall and Inglis; some of them were still hand-coloured as late as 1904. By the end of the nineteenth century the firm mainly supplied games and toys which were sold to wholesale warehouses. They worked from The Steam Works, Dame Street, Islington, where they were still producing dissected 'Counties of England' in 1910. A trade magazine of this period commented that 'The expert fret cutter, Peacock Jnr, superintends the work.' The majority of Peacock's games and puzzles made in the early twentieth century were sold by Hamley's toyshop in London.

William Darton Jnr succeeded his father in the family business of Holborn Hill around 1804, and the firm continued to work until the 1860s. The Dartons made their puzzles mainly as educational or moral aids and continued on these lines even when others were turning to more frivolous types. William Darton Jnr, working from Ludgate Hill, published a very large number of table games as well as dissections. His amusing 'Assembly of Old Bachelors and Old Maids', published in 1810, was especially interesting for being so completely out of character with the rest of his work.

'The Novel and Elegant Game of the Basket of Fruit' or 'Moral and Intellectual Dessert', in its original slipcase and with the book of rules. Published by William Darton of Holborn Hill, 1822. (Bethnal Green Museum.)

A set of hand-coloured picture blocks contained in a blue box with gold decoration. Unmarked but with the original price of 3/2d. It illustrates how outdated prints continued to be used for toys as the earliest in this set date to *circa* 1820 while the latest belong to the 1860s. Length of box 16·5 cm. (6½ in.).

Block picture puzzles appear to have been introduced in the early nineteenth century, but examples made before 1840 appear only occasionally. The six different pictures became easier to assemble as the century progressed, for the separate segments became more positively identifiable. One early nineteenth-century hand-painted set in my own collection shows almost indistinguishable birds against a uniformly green, leafy background, making it almost impossible to assemble since the picture guides are missing. Religious subjects were highly popular by the last quarter of the nineteenth century, and the very attractive bright lithographed colours often combine strangely with the solemnity of the subjects. Many of the late picture blocks are extremely appealing and show children playing with toys or baskets of kittens or flowers, and though often unattributable they frequently command higher prices than earlier, hand-coloured work. For very young children these pictures sometimes took the form of alphabets, a type of block that had been produced for several centuries in ivory and bone as well as wood. Large alphabet letters were printed by firms such as Raphael Tuck, who also produced colourful scraps for assembling into collage type pictures.

Picture blocks, by the end of the 19th century, showed brightly lithographed scenes that fired the imagination of the child. An umarked set showing wild animals. *Circa* 1895.

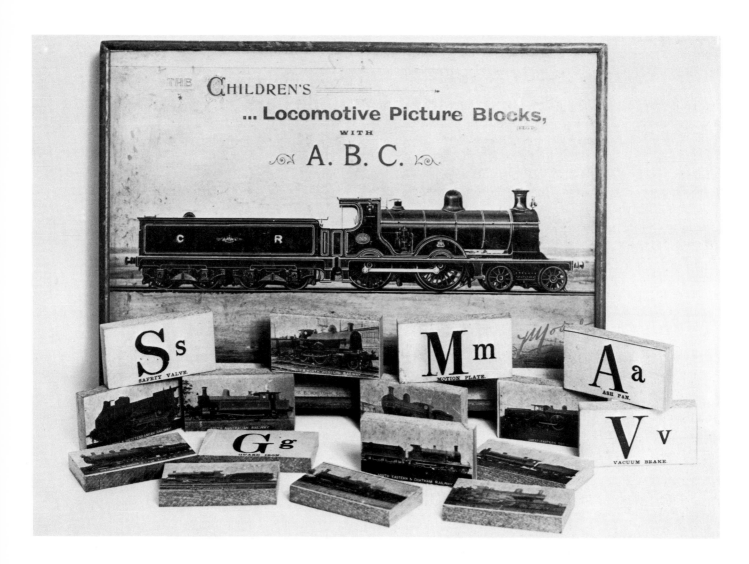

Locomotive picture blocks with the A.B.C. on reverse side. The illustrations are surprisingly complex for a simple learning exercise. *Circa* 1898. Width 37 cm. (14½ in.).

A set of Railway Picture Blocks with prints by Alf Cook Ltd, Leeds. *Circa* 1907. Width 26 cm. (10½ in.).

Playing cards

It was not uncommon in the mid-eighteenth century to see children playing with the same packs of cards that were used by their elders, but nineteenth-century morality caused a shift away from this practice and towards sets that were specifically designed for the young. A few packs were somewhat doubtful in intention, such as a set of costume cards produced by O. Gilbert and B. O. Grimaud of Paris representing monarchs French and foreign, past and present, as well as British nobles. Jazaniah Ford of America, also in the early nineteenth century, printed a set of court figures in Algerian uniform. An Augsburg set of the same date showed men and women of different classes of society.

Children in Europe and Britain were regaled with sets of cards. Between 1815 and 1826 two New Testament packs were issued in Milan, published respectively by P. and G. Vallardi and G. Arotta; these were followed by a quartet teaching Grecian, Roman and ancient history, as well as geography, all of which were actually copies of earlier French games. A few sets were

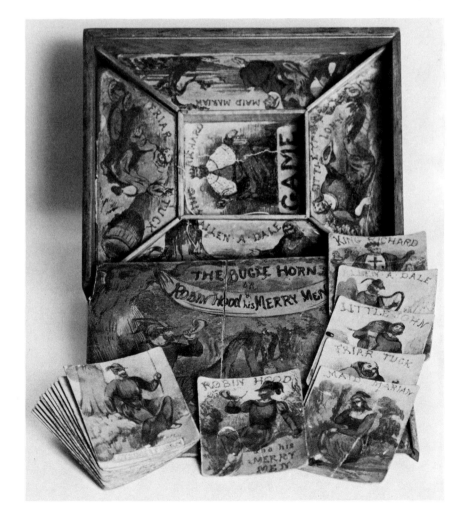

'The Bugle Horn or Robin Hood and His Merry Men. A Mirthful Game'. Very effectively and colourfully hand tinted. It is without instructions but the cards pack away into the central compartment. *Circa* 1830. (Collection Betty Harvey-Jones.)

'The Fancy Bazaar of Aristocratic Trades'. Hand-coloured lithographed cards. Published by E. & M. A. Ogilvy. *Circa* 1855. Size of large cards 15 × 12 cm. (6 × 4¾ in.). (Bethnal Green Museum.)

especially designed for school use, such as cards printed in 1825 for the 'Use of Miss Bradley's School, Priory, Lincoln', in this case a history of England and another of France. Among other classifications of subject matter around this time were 'Geographical, Philosophical, Astronomical, Scriptural and Botanical; Asiatic Costumes; Chronology of the Sovereigns of England'. One example showed 'Authors, their Birth Place and Fame; embracing the Birth place of the Principal Standard Authors and the names of their most popular works'. These sets were published by such firms as H. Greenwood of London, Oliver and Boyd of Edinburgh and James Robertson and Co. of Dublin. The 'Game of Quartettes No. v' was published around 1835 by all these companies simultaneously. In 1836 there appeared the 'Royal Historical Game of cards showing in 45 cards portraits of English monarchs from William I to Queen Victoria'; this was invented by a 'Miss Jane Roberts'.

One of the most attractive Regency packs was contained in a small metal box resembling a bronze medal. On opening this a set of historical cards based on the chronology of the Kings of England is found. Although most games and cards had been imported in the eighteenth century, American playing cards were advertised in 1808 by Inskeep and Bradford, while in the same year a New York store was offering 'Eagle Playing cards from the best manufactory in the United States'. In Boston around 1811 geographical, geometrical and alphabetical cards were available, and from 1843 a number were printed at Salem in New England. In Philadelphia in 1845 a set was published called 'The New Impenetrable Secret or Young Ladies' and Gentlemens' Polite Puzzle, being an entirely new set of entertaining cards, ... the whole designed while they amuse and entertain to establish the principles of virtue and modesty in the minds of both sexes'.

Lewis I. Cohen published his first set of cards in America in 1832 and after developing and improving colour printing, retired in 1854 leaving the company in the hands of his son and nephew who formed the company of Laurence and Cohen. In 1871 three cousins were taken into the firm and it then became known as the New York Consolidated Card Company, producing numerous sets of cards for the specific use of children.

There was a vast output of children's card games of an almost purely amusing kind after 1870, including nursery rhymes, variants on the Happy Family theme and many connected with animals. Instruction was not always completely absent; for instance a set produced by J. Jaques and

'A Capital Round Game. The most popular game ever published. Cards of Grotesque Characters, beautifully coloured. Published only by John Jacques and Son Ltd. London'. The pack of 32 was entitled 'Snap'.

2 READING

The principal manufactures are Ribbons and Biscuits
Engineering Works
POPULATION, 75,200

9 PLYMOUTH

THE OLD EDDYSTONE LIGHTHOUSE
Now removed to the Hoe
Naval Station, Dockyard and Arsenal
POPULATION, 112,030

8 BATH

THE ABBEY CHURCH AND GUILDHALL
Bath is famous for its Hot Springs
There are fine specimens of old Roman Baths
POPULATION, 50,720

5 CHICHESTER

THE CATHEDRAL
The Chief Town of Sussex
POPULATION, 12,590

6 WINCHESTER

THE CATHEDRAL
One of the most ancient towns in the kingdom
Egbert was crowned here
Brewing, Malting, Agricultural produce
POPULATION, 23,370

5 BRIGHTON

Queen of English Watering Places
POPULATION, 132,000

4 DOVER

DOVER CASTLE AND SOUTH FORELAND CLIFFS
The Coast of France can be seen from these Cliffs in clear weather
Packet Station   Has large Docks
POPULATION, 43,640

9 EXETER

The ancient seat of the West Saxon Kings
A Cathedral City
Iron and Brass Foundries
POPULATION, 37,280

8 CLIFTON

NIGHTINGALE VALE
Clifton is celebrated for its M
and is a place of fashion
POPULATION, 4

6 SOUTHAMPTON

6 ISLE OF WIGHT

4 CANTERBURY

1 LONDON

The largest City in the World
POPULATION (INNER LONDON) 4,800,000

The COUNTIES OF ENGLAND
A Geographical Game.
4th Series
JAQUES & SON, LTD.
LONDON.

Sons of London taught 'The Counties of England'. Ralph Dunn and Co. of the Barbican, London, published 'Word Making and Word Taking', a game aimed at all ages. A very large number of card games were printed in Germany but published in England, such as 'National Misfitz', described as 'the most interesting of the Misfitz series' and published by C. W. Faulkener and Co., London E.C., but printed in Saxony. This series included 'Animal and Society Misfitz', as well as a nursery rhyme set and a 'Golly Misfitz', which assembled into a procession of dolls. Other games published by Faulkener included 'Bargains', 'Fairy Tales' and 'Hurry Up Misfitz', the latter published in 1907 and portraying humorous scenes of street life. This firm worked from 41 Jewin Street. Earlier in the century it had produced the very colourful game 'Zooloo', with circular cards. 'Circulating Library', 'Cheating' and 'Musical Notes' (the latter described as 'one of the most useful vehicles for teaching the staff notation ever invented') were also among their products, as were 'The Stock Exchange', 'Psycho, a weird and wonderful fortune-telling game', 'Cat and Mouse', 'Fighting for the Standard' and 'House of Commons'. The list serves to give some idea of the vast range of subjects produced by a single company.

Opposite 'The Counties of England', a geographical game published by Jacques & Sons Ltd, London. Fourth Series. 47 cards plus a key and a paper instruction sheet. To be played in the Happy Families manner. *Circa* 1907.

'Minoru. The New Race Game. The Double Event Edition' by John Jacques & Son Ltd, London, based on the Derby of 1909 when Edward VII's horse Minoru won. (Bethnal Green Museum.)

'National Misfitz' published by C. W. Faulkner & Co., London E.C., and printed in Saxony. Height of box 21 cm. (8¼ in.).

Table games

As firms became more aware of the rapidly changing environment, topical toys were produced, such as an aeroplane game issued in 1909 including every known flying machine. 'Pip-Pip', which was sold at the same time, was a street motor race, while 'Fly To' incorporated a balloon race. 'Mark Over' was described as a sportsman's game and was sold by J. Jacques and Son who claimed that it was the only game produced that involved shooting at a moving object. The guns were loaded with rubber bands and the object was to shoot as many discs as possible while they rolled across a table.

'The Camel and its Utility. Images of African Moving Horsemen'. Hand-coloured lithographs mounted on card. The camel is jointed to allow for changes of position. German, *circa* 1860. Size 31 × 24 cm. (12¼ × 9½ in.). (Bethnal Green Museum.)

Among the more lively of table games is Lamplough's Gold Medal Model Cricket Patent Number 1258 with printed tin figures, felt-covered wicket and a cardboard boundary fence. The balls are bowled by means of a spring. *Circa* 1905. Size of box 28 cm. (11 in.).

A game that was possibly of more amusement to adults was 'Auction' by Henry Reason. Each player was given ten counters to buy cards (showing old clocks, brass fenders, etc.) that were sold to the highest bidder. A similar game, contained in a richer wooden box with an attractive label showing an auction in progress with instructions in German and French, was published some fifty years earlier with very small cards some 3·0 cm. ($1\frac{1}{4}$ in.) square.

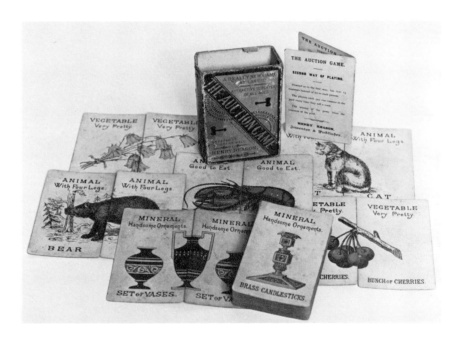

'A Really New Game at Last. The Auction Game', published by Henry Reason who also invented it and sold it from Rose's Toy and Fancy Repository, 203, Sloane Street, London. Printed by Baddow of Brighton. Played with cards and counters. *Circa* 1860.

'The New Game of Fortress and Siege', with English Grenadiers on the lid, though different pictures would probably be used for various countries. Played as a type of draughts with wooden men. It has a heavy paper covered board. Marked 'W. S. Bavaria.' *Circa* 1870. Box 34·2 cm. ($13\frac{1}{2}$ in.).

'Markover, The Sportsman's Game. Published by J. Jacques & Son Ltd, London'. The only game produced which features shooting at a moving object. A screen is also contained in the box. *Circa* 1895. Size of box 22·5 cm. (8½ in.).

Roberts Brothers of Gloucester was founded in 1891, mainly because H. O. Roberts had devised a new game that no manufacturer would produce, despite its obvious appeal among his friends. Eventually he found a publisher (Messrs Ordish) who would not manufacture but insisted that Roberts should carry out this part of the operation himself. The game in question, 'Philadex', became very popular. Roberts now took his brother into partnership, and as the work expanded a new factory, the Glevum Works, was built in 1902. In 1908 they bought up Woolley and Co. of London, an old-established firm, and took over the most important of their lines. By 1909 some two hundred gross of boxes were produced each week and their games included the ever-popular 'Happy Families' that was printed as one large sheet, rolled under pressure to give a high glaze, and each card then punched out by machinery. Electricity was used in the wood-working shops from 1910 in the manufacture of jigsaws and picture cubes, as well as for sanding. Once, as a special display, a complete set of picture blocks was made for a customer in five minutes. A report on the company makes an interesting comment about draughtsmen: 'The idea is prevalent that the Germans beat us at this business, but as a matter of fact they buy large numbers from us, box them and send them back.'

Another well-known English producer of board and table games was Chad Valley, whose 1897-8 catalogue gives some idea of the range produced; their games included 'Lotto', sold cheaply in a smart card travelling trunk, 'Karoo', 'Kismet', and 'Our Pets Lotto', attractively packed but with its educational aim lurking beneath—'It serves at the same time to commit to memory with pleasure the so much dreaded multiplication table.' Their 'Merry Game of Laripino' was much more interesting and involved a board in the centre of which stood a cardboard chute; down this marbles were rolled into numbered hollows. 'Storming the Citadel' was even more adventurous. A tower was constructed and ladders were set against arched windows; with a flat coin marbles were propelled up the ladders and into the citadel.' On the cover was seen a group of fiercely attacking soldiers, giving a very misleading idea of the contents though it was without doubt much more exciting than the majority of games made in the nineteenth century.

The 1920s and 1930s saw a much greater awareness of the actual needs of children at specific ages, and old catalogues show sub-headings such as 'Early Educational' or 'Constructive'. In 1939 Chad Valley reprinted 'English Table Games designed from the old-fashioned editions as published in the last century'. These reproductions were packaged to resemble bound books and were designed for the appreciation of adults, who were expected to store them in a bookcase. When the book was opened, the playing board could be unfolded. These sets could have sold only in a relatively small quantity, as the Second World War halted such frivolities and the factory was diverted into the war effort.

Many old games are still of interest to adults of today: *The Antique Dealer and Collector's Guide* published a special set as part of a 'Playthings Past' edition in 1974. The collectors of antique games rarely play on the old boards, because of the risk of damage, and so the reprinting of them gives the curious the chance to experience the serious amusement of the late eighteenth and early nineteenth centuries.

Toy animals and their settings

MODEL scenes involving animals held an obvious fascination for children in towns as well as country districts, and to feed this natural interest toy-makers created farms, zoos, menageries and hunting groups. These were often made of wood and were produced in the main by Tyrolean and Alpine carvers.

Crèche settings

Small crèche settings were assembled in all but the poorest of Catholic homes, and the children eagerly assisted in their arrangement. The animals

A Bavarian crib of folding type almost certainly printed by Raphael Tuck. Late 19th century. Height 41 cm. (16 in.).

and figures gathered around the manger were added to each year. Animals made for such scenes were usually larger than those packed into farms and arks, and were often carved in much more detail. The distinctive fur of various animals was cleverly imitated. The most expensive were correctly painted but cheaper versions were left plain. When not in use they were often packed away in the box-like bases of crucifixes. Each year, a few weeks before Christmas, a crib market was held in Munich near the old Sendlinger Tor near Sonnenstrasse. The scene as it was around 1910 was described by Maximillian Krauss in an article in *Moderne Kunst in Meister-Holzschnitten,* published shortly afterwards:

> The market had to compete with the thunder of streetcars, automobiles and waggons. This was the season when the children of Munich took their families' cribs from store and set them up in the corner of a room, and they would visit the crib market to find additions and replacements. At the market could be found palm trees and cypresses, fragments of classical temples, buildings in Gothic, Roman and Baroque styles, and a variety of small objects such as wells and sections of stone walls that could all be used to create a more realistic setting. Many of the pieces were decorated with coloured sand that glittered in the light like crystal.

Although carved wooden cribs had been very cheap in the eighteenth and early nineteenth centuries, the woodcarvers were by this time supplying the artistic market and their well-made animals and figures were too expensive for the ordinary child. Among the finer items were splendid carved crib figures:

> real little works of art from the wood-carving studios of Oberammergau and Berchtesgaden, beautifully painted and in expensive costumes, and with them wonderfully carved animal figures, prancing horses with rich trappings and mustard-coloured camels loaded with packages. There stand the little ones and look at these marvels which are, for most of them, unattainable, and there creeps into a poor child's heart, perhaps for the first time, a feeling of bitter disappointment.

As an alternative such a child bought the cheapest wax figures. In the wooden booths of the market were rows of shepherds with wax faces and hands, as well as hundreds of small heads for the central characters around the manger. Replacement hands, heads and feet were sold in great number. The Christ child himself was available in 'a thousand different versions'. Figures of angels hung from the ceilings of the booths, or were packed in groups in boxes; the light was reflected from their costumes and from the golden Christmas stars, 'as if the whole of Heaven came down to the crib market to be sold'.

The majority of surviving household cribs are of carved wood. They are often extremely difficult to date accurately as craftsmen have worked in a similar manner to the present time. Rows of angels, animals and figures for cribs are still made by the Tyrolean woodcarvers, as well as effective stables. They are necessarily expensive, especially when painted. The reference to wax in Krauss's article is extremely interesting, as very few of the household type have survived from this late period; the number of replacements offered by the stall-holders clearly indicates the fragility of wax items. Throughout the description the emphasis is upon the fact that this is very much a children's market, and it is the children who are buying the figures for their own cribs. This suggests more of a play context for the settings than one might at first consider likely.

Noah's arks

Noah and his ark was a theme favoured by artists from medieval times, as it offered a subject that included not only familiar domestic beasts but also exotic animals that were known only by description and by drawings (which were often incorrect). The Old Testament story promises deliverance for the just and reminds man of God's concern that no living creature should become extinct. A similar story is found in the mythology of Japan and China, where the central character is known as Fohi. It is probable that model arks were made of various substances during the Middle Ages. One of the earliest recorded is that owned by Elizabeth I, who used a silver salt in the form of an ark that contained a chessboard. Individual examples of small wooden animals can be found in several German museums. Lions, tigers and buffalo were all carved by sixteenth-century craftsmen, and it is possible that some of these were intended for arks as well as crèche settings. The ark, however, does not appear ever to have been considered as a devotional object.

Individual examples of craftsman-made arks are to be found in most European countries but are extremely difficult to date. The vast majority were made in Germany, and are included among the toys known as 'Nuremberg ware'. So popular were these cheap wooden toys that merchants were forced to employ craftsmen from further afield, and examples made in Altdorf, Sonneberg, Berchtesgaden and the Erzgebirge were all termed 'Nuremberg' as well. Catalogues were produced by the end of the eighteenth century. Because the requirements of customers in other countries were met, the regional differences between craftsmen were eventually stifled, which now makes it difficult for a collector to identify the area of origin of such toys.

Georg Lang, the largest Oberammergau merchant, began to develop new marketing methods around 1750; eventually he closed down the agencies manned by his own employees in other countries and relied instead on local merchants who perfectly understood the needs of their own customers. During the second half of the eighteenth century, popular art flourished in south Germany and Oberammergau merchants set up business houses as far apart as Cadiz, St Petersberg and Copenhagen. The making of toys was all-important in this region until the end of the first quarter of the nineteenth century. In 1821 more than a hundred carvers were employed by Lang, many being members of the same families. In 1879 a traveller visited an elderly German lady who had been taught by her mother to carve six animals: 'They were a dog, cat, wolf, sheep, goat and elephant. She had cut these all her life and could not cut anything else. It was her trade. And she had taught her daughter and granddaughter as a life's work to cut these six animals. In one house they will perhaps paint nothing but grey horses with black spots, in another only red horses with white spots.' (C. Mateaux, *Wonderland of Work,* London 1883). However, after 1860 the toy production of Oberammergau declined as metal toys from other parts of Germany became more popular (although animals for the devotional settings were made in even greater quantities than before).

Wood was not invariably the material used for the inhabitants of arks. From around 1740 Sonneberg craftsmen had begun to use a mixture of rye flour and glue water that could be moulded into the shape of small birds and animals. A wire or wood armature was required for larger figures. This brotteig substance was fragile and tended to be eaten by insects, so a stronger form was made by the addition of kaolin around 1815; this improved mixture was first used by Friedrich Müller, who saw possibilities here for a simple mass-production technique using moulds. Composition figures of this kind were sometimes made even more realistic after 1856 by flocking the surface. Because such figures were cheap, they threatened to rival traditional carved animals. However, the wood-workers survived by developing the wooden-ring method of cutting, as first used by a Seiffen turner. Logs of pinewood, carefully chosen and without knots, were soaked in water for several weeks and then sliced into rings which were shaped on the lathe into the approximate outline of an elephant or dog. Another worker would then cut the circular outline into segments, one animal being produced at each cut. The finishing, which included rounding the edges and cutting the legs, would then be completed by hand. Tails were often glued on, as were long manes or ears—though a more ambitious worker might carve the outline of a bird's wing, or suggest the texture of a lion's mane by working at the surface.

In the Groden valley animals were at first sent away for decoration, as painting was not a traditional craft. All the animals intended for arks are thought to have been painted before sale until the mid-nineteenth century, but after this time the carvers of Oberammergau began to leave them plain. In other regions, however, the practice of painting continued. The small animals were known as 'penny beasts' by the merchants, but 'misery beasts' by the peasant carvers who worked long and boring hours for a pittance. There is an interesting divergence of standard between the well-carved animals that were made at Oberammergau and the very crudely constructed arks in which they were housed, though it is possible that this is because only a few particularly bad examples have survived. A very simple ark from Nuremberg can be seen at the toy museum there; it contains 124 animals as well as Noah, his three sons and their wives, and was made by G. N. Renner and Co. of Nuremberg.

Animals were packed by the distributing merchants into either arks or

An extremely complex straw-work Noah's Ark made in the Erzgebirge region in the mid-19th century and containing the usual carved Penny Beasts.

chip-wood boxes. As the same figures could often be used in a zoo, farm or menagerie, the merchants were able to assemble them according to orders, so that a single ark would contain the work of many carvers. Even after an ark had reached its child-owner, the contents were frequently added to as they became lost or damaged. One early nineteenth-century ark I once owned contained animals of wood, papier mâché, metal and even celluloid, each added by successive generations of one family.

When the owner of Cremer's toy shop in London visited Saxony in 1875 he disapproved of the fact that the birds and insects were so much out of scale with other animals, such as the elephants. Rather than accepting the primitive charm of this arrangement, Cremer saw a sinister significance: 'It may have happened that the Saxon toy-men wished thus to impress the infantile mind that in the antediluvian epoch Nature now and then indulged in a wild freak.' Cremer was somewhat appeased by the promise that the craftsmen would supply a 'just proportion' in their future arks. British buyers were also constantly astonished by the way in which whole areas of Germany seemed dedicated to the production of a single type of toy. In a report of 1910 we read that 'Lately Fürth, six miles from Nuremberg, is almost completely devoted to the making of Noah's arks and puzzles.'

Both cribs and arks were sometimes made of paper but the survival rate is low, as they were soon damaged. An interesting panorama, published by John Betts, was sold at Christie's in 1976. This was basically a hand-coloured print, mounted on card, showing realistic animals grouped in front of a large ark. A sheet of paper moved behind a rectangle cut away from the print at the ark's entrance, so that the effect was given of pairs of animals passing through. The panorama was wound on wooden rollers concealed behind the picture. On the back was written 'Betts Large

A realistically modelled ark with figures mounted on a wheeled base. The ark and figures are made of composition on wood. Late 19th century. Length 76 cm. (30 in.).

A Gothic style wooden ark made by wounded British Soldiers during the First World War. Length 46 cm. (18 in.).

Pictorial Noah's Ark. Including a train of animals six yards long and accompanied by a book with the natural history of every animal in the pen . . . Published by John Betts. 115 Strand'. As Betts moved to the Strand in 1845, some help in dating is given. This panorama, showing the male and female of each species, was intended as a teaching toy, whereas the majority of arks were created purely for enjoyment.

As many as 370 figures are sometimes contained in the German arks. Most stand on fragile legs, but those from Oberammergau were often given more secure rectangular wooden bases. Dr Manfred Bachmann comments that Halbach, near Olbernhau, where chip boxes were once made, specialized in the making of arks from the mid-nineteenth century. In this area, there are twenty-four firms, many of them making nothing but arks in a wide variety of shapes and sizes. They were sent from small factories to decorators who painted them at home, and the work was then carried back to the town in large baskets. All these arks were provided with the traditional dove bearing an olive leaf, either painted or carved on the roof. The new demand for realism is seen in many mid-nineteenth-century arks, particularly those with composition animals, which often conform to some scale and have a much more realistic finish, with turned heads and open mouths. As composition figures crumbled away if left in a damp place, their number is often much depleted.

Bestelmeier had offered a variety of arks in his 1793 catalogue and the larger ones, besides holding a large number of animals, also contained several rooms as well as kitchens and stables, rather like the German cabinet dolls' houses of an earlier period and certainly more like the Biblical description of the vessel than the hut on a raft-like base that developed later.

No examples of such arks in the grand manner have survived. Of course, the majority of the arks were purely table or floor toys, and would have met with disaster if floated. A few were given iron wheels so they could be pulled along., However, the 1793 catalogue also catered for children of more rational taste, and some very small heavily varnished floatable arks were advertised. Even these contained around a hundred figures. Later makers added to the boat-shaped bases small houses that were modelled on the cottages and farmhouses they saw around them, and to some extent these suggest the architecture of the area where they were manufactured.

The actual design of arks has remained almost constant to the present time. A porch is always necessary and there is rarely any attempt to organize the interior of the hut. The stencilled surface decoration often provides the main variant: some are given windows with an almost *chinoiserie* fret, while others are pure Gothic. Two storeys are sometimes painted on larger arks, but the interior still remains box-like. Bavarian examples usually have a removable sliding panel at the back which is almost invariably lost! The hinged roof seems to have become even more popular by the mid-nineteenth century. A few Edwardian arks were given ratchet mechanisms, so that the animals appeared to be climbing the steps while Noah raised his arm as each beast went by.

After the introduction of lithography, coloured paper was sometimes applied to the wood but never with a great deal of success. The medium was more suitably used when the complete ark was made of lithographed

Mid-19th century Bavarian ark of very similar construction to that illustrated in colour. This example is painted in orange, yellow and black, with Chinoiserie style windows and a sliding panel at rear. It has about 110 inhabitants.

board. Printed arks of this kind are usually composed of a flat raft with a simple hut on it, and realism is completely dependent upon the surface design. Even lithographed arks of this type originating in France are still found to contain the German 'misery beasts'.

A few very well-constructed arks are found that are decorated in part, or sometimes completely, with straw work. Antique dealers frequently offer these for sale under the title of 'Prisoner-of-War Work', though they are in fact finished by a technique that was particularly favoured in the Erzgebirge region. The design which has great assurance was effected by gluing straw, stained in rich, natural colours, to a pine base. Arks of this type in good condition command the higher prices, as do those with delicately inlaid wood known as 'Tunbridge ware'. These smaller arks, a few of which might have been made at Tunbridge Wells, often have the appearance of models rather than toys and can be distinguished from German examples by the heavier wood used in their basic construction. Various American firms also made arks, but as many of the workers there had emigrated from Germany, it is sometimes difficult to be sure of the origin.

Among the tin toys offered for sale by Johann Heinrich Ramm of Lüneberg were a menagerie and an ark, the latter complete with thirty-two pairs of animals. These are of great interest as so few toys of this type were made of tin, since manufacturers of tin toys were eager to keep completely up to date. Printed paper arks, to be glued to card by the child before cutting, were also made, though it is those produced by Epinal that are now most frequently found. Although the ark is considered primarily as a nineteenth-century toy, Gamages still offered a very good range in their 1913 Christmas catalogue, including a 'New Stable Ark'; this was very reminiscent of those seen in the Bestelmeier catalogue, and was composed of stabling for animals in the hull, stairs to deck level where there were more stables and yet more stairs to the attic where Noah and his family sat at table. This toy, containing thirty-six animals, eight attendants and furniture, was 79 cm. (31 in.) long in its largest size. Others in the same catalogue included a few with flat boat shaped bases containing as many as 112 varnished animals.

The First World War halted the supply of traditional German toys and the organizers of work for wounded soldiers and refugees sought to satisfy the demand. Disabled ex-servicemen made, in particular, arks of Gothic design in very lightweight wood, usually stencil-decorated in black and orange on a cream base. The animals and figures were very crudely carved and had none of the assurance seen in the German folk work. Noah and his family have a close resemblance to crib figures, and it seems likely that these also might have been assembled. These toys, often with a carol or prayer pasted inside the roof, look much older than their actual date, and are often seen in antique markets described as nineteenth century.

Belgian refugees were also persuaded to manufacture arks and their work is characterized by the crossed flags of England and Belgium. These

An ark made by First World War Belgian refugees. The door bears the date 1915 and on either side of it are painted the Rippon Horn and the crossed flags of England and Belgium. The ark and occupants slot into a grooved board. Noah and his sons wear Belgian army uniform. There are 45 animals. (Collection Mrs A. M. Morris.)

It is not always easy to date home-made toys purely on appearance, as is evidenced by this carved red and blue ark carved by the author's father, 1968. Length 51 cm. (20 in.).

arks were made with much more attention to detail, but with an equal lack of skill in the swift carving of animals. Their construction was part of a drive to provide the refugees with 'remunerative employment that would give them occupations without competing with British labour'. The *Yorkshire Post* of 1914 stated that none of the men involved in the project had ever made a toy before but they were succeeding in turning cigar-boxes into a variety of playthings. The men in Yorkshire were organized in their labour by the Rippon Arts and Crafts Society: 'At present only half a dozen men are employed in the work and two of these may be called to the front at any moment.' Their toys are recognizable by the crossed flags and the further decoration of a 'Rippon Horn'.

A great source of designs not only for arks but also for menageries and zoos was *Hobbies* magazine, a weekly paper published in Norwich, that issued a big Christmas edition with up-to-date information on stock. Many items for construction by home craftsmen were offered for some years, so that as late as 1940 a fretwork ark was advertised in high Art Nouveau style. The sides were decorated with cut-out leaves and animals and must have looked extremely effective when assembled. The fretworker was supplied with coloured woods for making the animals themselves. Another ark, offered as a special gift in the 1937 catalogue, incorporated the phrase, 'Mr Noah he built an Ark' in the design of the hull. Satin walnut was provided for the main work, with whitewood for the ornamental overlays. It was suggested that the paper cutting guides on the animals should be left on the wood and painted. Special grooved moulding was sold on which the animals could be stood.

Farms, menageries and zoos

Farms and menageries were also made by the German makers of arks, and some idea of origin is sometimes given by the regional styles of the buildings. Farms have survived in considerably smaller number than arks and could never have been as popular. They also suffered speedy loss, as there was no appropriate container in which they could be packed away at night. Groups of animals were sold neatly packed in oval or round chip boxes and it is often surprising to see the number of small items, including trees and fences, that could be grouped together in the smallest boxes. The trees were cleverly made, by simply shaving slices of wood downwards along the trunk to give the effect of foliage. Small individual sets were sold,

The groups of figures are fixed in position in this carved wooden farm of mid-19th century Bavarian origin. (Collection Betty Harvey-Jones.)

such as a group of sheep with their shepherd. One set contained only cows in a variety of postures. A complete farm from a Grunhainichen sample book of 1860 contained an impressive farmhouse, a stable, farmer and wife, a group of trees and fifteen assorted animals. The arranging of the small-scale farms must have absorbed a child's attention for several hours, as all the fences and buildings had to be logically arranged and the animals were often so delicately balanced that one fall caused a whole row to tumble—a problem that was shared with Noah's arks. The arrangement was sometimes made easier by placing all the figures of one type on a small flat board, as in the illustrated example, though these glued-down figures can hardly have provided a very satisfactory toy.

During the nineteenth century there was considerable public interest in wild animals that were brought back from exotic countries and put on general view. A Waldkirchen sample book shows a most elegantly designed menagerie dating to around 1840, with a Grecian statue standing in the centre and neatly chained elephant, camel and tiger standing amicably outside their huts. The zoo-keeper held a monkey on a chain and the set also included trees and fences. Some of the larger menageries made in the Erzgebirge were in a realistic manner, with lions, for instance, that have quite ferocious faces. Considering the vast output of these toys, few have survived intact. Despite this rarity, they do not command high saleroom prices, as few collectors have the space to display several hundred small pieces.

Of much greater general interest to the collectors of antique toys are the animals made by Johann Hilpert of Nuremberg, whose delightful monkey group, showing the animals in various positions and dating to the 1780s, is best known. His lead models of animals, such as leopards and horses, were of the highest quality and made to show even the detail of an animal's rib-cage. Johann Ludwig Stahl, an agent, shows a variety of such figures in an 1805 catalogue, and their very artistic rendering of posture indicates they were manufactured from Hilpert's moulds. Hunting and crib scenes, as well as rural settings and the monkey sets, were included. Ernst Heinrichsen made a number of tin scenes in various sizes, including a field with horses and a poultry yard. Several other tin-workers made scenes of this type, often working from the animal drawings of recognized artists, which is why their work is so lively.

At Christmas 1908 in Hamburg, Steinberg and Co. copied the famed 'Hagenbecks Tierpark', the large show of wild animals set up by Carl Hagenbeck, the great dealer in such beasts. Animals made by several German firms were included in the arrangement, and among them were examples made by Berthold Krauss of Wive und Sohne, who made figures and animals of all descriptions from leather, felt and papier mâché. One firm that specialized in circus toys was Louis Lindner and Son of Sonneberg, who sold a range of animals, clowns and all their accessories. In France s.f.b.j. also produced a large range of farms and menageries, as well as the dolls for which they are better known. A most attractive tin menagerie was sold by Märklin in 1891. This was set out on a flat base with a duck pond. In the background was a bird table and there was a fine cage containing other exotic birds.

The great urge to impart useful knowledge was not far from the minds of the toy-makers, and Chad Valley's 'Home Zoo', advertised in 1914, contained twenty-six different animals that formed a complete alphabet, with accurate descriptions in rhyming verse: 'Each zoo contains a set of realistically portrayed animals with scissors, wheels, glue, etc. for cutting out.' The better-quality sets included cages for the animals. Gamage's 1913 catalogue also illustrated many boxed sets of animals, especially farm beasts, many of which were sold unpainted. Some were made of composition, and included a shepherd with his dog and sheep, a boxed menagerie, and a farmyard with fences and trees.

A child's enjoyment was traditionally derived from the arrangement of immobile figures, and it was not until 1903 that any real advance was made in the direction of greater complexity. In that year Albert Schoenhut registered his 'Humpty Dumpty Circus'. The Schoenhut family had worked as woodcarvers and toy-makers in Germany for generations before emigrating to America to continue their work as toy-makers. The first playthings they made there were pianos. Their business soon expanded, and among the ideas that they were offered by eager inventors was that embodied in their famous circus. There is a tradition that the inventor insisted on selling the idea to Schoenhut for a quick hundred dollars, instead of going for the obvious long-term advantages of a royalty based transaction. The small group that was acquired by Schoenhut included a clown, chair and ladder, but other characters were soon added so that a complete circus could be assembled. The registered version of 1903 had twenty figures, each of them in wood and provided with six joints so that a variety of amusing positions could be attained. The clowns balanced on the rungs of chairs or ladders by means of deep slits that were cut in their hands and feet. The durability of these figures is evidenced by the number that are still found in good working condition.

As the 'Humpty Dumpty Circus' was so absorbingly different from the traditional toys, it was soon a great success and is one of the few American-made toys that was exported in really large numbers, so that examples can quite easily be found in Europe. Thirty-three animals and figures were included by 1913, as well as tables, weights and wheelbarrows, all of which could be individually purchased. The complete set, which occupied a circus ring of some 61 cm. (24 in.), was housed in a collapsible tent, decorated with the flags of all nations. The male figures—ring-master, acrobat and lion-tamer—were all basically the same but with different costumes and heads of bisque or composition. The figures most frequently found now are the clowns, elephants and donkeys; the sea-lions, kangaroos and polar bears are very much rarer, as are the china-headed figures such as the lady acrobat. The large boxed sets, originally accompanied by a book of illustrations and rhymes, with photographs of the various tricks that the toys could perform, are now only very occasionally found complete.

Figures from a William Britain's circus including a very beautifully coloured white and blue rearing horse. *Circa* 1936.

Opposite above Part of a metal farm made by William Britain and collected between 1930 and 1940. The variety of animals and equipment is vast.

Opposite below A zoo made by William Britain with the original wooden animal houses. *Circa* 1935.

Several generations of children considered the name William Britain almost synonymous with farms and zoos, for the hollow cast products of this company finally ousted the German carved animals from British nurseries. Britain's made a staggering range of animals specifically for circuses or farms, and despite the very low prices for which they were often sold, the modelling was realistic and the colouring correct. The farms were first made in the 1930s but remained popular years later. The last catalogue printed before the Second World War commented: 'The ever increasing call for the "Model Home Farms" shows that it continues to hold a high place in the public esteem. It is just that kind of toy that can be played with equally well by the youngest or oldest child, not to mention a large number of grown-ups, and the fact that it can be added to at will, and is so infinitely varied.' The items available for the farm cccupied twenty-nine pages of the catalogue and included a chicken house and run, glasshouses, six- and ten-wheeled lorries, a horse-drawn timber carriage with a real log, trees of various kinds, and horse-drawn ploughs. The farmhouse, which has rarely survived, is an idyllic half-timbered building with a sliding door at the back. Boxed presentation sets of various farm people, including a blacksmith and a dairyman with yoke and pails, as well as sets of animals, were all available for this curiously old-fashioned toy, though the majority of children acquired the lead animals a few at a time. These farms sometimes grew to quite astonishing sizes, augmented with the more expensive pieces at Christmas and birthdays. As the figures were strong, they have survived in considerable number so that it is not too difficult to acquire pieces.

Great emphasis was placed by Britain's on the educational nature of their zoo settings. The pictures of individual animals were accompanied by short

A modeller at work on a detailed figure such as those seen in the zoo. (By courtesy of William Britain's.)

informative paragraphs which were very reminiscent of the Victorian board games; one example reads as follows: 'Guenon Monkey. (Walking) (Cercopithecus). These monkeys are found only in Africa and comprise several varieties. They are vivacious and intelligent creatures and are the species carried by the street organ player. The word "Guenon" is French and means to grimace.' Included among the zoo series was a realistic Noah's ark some 30 cm. (12 in.) long and containing pairs of elephants, rhinoceroses, polar bears, lions, llamas, wolves, monkeys, storks, kangaroos, brown bears and penguins, as well as Noah and his wife. Complete arks such as these are now very rare and would make interesting acquisitions. The production of hollow cast-metal animals did not cease until the 1960s, so many of the more common models can still be found with little difficulty, providing a worthwhile collecting field for the new enthusiast.

Appendix: on collecting

The fascination that is exerted by antique toys over all types of people has caused a rapid increase in the number of collectors. As rare pieces disappear from the market the prices of finer examples inevitably escalate. There are, however, still many fields of toy collecting in which prices have not appreciably risen, such as wooden carts and horses, and table and board games of the late Victorian and Edwardian type. Pieces made in the 1920s and 1930s are also very under-appreciated, and a collection of, for instance, educational toys made at this time could be extremely interesting. Dolls, dolls' houses, trains and tin toys are extremely popular, and the impecunious would be advised to choose a less crowded area.

Condition, as with any antique item, is important, and the temptation to buy a damaged piece in the hope that it can be restored should be avoided, as professional restoration is not cheap and is sometimes unsatisfactory. Great discretion has to be exercised before deciding to restore, though generally damage occasioned by normal play, such as that on the base of a horse or the cracking on the head of a waxed composition doll, is simply evidence of age and is best ignored. A doll's house, however, that had been unsuitably re-papered by a recent owner will repay stripping down to the original covering, or if necessary re-papering in old papers. Tin toys are frequently chipped, though again, unless they are in very unsightly condition, it is inadvisable to strip and re-paint: a collector will usually prefer to buy an item in its original damaged state than to accept another person's restoration, which might be less skilled than his own.

If intending to spend a large sum on an acquisition without specialist knowledge, it is advisable to buy only from an established dealer who is prepared to give a full description of the piece on the receipt. Auction room bargains in specialist sales are only very rarely found by the novice, as many knowledgeable dealers and collectors will have thoroughly examined all the items. I often see prices reached at auction that are far in excess of those asked by shops, and an acquaintance with prices of particular attributable objects is necessary before bidding. Quite often the pretty doll or toy that catches the eye has a relatively low value, making it inadvisable to simply buy 'just what I like'.

It is not a good idea to ask a local museum for advice on acquisitions, as their knowledge is necessarily of the more general type. Usually established collectors or dealers are much more reliable, as they are continually backing their judgement with their own money. It is better to pay a valuation fee than to obtain free advice that may be unreliable. A cheaper means of gaining advice, however, is by joining one of the collectors' clubs, as even in a small group there will usually be a wide range of knowledge.

Opposite A sheet of paper with dressing dolls printed and published by Gustav Kühn of Neu-Ruppin and with the number 8844. Late 19th century.

Bibliography

Altes Spielzeug aus Basel, Historisches Museum, Basel, 1973.

Aries, Philippe, *Centuries of Childhood*, Jonathan Cape, London 1962.

Athletics, Sports, Games and Toys, October 1895

Bachmann, Fritzsch, *An Illustrated History of Toys,* Abbey Library, 1966.

Bayne-Powell, Rosamond, *The English Child in the Eighteenth Century,* John Murray, London.

Bossi, Marco, *Autohobby,* Priuli & Verlucca, n.d. (*circa* 1976).

Bing, Gebrüder, catalogues 1906 and 1909; English catalogue 1912.

Boehn, Max Von, *Dolls,* reprint, Dover, London, 1972.

Britains Toy and Model Catalogue 1940, reprinted Almark Publications, England, 1972.

Britains, William, Ltd, catalogue 1905, reprinted Britains Ltd, 1972.

Chad Valley Ltd, catalogues 1897–1954.

Coleman, D., E. and E., *The Collector's Encyclopaedia of Dolls,* Robert Hale, London, 1970.

Cook, Olive, *Movement in Two Dimensions,* Hutchinson, London, 1963.

Culff, Robert, *The World of Toys,* Hamlyn, Middlesex, 1969.

Daiken, Leslie, *Children's Toys Through the Ages,* Hamlyn, Middlesex, 1963.

Dean's Rag Book Company, catalogues 1911–1938.

Gamages Christmas Bazaar, 1913; reprinted David & Charles, Devon, 1974.

Garratt, John G., *Model Soldiers, A Collector's Guide,* Seeley, Service and Co. Ltd, London, 1965.

Gerken, Jo Elizabeth, *Wonderful Dolls of Papier Mâché,* Doll Research Associates, 1970.

Great Toys of George Carette, The, catalogue 1911; reprinted new Cavendish, London, 1976.

Greilsamer, Jacques, and Bertrand Azema, *Catalogue of Model Cars of the World,* Edita Lausanne, Switzerland, 1967; UK edn Patrick Stephens, Cambridge, England.

Gröber, Carl, *Children's Toys of Bygone Days,* Batsford, London, 1928.

Hannas, Linda, *The English Jig Saw Puzzle,* Wayland, Sussex, 1962. *Two Hundred Years of Jig Saw Puzzles,* London Museum catalogue, 1968.

Hillier, Mary, *Automata and Mechanical Toys,* Jupiter, England, 1976. *Dolls and Dollmakers,* Weidenfeld & Nicolson, London, 1968.

Hobbies Handbook, 1934, 37 and 40, Hobbies Ltd, Norfolk.

Hornby, Frank, *The Life Story of Meccano,* facsimile reproduction from magazines 1932/1953, New Cavendish, London, 1976.

Jackson, F. Nevil, *Toys of Other Days,* reprinted White Lion Publishers, London, 1975.

King, Constance E., *A Collector's History of Dolls,* Robert Hale, London, 1977. *Dolls and Dollshouses,* Hamlyn, Middlesex, 1977.

Levy, Allen, *A Century of Model Trains,* New Cavendish, London, 1974.

Low, Francis H., *Queen Victoria's Dolls,* Newnes, 1894.

MacClintock, Marshall and Innez, *Toys in America*, Public Affairs Press, Washington, D.C., 1961.

Märklin, *Technical Toys in the Course of Time*, catalogues 1859–1902; reprinted Hobby Horse, 1975.

Marshall Field Toy Catalogue, 1892–1893, edited by Dale Kelley, Wallace Homestead Book Co., Iowa, 1967.

Moderne Kunst in Meister Holzschnitten, published Richard Bong, *circa* 1910.

Mogridge, G., *Sergeant Bell and his Raree Show*, Thomas Tegg, Cheapside, London, *circa* 1845.

Oberammergau Folk Museum Guide, published by Community of Oberammergau, 1963.

Ortmann, Erwin, *The Collector's Guide to Model Tin Figures*, Studio Vista, London, 1974.

Pressland, David, *The Art of the Tin Toy*, New Cavendish, London, 1976.

Reder, Gustav, *Clockwork, Steam and Electric*, history of model railways, Ian Allan, London, 1972.

Remise, Jacques, and Jean Fondin, *The Golden Age of Toys*, Edita Lausanne, Switzerland, 1967.

Roe, F. Gordon, *The Georgian Child*, Phoenix.

Roh, Juliane, and Claus Hansmann, *Altes Spielzeug*, Bruckmann, Munich, 1958.

Schoonmaker, Patricia N., *Research on Kämmer and Reinhardt Dolls*, published by author, U.S.A., 1965.

Speaight, George, *The History of the English Toy Theatre*, Studio Vista, London, 1967.

Index

Page numbers in italics refer to illustrations

Ackerman and Co 89
Adventures of Two Dutch Dolls and a Golliwog 146
Aircraft *69*
Airship Z VII over the Royal Train 90
Alabama Coon Juggler 59
Alexander Doll Co 145
Alfons and Gaston 154
All bisque dolls *129*
Alphabet blocks 221
  scraps *212*
Altdorf 234
America in General 20
American Model Builder 92
  Soldier Co 209
  Trotter *70*
Ammon, Johann Wolfgang 204
  C. 205
Amor Metal Toy Stamping Co. 144
Anamorphes, Les 91
Ancient Geography 20
Appenzell Historical Museum 186
Armour, miniature 10
Arnold Print Works 155, *155, 162*
Arotta, G. 223
Ars Magna Lucis et Umbrae 13
Art Fabric Mills 156
Assembly of Old Bachelors and Old Maids 219
Astleys Circus 30
Auction Game 229
Augsburg 10, 11, 12, 82, 102, 223
Aunt Jemima 156
Auria, Raffaele d' 29
Auto über Land und Wasser 60
Automata 8
Aux Nations 160

Baby Bumps 141
Baby Houses *13, 14, 15*
Bachmann, Dr Manfred 237

Barbara Bear 149
Barcelona Exhibition 1886 52
  1888 52
Bärenjahre 151
Barfoot, J. W. 219
Barnum, S. O. and Son 70
Bassett Lowke 58, 61, *74*
  Wenman J. *68*
Bateman, John 67
Baxter, George 211
Bayerische Nationalmuseum 10
Bearpit, The 148
Bears, mechanical 149, *148*
Bébé Bijou 126
Bébé Breveté 126, 127, *127*
Bébé le Teteur 128
Beecher 156
Beeson, James 68
Before and After Marriage 21
Belgian refugees 239, *240*
Bell and Francis 157, *158*
Bella, Stefano della 13
Belleville 64
Bello 155
Belton 122, 131, *130*
Bendigo Bear 151
Berchtesgaden 16, 30, 98, 233, 234, *30*
Bergmann, C. *171*
Berlin, Connecticut 25, 70
  Prussia 48
  Porcelain dolls 112
Berryman, Clifford 147
Besold, Carl Ludwig 205
Bestelmeier, Hieronymus 26, 85, 182, 186, 188, 237, 239
Bethnal Green Museum 31, 187, 188
Betsy Wetsy 143
Betts, John 236, 237
Big Theatre, The 83
Billikin 141, 153, *158*
Bing, Francis 58
  Gebrüder 48, 49, 51, 61, 66, 90, 93, 184, *54, 57, 74, 75*

Ignaz and Adolf 51, 58
  Stephan 58, 68
  Werke *53, 58*
Bingola 53
Biscuit tins 68, *67*
Bisque dolls *116, 123, 134, 137, 140*
Blackmore 185
Blackspot porcelains 112
Blampoix 126
Blucher 204
Boar Hunt, The 42
Bobby Penguin 160
Bobby Whitetail 158
Bogorodskoye 31
Bolo 157
Bonnet dolls 116, *115*
Bonzo 160, *160*
Borgfeldt, George *144*
Bottomley 194
Boudoir dolls 156
Bow-Wow 156
Bowles and Carver 21
Boys Christmas Presents, A 36
Brand, John 9
Brandenburg 58
Brassington and Cook 202
Brewster, Sir David 91
Britain, William 45, 206, 209, 244, *44, 45, 208, 209, 244, 245, 246*
British Legion Mascot 160
British Museum 8
British Toymaker, The 106
Brookland, The 46
Brotteig 98, 23, 58
Brown, George W. 70
Brownies 155, *155*
Bru, Casimir 120, 122, 126, 127, 128, 131, 143, *167*
Bub, Karl 58, 61
Bucherer 144
Bucking Mule 73
Bugatti 202
Burgkmair, Hans 10
Burlington Building Bricks 198

Buschow and Beck *145*
Butchers shops 187, 188
Bye-Lo Baby 144

Caesar, Julius 9
Camel and its Utility, The 228
Can't Break 'Em 145
Cantering Tricycle 38
Capital Round Game, A 225
Captain and Mrs Captain 154
Card games 12, *16, 17*
  teaching 13, 17, 223–225
Carnival dolls 156
Carpenter, N. *217*
Carrette, Georges 61, 68, 89, 91, 93, 184, 200–201, *57, 62, 77*
Carrington Bowles 19
Cars, child size *202, 203*
  sheet metal 51, 55, *51, 62, 65, 77*
Carter, F. *28*
Carts 8, *33, 34, 73, 176*
Cartwright 184
Caspar, Bertha 155
Catterfelder Puppenfabrik *136, 194*
Celluloid *145*
Central Fire Brigade 61, *75*
Chad Valley 68, 150, 156, 157, 160, 183, 184, 189, 196, 197, 230, 231, 243, *160*
Chamberlain and Hill 197
Chantecler dolls 131
  Hen 157
Chase, Martha 156
Christiansen, Ole Kirk 199
Chronological Tables of English History 21
Circus *244*
Citröen, André 65, 202
  cars 64, 65, 202
Cinematograph 93, *90*
Claretie, Léo 64
Climbing Nigger 59

Coaches 30, *30*
Cohen, Louis I 225
Colbert 11
Comical Street Cleaner 90
Complete Tour Through England and Wales 19
Compliment, The 79
Composition animals 235
        dolls 145, *100*
        toys 16
Concentra 57
Conservatoire des Arts et Metiers 64
Construction kits 55, 197, *192, 198, 199*
Cook, Alf, Ltd *222*
Co-operative Manufacturing Co 100
Counties of England 219, *226*
County Fair Tower 60
Cox, Palmer 155, *155*
Craft toys 195, 196
Crandall, Benjamin 38
        Jesse 34
Crane, Walter 26
Creedmore Bank *71*
Cremer 236
Cribs, household 233
        markets 233
        paper *232*
        wax 233
        wooden 233
Criss-Cross Spelling Slips 216
Cruchley, G. F. 219
Cruikshank, George 219
Cup and Ball game 10

D.E.P. *129*
Dairy Implements 184
d'Allemagne, Henri 64
Danel et Ci 131
Darton, William 21, 215, *214*, Jnr. 219
Dauphin, The 186
Davenport 191, *191*
Deans Rag Book Co. 145, 151, 157, *144, 159*
Décamps, E. 149
Deight, Robert 21
Delahaye 64
Delaney, Mrs Mary 190, 191
Delarge 64
de la Rue, Thomas 211–213, *146*

Delaunay 64
Denameur 126
Desvignes 89
Diabolo *9*
Dickie Blob 158
Dinky Toys 6, 69
Dionne Quinns 145
Dismal Desmond 158
Dissected Puzzles 20, *218*
Dog, Fin *46*
Dolls house dolls 14
        furniture 181
Dolly Dimple Flour 156
Dolly's Washing Day 184
Dover Toys 197
Dr. Quack 160
Dressel, Cuno and Otto 132
Dubois, I. E. 205
Dunn, Ralph and Co. 149, 189, 227
Dydee Baby 143

Earthenware dolls 8
Eden Bébé 168
Edgworth, Maria 37
Eeyore 159
EFFanBEE 145
Egyptian toys 8, 146
Elastolin 206
Elizabeth I of England 234
Ellis, Joel 99, 100
Epinal 196, 239
Erst Schweizerische und Spielwarenfabrik 35
Erzgebirge 186, 234, 239, 242, *235*
Eskimaux 154
Essex Bazaar 215
Esslingen 83
Eureka 203
European Geographical Amusement 19
European Tourist, The 213–214, *213*
Events in the Reign of Queen Anne 17
Evripose joints 151
Express mail van 56

Faber, G. W. *79*
Factories, tin 56, 57
Fairground engines 51
Falk, Firma 198
Fancy Bazaar, The 224

Fantascope 89
Farms *172, 241, 245*
Faulkner, C. W. & Co. 227, *170, 227*
Felix the Cat 158
Fiat 202
Fields, W. C. 145
Fiend of the Rocky Mountains 88
Finger Puppets 157
Finsburg, Samuel and Co. 148
Fleischmann 58
        and Blödel 155
Flip-Flap 48
Floor runners 49
Floresta Pluschwerk 155
Floss 156
Flying machines 51
Fohi 233
Ford, Jazaniah 233
Fort *174*
Fournier 120
Fox, George 215
Foxy Grandpa 156
Fr. H & C *110, 112*
Francis, Field and Francis 70
Frankfurt fair 28
Frederick the Great 16, 204
Freischutz, Der 85
Fretsawing machines 185
Fritz, Emil 49
Frog and Snake Bank 175
Fuller, S. & J. *121*
Furniture, ancient 9
        miniature 12, *15*, 184
        paper 14
        tin 15
Fürth 47, 49, 204
Fury, The 67

Gabriel, William 37
Gage of Liverpool 189
Galautee men 92
Gall and Inglis 219
Galloping Gig 40
Gamages 40, 157, 179, 187, 196, 198, 239, 243, *66, 193*
Game of Basket of Fruit 220
Game of Fortress and Siege 229
Game of Quartets 224
Game of Snake 19
Garages 55
Garrett, J. 205
Gaultier, Abbé 19
        Fernand 120, *118*

Gee-Swing 41
Gem Mangle 184
Gendron Wheel Co. *202*
Geography of England and Wales 21
George IV, Coronation of 82
        of England 105
Germanisches Nationalmuseum 28
Germany, Crown Prince of 42
Gesland dolls 118
Giengen am Brenz 151
Gilbert, O. 223
Gissey, Henry de 12
Glass miniatures 25
Glevum Works 190, 230
Glove puppets 85
Göbl, Andreas Benedictus 17
Gold Medal Cricket 228
Goldilocks 156
Golliwog Round Game 146
Golliwogs 45, *146, 147*
Gonks 160
Gooch, C. 109
Goodyear, Charles 143
Googlies 140, 141, *132*
Gorham, John *91*
Gottschalk, M. 85
Graeffer, F. 35
Gramophones *53*
Grandjean 126
Gras, Henri le 12
Gratieux, Fernand *9*
Gray Cast Iron Casting Co. 209
Great Exhibition 106, 213
Greek dolls *8*
Green, J. & Co. 202
Green, J. K. 85, 87
Greenly, Henry 68
Greenwood, H. 224
Griener, Ludwig 99, *99*
Gretchen 142
Grimaud, B. O. 223
Grocers shops *186, 189*
Gröden 16, 98, 235
Grödnertal dolls 97, 187, *30, 97*
Grünhain 51, 242
Gustav the Miller 59, *61*
Gunthermann *195*
Gutta percha 143
Gwenda Toys 183, 184

Haberdashers shops 185
Haffner, Johann 205

Hagenbach, Carl 243
Hamley Bros. 157, 219, 32
Handwerck, Max 133
Hans 142
Hardware and Woodenware
   Manufacturing Co. 180
Hausser, O. & K. 206
Hautsch, Hans and Gottfried
   11
Hayes, Will 158
Heal, Ambrose 37
Hebbard, Mrs 85
Heinrichsen 204, 205
Hermes 8
Herrad, Abbess 10
Herroard 11
Hesse Cassel 189
Hessmobil 63
Heubach, Gebrüder 122, 140,
   141, 140, 142
Heyde, Georg 206
Heyden, Jacob von der 10
Higginson, Rev. John 24
Higgs, William 96
Hill, John and Co. 209
Hilpert, Johann Gottfried 16,
   42, 46, 204, 242
Hispano-Suiza 64
Historical Pastime 217
Hobbies Magazine 241
Hobby Horses 9, 26, 28
Hobgrates 18
Hodgson and Co. 87, 82
Hoffman, Solomon 145
Holdfast 184
Holman Hunt, Diana 35
Holzschürer 10
Home Zoo 243
Hornby 69
   Frank 69, 197
Horner 89
Horsman 141, 145
Hortus Deliciarum 10
Hotchkiss 64
Houses, baby 13, 13, 14, 15
   cabinet 13, 28, 177
Hughes, Henry H. 157
Humpty Dumpty Circus 243
Hunting scenes 10, 44, 45
Huntley and Palmer 68
Huret 118, 120, 143

Ideal Novelty Co. 145
Ideal Toy Corporation 145, 147

Infant Jesus figures 102, 103,
   125, 7
Inskeep and Bradford 224
International Card Co. 212
Ives, Edward 70, 71
   Blakeslee and Williams 71
Ivory dolls 24
   toys 25

J. de P. 64, 65
J.E.P. 64
Jakobsen and Prior 88
Jameson, J. H. 85
Jaques, J. & Sons 225, 228,
   225, 226, 227, 230
Jeffreys, John and Thomas 19
Jeu de Fortification 13
Jeu des Rois de la France, Le 13
Jigsaw Puzzles 219, 170, 218
Joiboy Toys 201
Jones, Owen 213
Jouets de Paris 64
   en Paris 64
Journet, R. 197
Journey to the Pole 60
Journey through Europe 19
Jumeau, Emile 120, 122, 126,
   128, 129, 131, 168, 169
Jupiter 9
Juvenile Drama 85

Kaleidoscope 91
Kaleidoscope top 91
Kämmer and Reinhardt 135,
   139, 141, 142, 143 145, 138,
   139, 142
Kaulitz, Marion 139
Kelloggs 156
Kendrick, R. F. & W. 38
Kestner 135, 142, 171
Key to the Old Testament 21
Kindner und Briel 189
Kinegraphone 90
Dircher, Athanasius 13
Kitchens, American 182
   Nuremberg 183, 181
Kites 10
Kliptiko 198
Knickerbocker Speciality
   Co. 156
Knockabout Toy Sheets 157
Knopf im Ohr 151
Knucklebones 11
Kolman 10

Konstamm, Moses 48
Kookie 156
Köppelsdorf 139
Krackjack 153
Krauss, Berthold 243
   Maximilian 233
Kress cabinet house 28, 102,
   125
Krüse, Käthe 154
Kuhn, Gustav 83, 249

Landmann, J. J. 188
Lane, Lupino 158, 159
Lang, Georg 234
Langenthal 35
Lanternier, A. 122
Lapierre, Auguste 122
Laura and Lieselotte 60
Laurence and Cohen 225
Laurie and Whittle 215
Lawrence, J. W. 45
Lead flats 185, 205
Lechner, Alois 206
Lego 199
Lehmann, Ernst Paul 58, 61,
   59, 60, 61, 73
Leipzig 139
   Fair 48, 50, 151
Leliocinegraph 89
Lenci 156
Lessons for Young and Old 21
Lethieullier, Sarah 13
Lifelike Teddy Bear 148
Ligne, Prince de 13
Lindner, Louis and Sons 34,
   189, 242
Lines Bros. 40, 179, 193, 203
   G. & J. 40, 176, 179
Lion Mangle 184
Lithographed dolls' house 179
   games 21
Little Artist, The 21
Little Elecroplater 201
Little Henry 121
Little Wade 156
Lloyd, R. L. 87
Lloyd loom 194
Lockwood, F. & R. 215
Locomotive Picture Blocks 222
London Museum 37
   Stereoscopic Co. 91
   Wax Babies 108
Long, William 25, 34
Lord Roberts Workshops 157

Lorenz, Johann Gottlob 204,
   205
Loriot, A. 105
Lotto 211
Low, Francis H. 97
Lowther Arcade 26
Lucotte 205
Ludgate Hill 42, 45
Ludwig II of Hungary 10
Luton Museum 206

Macfarlane Lang 67
McLouglin Bros. 209, 216
Magic Disc 91
Magic Lanterns 13, 79, 92, 93,
   94
Magnetic Fishpond 171
Mannequin figures 102
Mansion of Bliss 215, 214
Mansion of Happiness 215
March, James 84
Marey, Professor E. J. 89, 90
Marienburg 85
Marionettes 85
Märklin, Carolin 49
   Eugen 49
   Gebrüder 49, 55, 58,
   183, 198, 243, 51,
   175
   Karl 49
   Theodor Friedrich
   Wilhelm 49
Markover 228, 230
Marseille, Armand 132, 139,
   140, 132, 140, 176
Marsh, Charles 108, 108
Marshall Field 70
Martin, Fernand 64
Marx, Louis 72
Mason and Taylor 100
Mason, Henry 100
Maudit, Vicomte de 158
Maximilian I 10
Meccano Guild 198
   Ltd. 69, 197, 198, 192,
   198
   Magazine 198
Medaille d'Or 129
Medici, Marie de 11
Meech, Herbert 109
Metal Doll Co. 144
Metal dolls 143, 143, 144
Mettoy Ltd 69
Michtom, Morris 147

Midland Tent and Strong Toy
    Co. 32
Mignon Theater 83
Mignot 205
Milbro Models 69
Military figures, ancient 9
Milliners shops 185
Mills Bros Model Engineers
    Ltd. 69
Milne, A. A. *159*
Mimi and Shah 158
Minerva dolls 143
Minoru 227
*Miscellanies for the Instruction of
    Infants* 21
Misery beasts 235
Misfitz Series 227, *227*
Model Home Farm 224
Model Rag Dolls 157
Model Theatre *83, 86*
Moden und Schittmuster
    Industrie 185
Mogridge, G. 81
Moko 48
Money boxes 72, *71*, 189
Monkeys, fabric *144, 153*
        mechanical 148, *59*
Montanari 106, 108
Montreuil-sous-Bois 122
Moody, C. 81
    E. 109
Moore, Coleen, Castle 177
Morrell, Charles 34, 187
Morris, Dr. Claver 103
Mother Goose 20
Mouse, Mickey 158
        Minnie 158
Müller, Friedrich 235
Munich 233
Musical Game 25
Musique d'Infanterie 207
Muybridge, Eadward J. 89
My Cherub 124
Myers, Joseph 87, 213, *213*

Napoleon 204
Nativity scenes 83
Neuburger, Daniel 102
Neumeyer, Fritz 80, *92, 93*
Neuruppin 83
New Game of Ladies Costumes 18
New Game of Human Life 19
*New Model Express Steam
    Locomotive* 55

New Model Motor Brougham 55
New Stable Ark 239
New Testament Packs 223
New York Card Co. 225
New York Herald, The 149
New York Rubber Co. 143
Newcomen, Thomas 56
Newton, T. 215
Niagara Lithographing Co. 156
Nicholas, Tsar 204
Noah's Ark Toy
    Warehouse 215
Noah's Arks *173, 235, 236, 238,
    240*
Nostell Priory 13
Nouveau Jeu d'Officiers 17
Nuremberg 10, 11, 28, 46, 47,
    50, 51, 58, 61, 85, 91, 103,
    182, 198, 204, 235
Nuremberg Exhibition 1882 52
        Flats *42, 204*
Nürnberger Spielwarenfabrik 51

Oberammergau 16, 29, 30, 37,
    98, 125, 206, 233, 235
Ogilvie, E. & M. A. *224*
Old Hall Earthenware Co. 191
Ole Bill 158
Oliver and Boyd 224
Ordish, Messrs. 230
Oriental 6, 190, *141*
Orleans, Duchess of 103
Osborne House 35, 187, 197
Our Pets 189
Our Soldier Boys 155
Outcault, R. 156

Paen Frères 144
Paine, James 13
Pandoras 102
Panoramas 82, 236, *217*
Panorama of Europe 217
Paper dolls 113, *113, 117*
        patterns 185
Papier mâché dolls 23, 98, 100,
    101, 163, 164
Parfumerie Régence 187
Parian dolls *121, 249*
Paris, Dr. J. A. 88
Paris Exhibition 1889 64
    1900, 52, 55, 68
    Exposition Universelle 129
Parisiennes 118, 143, *118, 119,
    120, 165*

Parke, A. 87
Parsons, Jackson 145
Patterson 70
Patterson Edwards 25, 32, 40,
    194
Paumgartner, Balthasar 28
Peacocks of Islington 189, 219,
    218
Peak, Frean 149, 189
Peck, E. S. 155
        William E. & Co. 149,
        193
Pedlar Dolls *15, 166*
Peepshows 13
Pellerin 187, *87, 207*
Penny Beasts 235
*Penny Plain, Twopence
    Coloured* 87
Penny Toys 42, *43, 44*
Perambulators 193–94, *194*
Perfection Art Dolls 144
Peter Pan and Wendy 160, *212*
Phantasmagoria of Robertson
    92
Phenakistascope 88
Philadelphia Exhibition 1876 38
        Tin Toy Manu-
        factory 70
Philadex 230
Phillip and Son 219
Piccaninny 155
Picture Blocks 221, *220, 221,
    222*
Pierotti 109, 125
Pilgrims Progress 21
Pirates of Florida Keys 88
Planck, E. 93, *66*
Plank horses 36
Plateau 88
Playmates 72
Pleasure Steamer, The 196
Plümiche, Carl Martin 16
Polich, Aug. 139
Polinchinelle et Arlequin *87*
Pollock, Benjamin 87, 88
Polyramas 87, *82*
Pooh Bear 159
Pope Joan board *18*
Popeye 158
Popski 158
Porcelain dolls *110, 111, 112*
Possum, Billy 148
Potter, Beatrix 150
Praxinoscope 89

Prince Imperial, The 39
Prismatic Dioramas 87
Prisoner of War Work 239
Proteau Views 219
Pullalong toys 8, *33, 47, 71*
Punch and Judy 191, *78*
Pushalong toys 155, *32, 29*

Queen Anne Dolls 96, *96*

Rabery et Delphieu 131, *126*
Rag toys, advertising 156
        printed 155, 156
Railway scenes 219, 222
        stations *56*
Ramm, Johann Friedrich 42,
    239
Raree Men 81
Rattles 8
Reason, Henry 229, *229*
Red Riding Hood 154, *155*
Redington 87
Regency toys *182*
Reka Co. Ltd. 42, 209
Renault taxi 64
Renner, G. N. 235
Reynaud, E. 89
Rheinische Gummi und
    Celluloidfabrik 145
Richter, Johann 60
Riedel 85
Riemschneider 83
Rijksmuseum, Amsterdam 102
Road to Rome 82
Roberts Bros 230
Robertson, James and Co. 224
Robin Hood and His Merry Men
Rochett, William 103
Rocking horses 25, 45, *35, 38, 41*
Roger, Nicholas 11
Rogers *191*
Rohler, Walter 85
Rohmer, Mme. 118
Roithner, Hugo 193, *27*
Rooney, Benjamin T. 70
Roosveldt, President
    Theodore 147
Rossignol, Charles 64
Route of the Overland Mail 82
Royal Dolls, The 160
Royal English Mail Van 55
Royal Game of Goose, The 17
Royal Historical Game, The 224
Royal Scot *74*

255

Rubber dolls 143
Run, Neighbours, Run 82
Russian toys 31
Russian wheels 49
Ruyter, Margarete de 102

S.F.B.J. 122, 131, 136, 142, 154, 242
Sandrart, Joachim von 102
Satirical Panorama of a Misspent Life 82
Sayer, Robert 20
Scale: Berlin 204
    Hanover 204
    Heinrichsen 204
    Nuremberg 204
Schneegass 181
Schoenhut, Albert 144, 243, *143*
Schoenner, Jean 93
Schramm, G. W. 194
Schreiber, J. F. 83, 85
Schreibersche Kindertheater 83
Schutz, Mathias 28
Schwarz, Henry 34, 38, 70
Schweinfurt 85
Science and Industry, Museum of 177
Seltz's American Boys Theatre 88
Sergeant Bell and his Raree Show 81
Sewing machines 185, *185*
Shadow theatre *84*
Sharp, Ann 103, 125
Shaw, William Thomas 89
Shipman, Charles 25
Shoofly 38
Showhorses 35, 40
Silbermann 206
Silver miniatures 182
Simmons and Co. 193–194
Simon and Halbig 122, 129, *176*
Simonne 120, *120*, *165*
Sir William Treloar Centre, The 157
Skaymo Ltd. *199*
Skelt, Martin 87
Skipping doll *100*
Slides, lever 94
    rackwork 95
    slipping 94
Slithead dolls 106
Smith Bailey & Co. 66
Smith, Celia M. *155*
Société Industrielle de Ferblanterie 64

Soldiers, composition 206
    jointed 10
    lead 16
    paper 16, 206
    silver 11
    wooden 206
Sonneberg 34, 98, 118, 140, 234, 235
Speaight, George 85
Spears, W. 195, *171*
Spenkuch, Georg 42
Spilsbury, John 20, 21
Spooner, William 219
Springfield dolls 100
Spurin, E. C. *184*
Square Lampascope 93
Squeak toys *146*
Stables 28
Stadtmuseum, Munich 102
Stahl, Johann Ludwig 243
Stampfer 88
Star Manufacturing Co. 40, 194
Statham, W. E. & Son 201
Stationary engines 56, 199–200, *57*, *66*
Steamtoys, Bing 54
    Märklin 50
Steiff, Margarethe 42, 147, 148, 149, 151, 152, 154, 155, *153*, *154*
    Paul 151
    Richard 151
Steinberg and Co. 243
Steiner, Jules 126, 128
Stereoscope 89, 91, *89*
Steudner J. Ph. 12
Stevens Model Dockyard 65
Stewart Reidpath 68
Stiegel, Henry 25
Storklegs engines 61
Stoves, model 72, *142*, *175*
Strasbourg 9, 14, 16, 83
Striedbeck, Jan Friedrich 16
Strobl, Andream 12
Stroboscope 88
Stromer, cabinet house 28, 37, 125
Strong toys 32, *27*
Struwwelpeter 152, *152*
Stump dolls *22*
Sunny Jim 156
Sutcliffe, J. 67, *67*
Sweden and Norway 20
Swift, The 67

Tatters 156, 160
    Little 156
Taylor, Luke 100
Teddy's Horse 38
Teetotum 19
Telephone sets 201
Telescopic View of the Great Exhibition 81
Terry, William J. 148
Thaumotrope 88
Thaumotropical Amusement 88
Théâtre Cinematographe 90
Théâtre Optique 89
Theobald, J. and Co. 93
Thuringia 131, 135
Tietz Toy Motor 49
Tige 156
Timor the Tartar 85
Tin flats 42
Tin Toys, American 25
    early 10
    kitchenware 181
Tinkle toys 16
Tiny Tots Sunday School 190
Toledo Metal Wheel Co. 194
Topliff and Ely Co. 194
Tops 9
Totum *see Teetotom*
Toy Trader, The 32, 42, 48, 50, 52, 131, 139, 148, 151, 152, 153
Trains, Bing 55, *58*, *74*
    Märklin 50
Trentsentsky 83, 87
Triang 40, 203, *203*
Trippel-Trappel Toys 157
Trix Trains 58
Troitse Sergeyev Monastery 31
Tru-to-Life 144
Tuck, Raphael 196, 221, *82*, *196*
Tunbridge Ware 239
Turner and Fischer 88
Turners 70
Tut-Tut Automobile 59

Uchatius, Franz 89
Uneeda dolls 143
Universal Director 20
Upppark 13
Upton, Florence 146

Vallardi, P. & G. 223
Various Employments 17

Vauban 11
Velocipedes 39, *39*
    American 38
Victoria, Queen 35, 97, 177, 187
Virtue rewarded and Vice Punished 215
Vischer, A. 143
Voltaire 16, 204

Waldkirchen 242
Wain, Louis *82*
Walker, Isannah F. 156
Wallis, John 17, 21, 215–217, *19*, *20*, 217
Wallis Bros. & Wickstead 201
Wallner, Anton 16
Waltershausen 135, 142
Warenhaus Tietz 49
Wax dolls 24, 102, 105, *104*, *107*, *108*, *109*, *125*, *139*, *175*
Webb, W. A. 87
    W. G. 87
Weiskunig, Der 10
Weiser, Gustav 91
Wellings, Nora *158*
Wells 68, *69*
West, William 85, 87
Wheel of Life, The 89
Wheeled toys 31
Wheelhouse, Mr. 106
Whieldon ware 190
White bisque dolls 113, *114*
Whyte, Ridsdale & Co. 141, 157, *158*
Wildey, Spence 156
Wolrab, Jakob 11
Wood, Basil Robert *30*
Wooden dolls 23, 26, *22*, *23*
    German 96
    waxed 98
    wire eyed 98
Woodman and Mutlow 21
Woolley & Co. 230
Work, Henry C. *73*
Württemburg 49

Zig-Zag 59
Zoetrope 89
Zoos 245, 246
Zoogyroscope 89
Zooloo *170*